Blackguards and Red Stockings

Blackguards and Red Stockings

A History of Baseball's
National Association, 1871-1875

by

William J. Ryczek

Colebrook Press
Wallingford, Connecticut

Library of Congress Cataloguing-in-Publication Data

Ryczek, William J., 1953-
    Blackguards and Red Stockings : a history of baseball's National
Association, 1871-1875 / by William J. Ryczek.
        p.   cm.
    Includes bibliographical references (p. 261) and index.
    ISBN 0-9673718-0-5 (60# alk. paper)   ∞
    1. National Association of Professional Base Ball Players (U.S.) – History.

Manufactured in the United States of America

Colebrook Press
56 Algonquin Drive, Wallingford, CT 06492

To my father, Frank Ryczek.
I learned the virtues of industry and integrity
from his fine example.

Acknowledgments

As I put the finishing touches on this manuscript, I realize that it has been more than ten years since the research for this book commenced. Any project of such duration requires the assistance of many people, far more than I am able to acknowledge in this brief section.

I wish to thank the staff of the Wallingford, Connecticut, Public Library for the use of their facilities and their assistance when needed; also for not asking why I was mumbling the contents of century-old box scores into my daughter's Fisher Price tape recorder (mine had broken); the staff in the dance section of the Performing Arts Research Center in New York (home of the New York Clipper); Mark Alvarez, for his thorough reading of the manuscript and assistance with the SABR Microfilm Lending Library; Fred Ivor-Campbell, for reviewing the manuscript; Bob Tiemann, for supplying me with portions of the Michael Stagno Collection and the fruits of his committee's statistical research; Giuliana Liseo and Wendy Callendar for critical last-minute software assistance; McFarland & Company, for publishing the work; Mark Rucker, for the photographs; and my good friends Bruce Barto and Mike Witkowski for reading the text in its early form and being honest enough to offer frank criticism.

Finally, my wife, Susan, an English major and fine writer in her own right. Her early attitude toward this project is summed up by a comment she made upon my return from a particularly grueling research trip to New York: "Is this ever going to amount to anything?" In the end, however, she offered much grammatical assistance and provided unwavering support in the face of numerous obstacles. Thank you.

Contents

Introduction

For its status as the first professional sports league, the National Association has been treated rather shabbily by baseball historians. The so-called *Ultimate Baseball Book* devotes less than half a paragraph to the league. Bob Carroll, in his article "For the Hall of Fame: Twelve Good Men," described a "sort of league called the National Association. It had a reputation that would embarrass the town harlot. Hard-drinking players were loaded on the field more often than on the bases, gamblers knew tomorrow's standing this morning and the whole mess was about as disciplined as the theater crowd when the Bijou burned down."[1]

While that may explain the formation of the National League by William Hulbert, the hero of Carroll's piece, it fails to explain why historians have uniformly dismissed the Association with a few stinging sentences.

The first time Wilbur Wright attempted to defy gravity, he crashed unceremoniously at the end of the takeoff ramp. Orville's miraculous flight three days later spanned 120 feet and lasted twelve seconds. Yet no one scoffs at them and compares their primitive aircraft to Boeing 767s. They were the first aviators, the pioneers.

Yet baseball's Wright brothers (George and Harry) remain relegated to the sport's shameful era, doomed forever to appear only in prefaces to the proliferation of histories of the National League.

Perhaps it was because until recently there were no meaningful statistics for the NA years. Even the recent exhaustive study by the Society for American Baseball Research is based to some extent upon estimates.

More than any other sport, baseball is a game of numbers. Even casual fans are aware of Dimaggio's 56-game hitting streak and Roger Maris's 61 home runs. Any baseball history is laced with a myriad of significant and obscure statistics which become embedded in the minds of serious fans.

But the NA was not a league of statistics. It was a league of people: people with human foibles, people with no road maps to guide them as they tried desperately to further the growth of their beloved game. The witty and sagacious Harry Wright, the irascible Rob Ferguson, and the old curmudgeon Henry Chadwick transcend statistics. Each was able to wield an influence over the loosely structured organization in a way that would be impossible in today's bureaucratic game.

Whether the NA is judged as a major breakthrough or an embarassing failure, its story is one that needs to be told. The little that has been written about the ancient league only whets the appetite for more. While Carroll may find the town harlot's reputation abhorrent, her story would certainly hold greater interest than that of the prim Hulbert. Yet everyone seemed embarrassed to tell the tale. As I read histories of baseball's early days, I found that none told the story of the league in sufficient detail to satisfy my curiosity. If a comprehensive history was to be written, it was apparent that I would have to write it myself.

And if I was going to write it, I was going to write it my way. While most "serious" historians, such as Seymour and Voight, concentate on off-the-field developments, I also wanted to include an account of the action between the foul lines. Many of the academic histories use baseball as a tool to show the development of American society. *Blackguards and Red Stockings* uses American society as a background to show its effect upon the development of baseball. While it is history, and it is documented, the work is first and foremost a *baseball* book, geared for the serious student of the game and yet, one hopes, readable enough for the interested fan.

The primary sources of information for this work were contemporary newspapers, journals, and correspondence. For periods beyond the 1871–1875 period, I have relied upon secondary sources. In order to reduce the amount of repetition within the Notes, I have abbreviated the sources cited to publication and date or author and page, unless a title is necessary for clarity. Further information on the sources is given in the Selected Bibliography.

So, here it is. The first (and probably last) history of the National Association, the first (and probably the most interesting) of baseball's major leagues.

Chapter 1

Opening Day

No one threw out a ceremonial first ball. Nary a celebrity vied for the honor of singing the national anthem to the less than 500 spectators. All the pomp and circumstance associated with opening day was missing from this, the first opening day.

There was only skinny 19-year-old Bobby Mathews of Fort Wayne, waiting to pitch to James (Deacon) White of Cleveland. Mathews was standing not on a mound but on a flat surface between two boards which marked the boundaries of the pitcher's position 45 feet from home plate.[1] Bill Lennon, his batterymate, stood well behind the bat, in deference to the fact that he was wearing no protective equipment. Standing alongside was the lone umpire, John L. Boake of Cincinnati.

Mathews raised himself up to his full five feet five inches, brought his arm back, whipped it forward, and sent an underhand delivery wheeling toward the plate. White watched it sail wide of the strike zone.[2] Spotting a fat pitch, the free swinging catcher uncoiled from his left-handed stance and lashed a hard drive to right field. By the time right fielder Bill Kelley retrieved the ball, White was standing on second base with a double.[3]

The date was May 4, 1871, the place Hamilton Field at Fort Wayne, Indiana, and the occasion was the first game in major league baseball's first season.[4] It was fitting that White and Mathews faced off against each other in the inaugural, for both were much more than historical footnotes. Mathews won 298 games in 15 years in the big leagues (the most of any pitcher not in the Hall of Fame) while White batted .347 in 5 National Association seasons and .303 in 15 additional major league campaigns.

White's heroics on this day, however, were short-lived. The next batter was Gene Kimball, who lofted a popup toward second baseman Tom Carey. Carey made a fine catch and doubled White off second. The inning ended when Charley Pabor fouled out to Lennon.

The game was still scoreless when Lennon led off the second with a double off Cleveland fireballer Al Pratt. Center fielder Art Allison saved a run with a splendid running, one-handed catch of Carey's fly ball, no mean feat for a man without a fielder's glove. With two outs, Joe McDermott stepped to the plate.

The center fielder was a New Yorker who had been a last minute addition to the Kekiongas after breaking his contract with the Brooklyn Atlantics.[5] Just prior to the start of the season, Fort Wayne had issued a challenge to competing teams by means of a very formal engraved invitation.[6] The team roster was printed on the card, with the exception of McDermott and T. J. Donnelly, whose names were roughly penciled in at the bottom. Both latecomers made it to Fort Wayne in time for the opener and now McDermott was at the plate with a runner in scoring position. His single chased Lennon home with the first run. It was McDermott's only hit of the season, and one of ten in his big league career, but it drove in the first run in major league history.

In the fifth, Bill Kelley singled for Fort Wayne. He reached third on two passed balls by catcher White, normally a defensive stalwart, and scored on an infield out, increasing the lead to 2–0.

Cleveland put up a brief struggle in the top of the ninth. White led off with a single, but was thrown out by center fielder McDermott when he unwisely tried for his second double of the game. With two out McDermott, once again in the midst of a key play, dropped a fly ball which would have ended the game. His muff proved harmless, as Mathews bore down to strike out Allison, making underdog Fort Wayne a 2–0 winner in America's first major league baseball game. Although the rules called for the Kekiongas to bat in the bottom of the ninth despite their lead, a spring shower drove everyone to cover and umpire Boake called the game.

The Forest Citys of Cleveland versus the Kekiongas of Fort Wayne[7] hardly had the makings of a classic opener. It was not meant to be, but became the opener by accident. The schedule contemplated that the opening game of the season would be a gala affair pitting the star-laden Boston Red Stockings against the Olympics of Washington. The carefully laid plans for opening day failed to unfold as Washington was hit with a rainstorm that washed away the game and thrust the unknowing Forest Citys and Kekiongas nines into the spotlight.

It had not rained in Fort Wayne, the teams had played, and the first season of the National Association was under way. Before the league closed its final campaign less than five years hence, more unusual occurrences had both graced and plagued the Association than the Kekiongas and Forest Citys clubs could possibly have imagined.

Teams played on fields containing trees and water hazards. Players, in this prereserve clause era, jumped freely from team to team, with one club moving in its entirety to another franchise. Teams came and went as frequently as the players, as financial instability was a way of life and no prospective entrant, no matter how lacking in talent or funds, was turned away if it was willing to put up the $10 entry fee.

While the players were professionals, management was strictly an amateurish proposition. The full name of the NA, the National Association of Professional Base Ball Players, was prophetically descriptive, as it was truly a league of players, not of clubs. Managers merely provided a stage upon which players directed, produced, and performed. Many were unforgettable characters who marched to the beat of their own percussionist, and some did not always act in the best interest of their team. Indiscretions were overlooked, talented athletes were afforded numerous chances, and (not surprisingly) very little profit was recognized by any of the stockholders.

As a result of the loose organizational structure, the NA produced five years of baseball unlike any five years in any subsequent major league. Ignorant and sometimes biased umpires created havoc with totally irrational decisions. Games took place with nine players versus eight, as piqued athletes jumped teams at their whim. There were arguments over equipment, rules, playing sites, and a myriad of other issues, as the emerging rules were often inadequate to deal with novel circumstances.

Although each of these factors, compounded by uncontrolled gambling, drunkenness, and persistent rumors of fixed games, brought the league to the brink of extinction, none was sufficient to bring about its demise. The mortal blow came not from any of the shadowy figures who populated the NA, but from the one team considered a paragon of virtue.

In May 1871, the outlook was much more sanguine. A new league, a crisply played 2–0 game, and the prospect of the first organized pennant race gave no foreshadowing of the adventures yet to come. May 4 was the starting point, but it was also the culmination of a long journey.

Chapter 2

Elysian Fields
to Fort Wayne

The journey to Fort Wayne began, according to romantic legend, in the heart of Leatherstocking country, Cooperstown, New York. General Abner Doubleday, baseball's supposed inventor, was more reliably reported to have sighted the first Union cannon fired at Fort Sumter. His claim to military legend is much stronger than his hold on baseball immortality, which is based upon the recollections — 60 years after the fact — of an aged, somewhat senile acquaintance of Doubleday's named Abner Graves and the presence of a moldy, dilapidated baseball in Graves's possession.[1] Any credence the tale might have is tarnished by the revelation that, at the time Doubleday was supposed to have been on his hands and knees laying out the diamond, he was not even in Cooperstown, but was a cadet at West Point.[2] Further, none of Doubleday's acquaintances ever remember hearing the general utter a single word about the sport he had "invented." Although a prolific writer following his retirement from the military, Doubleday committed to paper nary a word on baseball.[3]

It is possible that Graves's comments were not entirely the senile ramblings of an old man. He may well have seen Doubleday explaining the game to a group of youngsters and believed that the general was inventing it.[4] In any case, his testimony was not something upon which to base definitive historical conclusions.

All of the above was conveniently ignored by the Mills Commission established by A. G. Spalding which, in 1908, declared that there was no doubt that Doubleday had invented the national pastime.

Substantive research has placed the origins of the modern game in metropolitan New York at the husky young hands of Alexander Cartwright. During the 1840s Cartwright's band of businessmen and artisans met during their leisure hours, divided into teams and played a congenial

4

match or two purely for the physical and social benefits. By 1842, they were gathering at what is now Madison Square at 27th Street and 4th Avenue, and by 1845 had moved uptown to Murray Hill.[5] The enterprising Cartwright suggested they form an organization, which took shape as the Knickerbocker Club. The Knicks were a social club first and foremost, and remained so — an anachronism in their later years — until their dissolution in 1882.

The Knickerbockers were a team of many firsts. Most important was the first set of standardized rules, devised by Cartwright himself. The Knicks also wore the first uniforms, including blue woolen pantaloons, white flannel shirts, and natty straw boaters which proved less than functional under game conditions.[6] They played the first game between rival clubs, losing to the New York Club by the embarrassing score of 23–1 on June 19, 1846.

After that debacle at the Elysian Fields in nearby Hoboken, the team returned to intramural competition for several years before gathering the courage to return to the field in 1851. They made amends for their previous showing with a victory over the Washington Club of New York.

During the 1850s, clubs began to organize and multiply in the New York area. While some, such as the Eckfords of Brooklyn, were made up of working men,[7] the overwhelming majority were for gentlemen and white collar workers only.[8] Professional players, of course, were not allowed.

In 1833 the Olympics of Philadelphia organized to play town ball, an unevolved form of the game popular in New England. Twenty-one years later, an unimaginative group of Bostonians organized the Olympic Club of Boston. The New Englanders played the game a bit differently from their New York cousins, allowing the pitcher to fire a small, light ball with an overhand motion. New York hurlers (using a heavier ball) were restricted to an underhand toss. In Boston a runner was declared out if struck with a thrown ball. This provision was mercifully eliminated from the rules when the New England and New York versions were merged.

By 1857 there were enough teams to warrant the formation of the National Association of Base Ball Players and the establishment of the first official code of rules. From 16 clubs in the first year, membership grew to 25 in 1858, 24 of which were based in New York or Brooklyn and one from Brunswick, New Jersey, a mere 30 miles from New York. Colleges and universities were also taking an active part in the new game. On July 1, 1859, the first recorded intercollegiate match took place at Pittsfield, Massachusetts, as Amherst College defeated Williams 66–32.

The growth in the number of teams provided the impetus for a new phenomenon, the tour. The first such journey was undertaken by the Excelsiors of Brooklyn, featuring legendary pitcher James Creighton, who toured upstate New York, Philadelphia, and Baltimore in 1860 and returned home undefeated. While Creighton's contribution to the game of baseball was immense, his career was fleeting. He was the first closet professional[9] and revolutionized the art of pitching with the fast underhand throw, which quickly replaced the lobbed "pitch." In October 1862, Creighton ruptured his bladder while hitting a home run for the Excelsiors. Carried to his home, he died a few days later at the age of 21.[10]

The tours of the Excelsiors and others aided in the growth of the game's popularity, bringing big-time baseball to many remote outposts. Further growth was engendered by the Civil War, which proved a blessing in disguise. Although President Lincoln's army plucked many a player from local teams, the army proved the ultimate melting pot. Small-town lads who had never heard of baseball met city slickers who showed them how to fashion a bat out of a broom handle and how to use it. The newfangled American game helped both Union and Confederate campaigners ease the drudgery of camp life. Bored prisoners often taught the game to their captors. A military game on Christmas Day 1862 at Hilton Head, South Carolina, was reportedly watched by 40,000 spectators. A. G. Mills and Nick Young, both future National League presidents, played baseball as Union Army recruits. The Civil War period also marked the final decline of cricket as an American sport, paving the way for baseball to become the national pastime.[11]

The increase in enthusiasm was evident immediately following the war. Although the drain in manpower caused the number of teams to drop from 54 in 1860 to 34 in 1861, membership soared to 91 in 1865 and exploded to 202 in 1866, the first full year of peace. Of the 202 teams, 73 were from New York alone.[12] In 1873 more games were played in Prospect Park in Brooklyn than had been played in the entire United States 10 years earlier.[13] By 1875 more than 1,500 teams blanketed the country.[14]

Enclosed fields began to make their first appearance in the Civil War era, with the Union Grounds in Brooklyn opening its gates in 1862.[15] The debut of the Capitoline Grounds, on the other side of town, was two years later.

The mid–1860s saw the dominance of the game by one of the occupants of the Union Grounds, the Atlantics of Brooklyn, who had been in existence since 1855. They won the national championship—which could be acquired by beating the previous champions in a best of three series—in 1864 and held it until 1867, when they lost the crown to the Unions of Morrisania, New York (now part of the Bronx).

The year 1867 marked another milestone in the growth of amateur baseball. The Washington Nationals, a team composed of government clerks and others which had been in existence since 1859, left Washington, D.C., on a 3,000-mile tour of the Midwest. Captained by George Wright, the Nationals were scrupulous in their amateurism. Not only did they refuse any share of the gate receipts, but the players insisted upon paying their own traveling expenses, which amounted to roughly $3,000.[16] As appeared to be de rigueur for baseball tours, the Nationals had a song composed to commemorate the event. Called "Westward Ho," the lyrics were as follows:

> Come all you jolly Nationals
> And fill your glasses up
> Success to all who toss the ball
> Be this our parting cup
> The banner floats the breeze upon
> Our comrades wait below
> Farewell awaits to Washington
> We're going Westward Ho.
> *Chorus:* When we went Westward Ho
>   When we went Westward Ho
>   We'll never forget the jolly days
>   When we went Westward Ho.[17]

Despite the awkward wording of their ditty, the team blew through unseasoned opposition, as expected, on their way to the culmination of the tour in Chicago. As a warmup prior to playing the mighty Chicago Excelsiors (with over 200 teams, original names were at a premium) the Nationals played the Forest City club of Rockford, Illinois, at Dexter Park in Chicago. Admittedly suffering from stage fright,[18] 16-year-old Rockford pitcher Albert Spalding and his mates fought their nerves as well as the opposition and defeated both. The local youngsters jumped to a 24–18 lead after six innings and held on for a shocking 29–23 upset. This proved to be the only blemish on the Nationals record and gave rise to a week-long celebration in Rockford.[19] It also marked the emergence of young Spalding as a pitcher of some repute. Within five years he was the top pitcher in baseball.

By the late 1860s many organizations were not as squeamish about professionalism as were the Nationals. With most of the top teams playing two or three games per week, it was nearly impossible for a prominent player to hold a full-time job. A talented ballplayer was generally not paid directly for his efforts on the diamond, but might get three or four times the going rate for a clerk in a store owned by one of the team backers. On game days, or maybe all days, the player would conveniently be excused from work. Rockford had "professionals" as early as 1865.[20] Infamous political manipulator William (Boss) Tweed, president of the New York Mutuals, provided employment for many of his players in the New York City coroner's office[21] and street cleaning department.[22] Coroner John

Wildey served as team president from the mid–1860s through the early 1870s. It was reported that $30,000 in municipal funds were paid to the Mutual players during Tweed's tenure as president.[23]

This closet professionalism was widespread and continued until 1869. Following the official recognition of professionalism at the 1868 convention, Cincinnati put an end to the sham by sponsoring an openly professional nine. The key members of the team were the Wright brothers (George and Harry, that is, not Orville and Wilbur). Harry was the captain and center fielder, all for a $1,200 annual salary,[24] while George was the shortstop and probably the most talented member of the team. The play for pay Red Stockings took the field on April 17, 1869, and easily dispatched a local collection of amateurs by a 24–15 score. Finding no serious competition in the Cincinnati area, the team set sail on their famous tour. They left in their wake 57 victories, 1 disputed tie, and no defeats.[25] The Red Stockings outscored their opponents by an astounding 2,395 to 574, led by George Wright, who had a .518 batting average, 339 runs scored, and 59 of the team's 169 home runs. The lowest average on the squad belonged to first baseman Charlie Gould, who checked in at a mere .453.[26] The Reds traveled nearly 12,000 miles — venturing as far west as San Francisco — played before more than 200,000 spectators, [27] and returned to Ohio as the undisputed champions of the United States. Aptly named president Aaron Champion was so ebullient he seemed unconscious of the fact that the season had netted a profit of only $1.39, partially due to the team's astronomical payroll of $9,400.[28]

The professionals stretched their unbeaten streak by winning the first 22 games of the 1870 season before meeting their match in the Atlantics, champions of the mid–1860s who were thirsting to reclaim lost glory. On June 14, before an estimated 9,000 fans at the Capitoline Grounds in Brooklyn, the Atlantics toppled the champions 8–7 in 11 innings on a triple by first baseman Joe Start and a throwing error by Cincinnati first baseman Charlie Gould.[29] Legend has it that the "tenth man" played a role for the victors in the form of a fan who jumped on Cincinnati right fielder Cal McVey's back while he chased Start's drive.[30] With the mantle of invincibility dislodged, the Red Stockings stumbled home with five more losses, never to take the field again.

With Cincinnati deposed, there was no clear-cut champion for the 1870 season. The Red Stockings lost the fewest games, the Philadelphia Athletics "had about the best record" and the Mutuals of New York lost the fewest regular match games.[31] And what about the Atlantics, who had struck the first blow to the Red Stockings? Chicago also laid claim to the title on the basis of victories over Cincinnati and the Mutuals. The Mutuals countered that their game with Chicago was an exhibition.

The distinction between regular match games and exhibition games was to be the bane of the professional ranks for some time, the nature of an exhibition being largely in the eye of the beholder, generally that of the loser. Alex Davidson, secretary of the Mutuals, claimed that New York had won the championship by beating the Atlantics, who had beaten the Red Stockings. At that time, the New Yorkers had challenged all comers to wrest the banner from them. When no one answered the call Davidson, according to his later testimony, then declared that all future games would be exhibitions. He claimed that he reached agreement with Tom Foley, manager of the Chicago club, that the game was not to be counted. Foley, of course, declared that nothing of the sort had taken place, and a Mexican standoff existed.[32]

This was not the first time that the annual championship had been the subject of dispute. In 1868, after splitting their first two contests, the Mutuals and Atlantics failed to meet in a third and deciding championship game. In 1867 the Unions of Morrisania dethroned the Atlantics by winning two of the three games played. The Unions, however, aside from their series with the Atlantics, had a rather ordinary season, losing four series to other clubs. By virtue of defeating the champions, however, they were considered the 1867 pennant winners. Esteemed reporter Henry Chadwick on that occasion had respectfully opined that there should be no champion that season, as a team losing a double series should not be allowed to claim the crown.[33]

The fact that the champion could only be unseated in direct competition encouraged the front-runners to avoid strong teams and play only the weak. It was obvious that a more definitive selection process was needed.

In the wake of the disputed 1870 championship, the fourteenth annual meeting of the National Association was held at the Grand Central Hotel in New York City. The *New York Times* declared the gathering an unqualified fiasco.[34] If so, it was not because of a lack of material for discussion. In addition to a pro/amateur rift, there had been an alarming tendency on the part of the state organizations to usurp the authority of the National Association on matters local in scope. Proxy voting had enabled certain clubs and individuals to accumulate unwarranted power, which was abused for their own benefit. At the 1870 gathering John Wildey of the Mutuals, along with Tom Foley and Jimmy Wood of Chicago, had effectively frozen out the amateurs by the judicious use of proxies.[35]

There was also the embarrassing matter of the missing funds from the Association treasury. Outgoing treasurer Morton Rogers claimed to have turned the money over to his successor, yet it remained unaccounted for. Incoming treasurer Conant was not in attendance to present his side of the story.[36]

The battle line was drawn immediately when Mr. Cantwell of Albany proposed a resolution which stated "that this Association regard the custom of hiring men to play the game of baseball as reprehensible and injurious to the best interests of the game."[37] There was lengthy and spirited discussion on the issue, with neither the professionals nor amateurs giving an inch. Wildey provided the most vociferous (if questionable) defense of professionalism.[38]

Although the resolution was narrowly defeated, the acrimonious debate was the crowning evidence that the nature of the game was changing and amateurs and professionals could no longer coexist in harmony in the same organization. Although there were hundreds of amateur clubs and only a dozen professional organizations, the pros were beginning to exert an influence disproportionate to their numbers. Professionals and amateurs alike left the Grand Central Hotel in an ill mood, each with the feeling that things would be different in 1871.

Chapter 3

Collier's Rooms

Union Square is a Greenwich Village landmark bounded by Broadway and 14th Street. Statues of George Washington and Abraham Lincoln, favorite resting places for the resident pigeons, stand watch at either end of the square. In the immediate area there is a plethora of antique stores — including one specializing in Chinese antiques — and the offices of the *Village Voice*, the organ of the radical left which seems to have gone the way of the love-in. One can discern all the earmarks of modern day America, including McDonald's, Wendy's and, until recently, May's Department Store, which lurked just around the corner on 14th Street. Most of these twentieth-century icons, however, are clothed in ancient garb, buildings that date back to the prior century. Some are restored, while others show the wear and tear of 100 years or more of constant use. From such buildings sprout signs proclaiming the existence of "Nick's Coffee Shop" and "Cheap Jack's" clothing store.[1]

In 1871 the area, although containing many of the same buildings, was much different. One block south of Union Square, situated squarely on the corner of Broadway and 13th was a building housing a saloon known as Collier's Rooms.[2] Like the intersection, the rest of the United States was far different in 1871. The population hovered at 38 million, with slightly fewer than 1 million residents occupying New York. Thirty-seven states had been admitted to the Union, including the reconciled former Confederate states. The country was still healing the wounds of the Civil War, which had ended only six years earlier. While the North was left relatively unscathed, the South remained a festering battlefield. The Ku Klux Klan rode openly and, many thought, heroically, as one of the last vestiges of the Old South. Former president of the Confederacy Jefferson Davis, released from prison, was president of the Carolina Insurance Company.[3] His conqueror, the hero of the Union Army, Ulysses S. Grant, occupied the White House. Nearly apolitical, he said little but kept a tight rein on the public purse. During his eight years in office, Grant reduced the national debt by $600 million.[4]

In New York, where baseball was flourishing, the infamous Tweed ring was beginning to unravel, culminating in an investigation that would send Boss Tweed himself to prison. The most significant historical event of 1871 would occur in Chicago near the end of the year and would have a crucial impact on baseball's first pennant race.

The postwar period was one of tremendous growth. The 1870 census indicated that the center of the country's population was in the vicinity of Cincinnati, Ohio,[5] origin of the famous Red Stockings. The rail system was under constant expansion to link the spreading population. In 1830 there were only 23 miles of track in the entire United States. By 1860 over 30,000 miles of track crisscrossed the country and 10 years later, despite the efforts of William Sherman and J. E. B. Stuart's cavalry, the figure had nearly doubled. Almost 8,000 miles of track were laid in 1871 alone.[6]

On the international scene, Otto von Bismarck of Prussia rode through the streets of Paris in triumph following the conclusion of the brief Franco-Prussian War. The French, wracked by internal divisions and socialist pressure, could only watch in meek submission.

March 17, 1871, was a rainy, stormy day in New York City,[7] as winter refused to yield to spring. Ignoring the inclement weather, the representatives of ten professional baseball teams met in Collier's Rooms to formalize their secession from the obsolete National Association.

The momentous evening had come to pass in a roundabout fashion. Nick Young, secretary of the Washington Olympics, suggested a gathering to formalize a playing schedule for 1871.[8] J. M. Thatcher, secretary of the Chicago club, opined that, since they were all together, the meeting should be used to formulate a code of rules and criteria for the selection of umpires.[9] That was all.

When the delegates convened at 7:30 P.M., it was obvious that the gathering would be of greater import than Young had originally intended. The *New York Clipper* saw the meeting as a parting of the ways between professionals and amateurs and would be satisfied with nothing less. "If the convention fails to organize a regular association on Friday night," declared Henry Chadwick in the *Clipper*, "their meeting will have been ... a failure."[10]

J. W. Schofield of the Troy Haymakers opened the meeting, but quickly stepped aside when James Kerns of the Philadelphia Athletics was elected chairman. Like any self-respecting secessionist, Kerns began by stating that the professionals had been forced to take action by the hostility of the amateurs, who had held their convention the previous evening at the Brooklyn headquarters of the Excelsior club.[11]

His point was much more than mere propaganda. Dr. L. B. Jones of the Excelsiors had sent a letter to the *Clipper* stating in its essence that baseball was a wonderful, all–American game that was being ruined by professionalism.[12] The letter was also signed by the Knickerbocker, Eagle, Gotham, Eureka, and other amateur clubs. The amateurs had then established their own organization which prohibited professionalism. The professionals had truly been backed into a corner. The bridge between the two groups was smoldering and would be fully aflame before the evening was over.

The delegates at Collier's commissioned Schofield, Alex Davidson, and the esteemed Harry Wright to draft plans for a counterblow.[13] They retired to another room and returned shortly with the recommendation that the delegates and their clubs form a National Association of Professional Base Ball Players, an unwieldy moniker that was referred to by abbreviation only or simply as the National Association. The trio also recommended the adoption of a constitution (which was never done) and the same set of playing rules adopted by the joint convention during the previous November.

The recommendations were greeted with great enthusiasm. Nine of the clubs were ready to elect officers. The Mutuals, who were on their own turf, claimed that they had not had time to consult their members and wished to defer the election. The majority prevailed upon them and the Mutuals agreed to allow nominations to proceed. In a heady atmosphere of utmost goodwill, Kerns was elected president, J. S. Evans of Cleveland vice president, Young secretary and Schofield treasurer.

The formalities dispensed with, representatives of the western teams began to make arrangements for their eastern tours. No tours were established for the eastern teams and no second tours were planned from the west. The revolutionary idea of a fixed schedule of games was never discussed and would not be instituted until 1877.[14] The remainder of the schedule would be patched together on a "catch as catch can" basis.

Problems were bound to arise with such a setup. Troy and Chicago, for example, had not scheduled any games with each other due to ill-feeling between the management of the two teams. Troy had signed former Chicago catcher Bill Craver, whom the White Stockings had attempted to expel at the November convention. It was also difficult to convince teams such as the Mutuals and Athletics who hailed from large population centers to visit towns like Rockford, where their share of the gate receipts might fail to justify or even cover travel expenses. If games were not played as required, a forfeit was in order, but it was often difficult to identify the sinning party, as both teams generally pointed fingers in the direction of the other. As a rule of thumb, the visiting team was generally acknowledged to have the obligation to see that the game took place.

One other detail remained undecided. After the acrimony of the 1870 season, a foolproof method of deciding upon a champion was a must. The proposals of Nick Young on this issue were adopted intact. Any club could be considered a contender for the championship by paying a $10 entry fee prior to May 1. Each entrant would play a best three out of five series with every other entrant, with the team winning the most games declared the champion. The entry fees would be used to purchase a streamer which the champion would have the honor of displaying at its home park throughout the following season. On March 17 this concept appeared unassailably clear. By October both reasonable and unreasonable men would differ as to its meaning.

With the business of the meeting concluded, the hosting Mutuals treated the assemblage to champagne, goodwill, and toasts to a lasting organization. The schism was now official. The old National Association was never again viable. The amateurs, thinking they had cut out the cancer sore which would shrivel up and die outside the massive host, had in fact signed their own death warrant. Numbers certainly favored the amateurs. The dozen pro clubs were dwarfed in magnitude by more than 500 teams which competed only for pride and pleasure. Quality prevailed over quantity, and despite occasional revivals of enthusiasm, amateurs would never again hold the preeminent position in baseball circles, passing from fashion as they bowed to the professional tide. The Amateur National Association failed to gain acceptance and expired in 1874. At its last meeting, the treasurer reported a cash balance of $4.05.[15]

Like the first game at Fort Wayne less than two months later, the formation of the new professional league was accompanied by little fanfare. Ten men on a rainy night in a New York City saloon had set the course for professional sports in America, an imperfect beginning to be sure, but a beginning.

Chapter 4

The Game

If America was different in 1871, the game of baseball was also a far cry from that which is played on the astroturf saucers of the 1990s. There were nine men and nine innings, but very few of the other trappings bore much similarity to the modern game. Even the name was different. The words "base" and "ball" were not merged until the twentieth century. During the nineteenth it was known as "Base Ball."

A good starting point to illustrate the differences is the pitcher-batter confrontation. It was more cozy in 1871, since the two antagonists were only 45 feet from each other, rather than the current 60 feet 6 inches. Players of equal height could stare each other directly in the eye, for there was no mound and no pitching rubber. Hurlers were restricted to an underhand delivery, supposedly a pitch (similar to a horseshoe pitch) rather than a throw. This rule was largely disregarded, as all of the top pitchers used an underhand snap throw (like that employed in fast pitch softball) which added speed to their delivery. Speed and changing speeds were the primary weapons of the NA pitcher. The pitcher was restricted to delivering the ball from below the hip, a regulation modified to include below the waist serves in 1877.

The curveball made its appearance gradually. In 1862 14-year-old Arthur Cummings noticed that a thrown clam shell exhibited a pronounced curve and wondered whether he could make a baseball perform similar tricks. By 1864, when he played with his first team, the Carol Park Juniors of Brooklyn, he had succeeded by snapping the ball off his fingertips, a skill he made known to the public three years later.[1] During Cummings's tenure, however, the curve was more of a curiosity and carnival stunt than an effective out pitch. Al Spalding, the premier pitcher of the era, never once spun a curve homeward.[2] His success was due to a fastball, an outstanding change up (or "dew drop" as it was known), sterling control, and about eleven runs a game from his hard-hitting mates.

15

Trick pitches, such as the spitball and emery ball, were not much in evidence, although Bobby Mathews is alleged to have thrown the wet one as early as 1868.[3] There was little need to deface the ball, for nature provided that convenience, as only one ball was used in most games.

No matter what pitches he threw, the hurler needed endurance. Most pitchers started every game and were rarely removed. Even allowing for the reduced strain produced by the underhand throw, it took a strong arm to pitch the 625 innings that Dick McBride of the Athletics hurled in 1870, or the 440 completed by Cincinnati's Asa Brainard.[4]

The term "tools of ignorance," used today to describe the catcher's equipment, was inapplicable in 1871, for there were no tools. There was certainly a case to be made for ignorance. The only protective device worn by the catcher was a mouthpiece employed in the vain hope of keeping one's bridgework intact.[5] Doug Allison and Nat Hicks claimed to have worn gloves as early as 1869,[6] and the Athletics' Fergy Malone wore a pair of light gloves in 1871[7], but no catcher used them on a regular basis. Although by 1875 journalists were urging catchers to wear regular gloves with the fingers cut out, actual usage was rare, which meant that the average backstop's hands were in tatters by mid-season. Some used chemical preparations[8] in an attempt to harden their hands, but to little avail.

The face received even less care than the hand, as the mask was not introduced until 1877. With no one on base, the catcher stood far behind the plate, but with runners on, he had to move up and take his chances. Likewise, with two strikes on the batter, it was prudent to move close to the bat to catch the third strike before it hit the ground. Wild pitches, foul tips, and errant throws all exacted their pound of flesh.

This was not unrelated to pitching strategy. Throwing 80-miles-per-hour fastballs directly to the grandstand served no purpose. A pitcher could deliver his heater only to the extent that his catcher was both willing and able to "face the hottest fire." The curveball presented even more of an adventure. If the ball hit the ground, the reverse spin made it almost impossible to stop. In an era of passed balls and stolen bases galore, one of the main precepts of pitching was to deliver a toss that the beleaguered man behind the bat was able to corral. Control and a change of pace were often preferable to raw speed, which was as dangerous to the catcher as to the opposing batter. The successful (and sensible) catcher helped his pitcher keep the batter off stride with trickery, rather than attempting to blow the ball past the opposition.

In an 1872 game the *Clipper*'s praise of Mathews' strategic ability and "headwork" was contrasted with George Zettlein's lack of these attributes. Troy's veteran 27-year-old right-hander relied upon speed rather than guile to such an extent that the *Clipper* described him as "a splendid army without a shrewd tactician at its head."[9]

A wily catcher might have compensated for Zettlein's lack of strategy. Troy, unfortunately, had Doug Allison behind the bat. Doug's forte was playing close behind the bat and taking a great deal of punishment without complaint. For his efforts, he garnered a greater number of foul tips than his contemporaries. The impatient Allison, however, was not one to guide his pitcher in working the ball up and down or in and out. This talented battery was not necessarily an effective one.

The successful pitcher also needed control, although it was not certain to what degree.[10] Umpires were commissioned to call balls and strikes, but were not required to do so on every pitch and were, in fact, prohibited from making a call on the first pitch until 1875. Starting with the second pitch, the fun began. If the batter swung and missed, it was a strike. A foul ball was not a strike. Base runners had to return to their base after a foul and could be put out if the ball was thrown to the bag before they tagged up. If a foul tip, a foul fly or a one-bounce foul was caught the batter was out. It was in the batter's interest to avoid any pitch thrown in his vicinity, since being hit did not entitle him to first base.

If the pitch was taken, the umpire needed to pull out the rule book. Each batter had the right to call for a high or low pitch upon stepping up to the plate. A high pitch had to be delivered between the waist and shoulders, a low pitch below the waist and more than a foot off the ground. If the pitcher hit the target and the batter declined to offer, the pitch could be considered a fair ball (a strike). Then again, it might not be, depending upon the umpire's discretion. If the pitcher missed the plate, the ball was not fair. This again could be called at the arbiter's discretion. Three pitches that were not fair were to constitute a called ball. Or was it three consecutive pitches that were not fair? This was not made clear to the umpires and was often interpreted according to their pleasure.

A ball that was not fair, however, was not to be confused with an unfair ball, which was something else altogether. An unfair ball was one which bounced in front of the plate, sailed over the batter's head or was otherwise so wildly delivered that it was unhittable. Every one of these was to be called a ball (in some years). Nine balls that were not fair, three unfair balls, or any combination of the above constituted a walk. It was no wonder that the beleaguered umpires often found themselves under attack by the sporting press for failure to call balls and strikes properly![11]

Some umpires still followed the custom of warning a pitcher or batter before calling balls or strikes. Adding to the arbiter's discomfort were the rule changes which came nearly every year in an attempt to improve upon this unwieldy set of standards. After most of these attempts the rule became even more muddled. In 1872 the umpire was expressly commanded to call either a ball or a strike on every pitch after the first. This commission was largely ignored, causing the *Clipper* to publish a statistic entitled "unfair balls not called." The totals for a single game sometimes reached into the 50s.

Despite the cumbersome ball-strike rules and occasional delays for umpires' rulings, games were played quickly. Most were completed in 2 hours or less, and it was not uncommon for a contest to end in less than 90 minutes.

An element of 1871 baseball that was wisely eliminated in future years was the "fair-foul." If a batted ball landed in fair territory it was fair, even if it entered foul territory before passing first or third base. A batter skilled at executing the fair-foul could make considerable hay on the bases as fielders frantically chased the ball into foul ground.

One aspect of the game which has remained unchanged is the distance between the bases, then as now set at 90 feet. What differed was the identity of the pedestrians along the basepaths. If one of the regulars had bad wheels, he could request a substitute runner. Since the limited rosters required that players suit up if no bones were sticking out, this privilege was used on a number of occasions. The substitute runner (who was selected by the opposing captain) stood poised in the blocks waiting for the batter to make contact, at which time he could light out for first base. Overeager courtesy runners had a tendency to jump the gun, breaking as the pitch approached the plate, causing passed balls and yet another thorn in the catcher's side.

The idea of the substitute runner was carried one step farther by the Philadelphia White Stockings during an exhibition game. Pitcher George Zettlein fanned and strolled back toward the bench, oblivious to the fact that the third strike had eluded the catcher. Teammate Denny Mack, ever on the qui vive, leaped off the bench and dashed to first, claiming the base to which his distracted teammate was entitled. A lengthy argument ensued, the end result of which was both Mack and Zettlein assuming seats on the bench.[12]

On at least one occasion, a forgetful batter broke for first base in tandem with his stand-in. Some pitchers, prima donnas even before the advent of the designated hitter, felt they deserved a courtesy runner on all occasions. An 1874 Hartford-Mutual game was delayed while the opposing captains debated whether pitcher Mathews should be allowed relief on the base paths. The Mutuals at first refused to play if the courtesy runner were not allowed, but relented and took the field nonetheless.[13]

In the absence of the designated hitter, the pitcher was expected to carry a fair share of the load on offense. Many pitchers played other positions when not in the box and virtually all were capable of making a respectable showing with the bat. The top 10 winners in league history all batted over .200, with Al Spalding leading the pack at .320, amassing 462 hits in 5 years. The composite average of the 10 pitchers was .243.

Courtesy batters could be employed if a player were temporarily incapacitated and unable to take his turn at the plate. A switch to a less physically demanding position — generally the outfield — was a common method of resting a slightly injured warrior. If a player was totally disabled in the course of a game, he could be replaced by a substitute. Injury was the only reason for which a substitute could enter the game subsequent to the fourth inning, an exception inserted to accommodate late-arriving regulars. Some captains were not above directing an ineffective player to feign injury in order to remove him from the game.[14] If an injured player, having retired from the field, regained his spryness, he could reenter the fray at any time.

Teams rarely had more than ten, or at most eleven, men available for play. When traveling, they brought only nine or ten to minimize expenses. If a player was unable to answer the bell, the captain was generally forced to hire a substitute in whatever city the team happened to be playing. The loss of a pitcher or catcher was particularly unfortunate, since these talents were at a premium. A substitute had to be brought in at another position, with one of the other regulars assigned to the battery.

The dominant theme of the game as it was played in the 1860s and early 1870s was scoring. The prohibition against overhand pitching, the limits placed upon the pitcher by his catcher's tribulations, and the handicap of fielding without gloves added up to an offensive-minded game. Perhaps it was a lack of defense instead, but the end result was a multitude of runs. During the 1850s and 1860s, when the competition was not always even, there were more striking examples of what heavy hitting and sloppy fielding could do to inflate the final score. The average number of runs scored increased consistently from 1857–67, then declined steadily thereafter.[15] The increase could be attributed to the use of a harder ball, while the later decline was due to improved fielding.

On June 8, 1869, the Niagara Club of Buffalo disposed of the Columbias of the same city by the tidy score of 209–10. The Columbias were holding their own (relatively speaking) until the Niagaras broke through for 58 runs in the eighth inning.[16] On May 13, 1870, Chicago slipped past the Bluff City Club of Memphis 157–1.[17] According to the 1891 *Clipper Annual*, teams had passed the century mark in runs scored no fewer than 25 times. The powerful Athletics accomplished the feat nine times in 1865 and 1866 alone.[18] During those years, Philadelphia sometimes played two games in a single day. In the course of one of their more successful double dips, Al Reach scored 34 runs, covering more than 2 miles in his trips around the bases. The Nationals of Jersey City were punch drunk on the last day of September 1865 after the Athletics hammered them for 25 round-trippers in a single contest.[19] Reach, a diminutive 5'6", slugged 37 homers during the 1867 season.[20]

Charley Pabor of Unions of Morrisania and Al Reach of Philadelphia Athletics (1870) (courtesy of Transcendental Graphics).

In July 1866 strongman Lip Pike of the Athletics at five feet eight inches (the first Jewish professional ballplayer) stroked six home runs, five in succession, in a game against the Alerts, a team which proved somewhat less than formidable.[21] His feat was eclipsed the following year, however, when the peerless one, Harry Wright (not known for his hitting) whacked seven against the overmatched Holt club of Newport, Kentucky.[22]

Despite these home run heroics, the concept of the dramatic blast over the outfield wall had not acquired the aura it would in the next century. Henry Chadwick emphasized "scientific batting" and belittled slugging as an attribute of the "old time muffin games." Most bats used by NA performers weighed in at 45–50 ounces[23] and the majority of players were content to put the ball solidly into play. The fences at the Union Grounds were erected primarily to keep out erstwhile freeloaders, as proprietor William Cammeyer was among the first to recognize the profit potential of the new sport. The idea of the fence as a home run target was diminished by the fact that those in the Union Grounds were all more than 500 feet from home plate.[24] Home runs were typically of the inside the park variety, except in Philadelphia, where the fences broke in sharply toward the foul lines.[25] A home run need not clear the fence, of course, and some round trippers were of a tainted variety, perhaps rolling under the barrier or bounding through a hole in the fence. A fair-foul driven into the crowd also provided an excellent opportunity for a home run.

Given the commonplace nature of offense, the club managers naturally placed an emphasis on premier defensive performers. In the modern game the difference between a top fielder and a poor fielder might be a .980 fielding percentage versus one of .950. In 1871 the difference might be one error per game versus three or four. As late as 1876, major league teams averaged six to ten errors per game.[26] Replacing a fumble-fingered or scatter-armed infielder with a sure-handed one could save a team one or two runs per game, since the majority of runs scored were unearned.

The 1875 Boston Red Stockings, the premier fielding team of the NA era, boasted only two players with fielding averages over .900, with defensive wizard George Wright posting an .882 mark.[27] Wright was the only shortstop of the bare-hand era to maintain a lifetime fielding average greater than .900.[28] Averages of less than .800 were common among infielders and catchers, with the highest fielding average by any NA catcher being .848 by Nat Hicks of the Mutuals in 1873.[29]

Many of the players considered to be of star caliber in the NA were known more for their fielding ability than for any prowess with the bat. Bob Ferguson, perhaps the finest third baseman of his time, had a five-year batting average of only .243. His skill in handling popups and line drives, on the other hand, was immortalized in the nickname "Death to Flying Things." His arrogant, domineering personality gave rise to other descriptions which stood neither the test of time nor the limits of decency.

Uniforms had come a long way from the Knickerbockers and their straw boaters. The players were typically clothed in high-collared, baggy, drab gray flannel. Teams were often identified by the color of their stockings, generally the only distinctive marking other than the team name or symbol across the breast. The garb of the Cincinnati Red Stockings, considered "flashy" in its time,[30] appears as dull as all the others in retrospect.

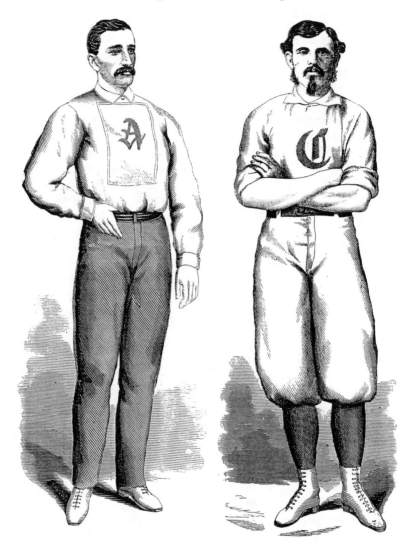

Bob Ferguson of Brooklyn Atlantics and Harry Wright of Cincinnati Red Stockings (1870) (courtesy of Transcendental Graphics).

Only rarely did a team venture beyond the norm, not always with success. The 1872 Lord Baltimores made a strong fashion statement when they took the field for the first time. Baltimore's players looked ridiculous, sporting bright yellow trousers beneath yellow and black striped silk shirts[31] with matching hats. A viscount's coronet on the left breast completed this haberdasher's travesty.[32] After their initial appearance, many eschewed the team's given nickname and referred to them as the Canaries.

In their second game they managed to make an even more garish appearance. Their own uniform stockings were not available, so they wore the neighboring Pastimes' red and black plaid hose, which blended nicely with their yellow and black uniforms.[33] Fortunately, the team played better than they looked, finishing a strong third.

While every team had a manager, he did not fulfill the same role as the field manager in today's game. The NA manager was a business manager who arranged games, signed players, and handled the club's finances. The captain was responsible for the on-field direction of the nine.

As a final insight into the game of 1871, one must consider the hold the game had on the American public. It was truly the only game in town. Some Ivy League collegians were beating each other senseless while chasing an irregularly shaped pig bladder, but no one paid much attention to this combination of rugby, soccer, and mayhem. James Naismith had yet to hang up his first peach basket.

Many of the popular sports of the antebellum era, such as horse racing and billiards, were strictly sedentary. Early Americans, whose rural lifestyle had provided regular and strenuous exercise in the course of satisfying daily wants, had little need for contrived exercise in the form of sport. In the first half of the nineteenth century, with increasing urbanization and the impact of the Industrial Revolution, workers found their limbs growing slack and nerves growing taut from numbing factory or office toil. Vigorous sport provided the opportunity for mental relaxation and improved muscle tone.

Moral justification for indulgence in the physical pleasure of sport arrived at the same time. The staunch Puritanism of the seventeenth century had softened in the eighteenth and virtually disappeared by the nineteenth. Although baseball was forbidden on the Sabbath in most areas, participation in sport itself no longer presented a moral dilemma. Journalists frequently trumpeted the physical and emotional benefits of a brisk game of ball, whether competitive or purely social.

The sports pages of the 1870s provided the reader with a knowledge of the aforementioned horse racing and billiards, along with other sports such as cricket, shooting, pugilism and pedestrianism (track). All of these games had originated in Europe and none had the popular appeal of baseball — the first truly American sport.

Today one can, during the month of October, see the opening kickoff, the first pitch, and the opening tip on the same day. In the 1870s the off-season was truly the off-season, punctuated only by a frigid practice game in mid–November, or possibly a game played on skates in the dead of winter. It seemed that America's appetite for baseball was insatiable.

Chapter 5

The Players

By May 1, nine teams had sent Harry Wright their $10 entry fee and were ready to compete for the first championship pennant. They lined up as follows:

Boston Red Stockings
Chicago White Stockings
Cleveland Forest Citys
Fort Wayne Kekiongas
New York Mutuals
Philadelphia Athletics
Rockford Forest Citys
Troy Haymakers
Washington Olympics

The Brooklyn Eckfords, which had sent delegates to the March meeting, declined to enter the competition. Troy, Rockford, and Fort Wayne are notable by their inclusion, since the nines represented relatively small metropoles compared to New York, Boston, and Philadelphia. The Rockford and Troy combines had a long and successful history, the Rockford annals including the aforementioned upset of the Nationals in 1867. Their size, however, would betray them.

Boston's Red Stockings represented the cream of the former champions from Cincinnati. Harry Wright was born in Sheffield, England, in 1835, the son of renowned cricketer Sam Wright. He arrived in the United States as a youth and began playing cricket with the St. George's Club in 1850.[1] By the late 1850s he had switched to baseball and performed with the Knickerbockers and Gothams in New York. Lured west in 1866 with the promise of a job as a cricket professional, he formed the Cincinnati Red Stockings the same year.

An 1871 Mort. Rogers baseball card of Boston catcher-outfielder Dave Birdsall (courtesy of Transcendental Graphics).

At the end of the 1870 season, during which the Reds had suffered six defeats, the citizens of Cincinnati, spoiled by the undefeated 1869 entry, began to find fault with the captain and his brother, star shortstop George Wright. They accused Harry of greed, mismanagement and controlling the salary structure of the sport. The officers disbanded the team, a fate Harry was suffered to learn through the newspaper.[2]

While the Red Stockings had worn out their welcome in Cincinnati, Boston was starving for a first-class ball club and had been trying to obtain the services of Harry Wright for two years. George Wright went to Boston and met with the organizers of the prospective Boston team, who asked him to send for Harry.[3] The elder Wright's prodigious organizational ability enabled him to form a team quickly. Between the official formation of the club on January 20 and the beginning of the season in April, he brought roughly half of the old Red Stockings to Boston. The remaining prodigals drifted down to Washington, where they joined Nick Young's Olympics, creating a natural rivalry.

Although his sponsors had raised $15,000 for salaries and expenses, Harry at first thought that, deferring to the Puritan atmosphere of Massachusetts, the club should be run on an ostensibly amateur basis.[4] After being convinced otherwise (in part by Al Spalding[5]) Wright arrived in Boston in mid–January, bringing along the Red Stocking name and, more important, brother George, first baseman Charlie Gould, and hard-hitting utilityman Cal McVey. George was 24 years old and had been playing baseball since 1863. A natural athlete, he was a dexterous juggler and later became a pioneer of American golf.[6] He had been the leading hitter in the country in 1867[7] and by 1871 was considered the game's best all-around player.

Harry Wright filled out the team by making a jaunt to Rockford and plucking the crown jewels from the poor Forest Citys—pitcher Spalding and speedy second baseman Ross Barnes—and taking along outfielder Fred Cone for good measure. Harry had not forgotten Cincinnati's 12–5 loss in 1870 at the hands of Spalding and the Rockford nine.

Barnes was a handsome bachelor who paid meticulous attention to his attire.[8] A favorite with the ladies throughout his tenure in Boston,[9] Ross could be a prima donna who occasionally required some harsh words from Captain Wright to put him back on the straight and narrow. Barnes and Gould had a serious personality clash which reached epic proportions in 1872 and apparently played a part in Gould's retirement the following season.[10] Veterans Harry Schafer, the Philadelphia Athletics' leading hitter in 1870,[11] and tough Dave Birdsall of the Morrisania Unions were the other regulars.

Washington's Nick Young signed former Cincinnati second baseman Charley Sweasy to captain the Olympics. He brought in tow the battery of

Asa Brainard, a veteran who had been playing ball since 1857, and cantankerous catcher Doug Allison. Brainard and Allison were quite a pair. The former was a Beau Brummel known as "the Count" who took great pride in his prodigious sideburns and liked to play billiards[12] and keep late hours. His character was less admirable than his pitching ability. While in Cincinnati, Brainard had married the daughter of a family with whom he had boarded and shortly thereafter fathered a child. Within a year he had deserted wife and child, leaving his son to die by the age of seven.[13]

The Count's concentration on baseball was not always what it should have been. George Wright recounted a story of Brainard's fascination with a rabbit that had bounded onto the playing field in the midst of a game. The pitcher fired the ball at the animal as it skittered between second and third base. The ball rolled free in foul territory as two opposing runners crossed the plate, adding another chapter to the Brainard legend.[14]

Brainard was a tribulation to Harry Wright due to his hypochondria, his proclivity for missing practice, and his erratic personal habits. The manager probably added years to his life by allowing the pitcher to become Young's problem. Spalding, a hard-headed, sober young businessman even at 21, was much more in tune with Harry's sense of discipline and gentlemanly conduct. When Brainard was signed by the Middletown Mansfields midway through the 1872 season, Wright commended Middletown manager Ben Douglas on a fine acquisition, but cautioned him to get all agreements with his new pitcher in writing. Harry also advised that a stern admonishment, accompanied by the threat of "no play, no pay" was required from time to time to keep the renegade Brainard in line.[15]

Allison was married and not a noted carouser like his batterymate, but he was moody and rebellious on the field. Young would have his hands full with these two. Brainard sat out one Olympic game due to "personal differences with other team members," a situation that was resolved only through the intervention of the club directors.[16]

Versatile Andy Leonard and balding third baseman Fred Waterman also joined Cincinnati South. Waterman was yet another who was prone to on-field displays of temper, but he had placed second to George Wright among all professional players in batting in 1870.[17] Leonard was an excellent outfielder, a fast man who got a quick jump on fly balls and had, according to Harry Wright, the most accurate outfield arm he had ever seen.[18] Young assembled a talented supporting cast and was ready to challenge the Wright brothers for the banner. Sweasy flamed the rivalry to greater heights by boasting that he could beat the Red Stockings with the amateur Olympics,[19] a remark he would have reason to regret. He was, in fact, of little use to the team all season; he developed a rheumatic illness that forced him to miss much of the season, keeping him on the sideline until August.

To house these newly acquired stars, Washington spared no expense in renovating their grounds at 16th and R streets. A new grandstand, spanning 60 feet behind the backstop, had been erected and the field had been reconditioned and resodded at the substantial cost of $4,000.[20]

In contrast to these ad hoc combinations, the Philadelphia Athletics had been in existence since 1860. During the mid–1860s they, along with the Atlantics, had dominated organized baseball, compiling an admirable 178–11 mark from 1864 through 1868.[21] Many veterans, such as pitcher Dick McBride, second baseman Al Reach, and first baseman Wes Fisler had been with the club for a number of years.[22] McBride was a former cricketer whose long sideburns completely encircled his sharp features. At 26 years of age, he had already played 10 years with the Athletics and, though possessing an explosive temper when riled and a sarcastic wit which did little to endear him to his opponents, was generally a cool performer in the pitcher's box. Reach had operated a successful sporting goods franchise since the 1860s that would later be gobbled up by his rival Spalding. He was a New Yorker who had openly accepted a regular salary since 1862. The slightly built southpaw began his playing career in 1858 and had played for the Athletics since 1865. He was the oldest regular at 31.

Weston Fisler was known as "the Icicle" since he never seemed to perspire, no matter how hot the weather or how intense the pressure. A shy, quiet man, he was a meticulous dresser who later opened a haberdashery shop.[23] At a mere 5′6″ and 137 pounds, he presented a bull's eye rather than a target for his infielders, but he was a strong hitter and a steady fielder. The son of the longtime mayor of Camden, New Jersey, he had played for a number of teams in the Philadelphia area before joining the Athletics in 1866.[24]

Another Camden native, handsome Johnny Radcliff, was the shortstop. They grew them small in Camden in those days. Radcliff could look Fisler dead in the eye, but outweighed him by three pounds. He had been the Athletics catcher for three years before moving to shortstop in 1870.

A heavy hitter and a nightmare for those compiling box scores was center fielder John (Count) Sensenderfer. A speedy baserunner and excellent outfielder who knew how to play the hitters, Sensy had joined the Athletics in 1867. As his nickname would indicate, he was a gentleman who possessed some musical ability as a pianist and singer[25] and was a favorite with the ladies — a quality which stood out in this rough-and-tumble era. He was also a .300 hitter.

The final Athletic veteran was left-handed catcher Fergy Malone, who had been with the team off and on since 1862. Born in Ireland, he had bounced back and forth between Philadelphia and Washington area clubs. A solid batsman, Malone had difficulty throwing and later in his career suffered from arm trouble[26] that caused him to be moved to first base.

With their veterans in the fold, the Philadelphians looked to Chicago to regain two prodigal sons who would complete the puzzle. Outfielder Ned Cuthbert had left the Athletics a year previously for the pecuniary rewards of joining the newly formed Chicago White Stockings. The Athletics wanted him back. So did Chicago. Cuthbert couldn't decide and signed with both teams. On November 22, 1870, he signed with the White Stockings for 1871. According to his later testimony, he signed only on the condition that he could convince his family to move to Chicago. When Mrs. Cuthbert balked, Ned decided that the contract was null and void and signed with the Athletics. His wife's will prevailed and, after much shouting and letter writing by the Chicago management, the agreement with the Athletics stood.[27]

Long Levi Meyerle, at 6'1" and 177 pounds, was a giant by 1871 standards. Awkward and something of a lummox in the field, he was the best pure hitter on the Athletics' team and in 1871 the best in the league. An excellent contact hitter, Meyerle struck out only twice in 55 National League games in 1876.[28] His fielding skills did not match his offensive talent. In 1874, while playing for Chicago, he made six errors at third base in a single game. A 22-year-old with a long, solemn and somewhat homely face, he had played for Philadelphia in 1869 before jumping to Chicago for the 1870 season for a $1,500 salary.[29] Levi returned to Philadelphia to become the Athletics' third baseman for 1871.

The overwhelming number of homegrown products made the Athletics unique among the NA members. They were familiar with each other's style of play and with McBride's pitching, and lacked the all-star nature of the other assemblages.

Fort Wayne's Kekiongas were of the other persuasion. They were a local team, but the locale was Baltimore. Nearly all their players, including star hurler Bobby Mathews, were drawn from the City of Monuments and were veterans of the old Marylands. There was nary a Fort Wayne native on the roster. The team had been hastily assembled, with the final four players added during the month of March.[30]

Cleveland had formed its first team in 1866,[31] added some paid performers in 1869, and had maintained an all-professional team since 1870. They had shown promise that year, but were a mediocre 9–11 against professional teams.[32] Fastballer Al Pratt, who had pitched 248 innings in 1870,[33] was back in 1871. Pratt was known as the "Five-Inning-Wonder," for his hard throwing and elaborate motion made him a softer target as the game wore on. His batterymate remained the peerless James (Deacon) White, a solid 175 pounder who was prematurely balding and sported a walrus-like mustache.[34] Holdover Jim Carlton manned first base, with pool shark Gene Kimball at second. Just before the start of the season, Cleveland signed John Bass of New York to play shortstop beside Ezra Sutton, who covered the

The NA's first batting champion, Levi Meyerle, who batted .492 for the 1871 Philadelphia Athletics (courtesy of Transcendental Graphics).

The 1871 Troy Haymakers: *Back row:* **Dick Flowers, Steve Bellan and Clipper Flynn;** *Front row:* **Steve King, Bill Craver, Mike McGeary, Tom York, John McMullin and Lip Pike (courtesy of Transcendental Graphics).**

hot corner in fine style. Sutton batted cross-handed[35] and thus had little power (although he hit the first two home runs in NA history on May 8[36]) but he was an effective spray hitter who was consistently close to the .300 mark. In left field was the former pitcher of the old Unions of Morrisania, honest, good-natured Charley Pabor, whose temperament was to be sorely tested when he captained the 1875 Brooklyn Atlantics.[37] Arthur Allison, brother of the renowned Cincinnati catcher, was the center fielder, while Elmer White (cousin of James[38]) and Caleb Johnson shared duties in right field.

The Troy Haymakers had likewise been formed in 1866, and had been operated by "Big John" Morrisey, a notoriously corrupt New York politician. In 1869 they had produced the only blemish on the Cincinnati record, a blatantly suspicious tie in which Troy captain Bill Craver had pulled the team off the field over a dispute regarding an insignificant foul tip (see Chapter 8).

The Haymakers chose to stand pat from their 1870 alignment, despite the loss of pitcher Cherokee Fisher. His duties passed to hot-tempered left-hander John McMullin, a hard thrower and capable batsman who was better suited to outfield play. Troy also featured the only Cuban-born player (and only Hispanic) in the NA in scatter-armed third baseman Esteban (Steve) Bellan. The remainder of the team was a very talented crew including

versatile captain Bill Craver — who was tough as nails — and Lipman Pike
of the six home run day in 1866. Mike McGeary, a catcher/shortstop who
excelled at handling foul tips, center fielder Tom York — who enjoyed
several solid years in the majors — and Steve King, the Haymakers' leading
hitter in 1870,[39] rounded out the team.

The New York Mutuals filled out their roster by gnawing on the carcass of the proud old Atlantics, acquiring such stalwarts as captain and
switch-hitting third baseman Bob Ferguson, veteran shortstop Dicky
Pearce, "Old Reliable" first baseman Joe Start, catcher Charlie Mills, and
infielder Charlie Smith. Pearce had been playing regularly with the Atlantics since 1856,[40] and, although he possessed only a mediocre throwing arm,
was the finest shortstop in the game in his prime. He was the first and
perhaps the finest bunter in baseball. Even at 35, he was a heady veteran
with several solid years ahead of him. Smith was also a Brooklyn veteran,
having joined the Atlantics in 1858.[41] Start had a remarkable career, spanning from 1860 through 1886, covering the amateur era, the NA, and the in-
terleague wars of the 1880s. He was a talented left handed hitter with good
power, a fine baserunner and an excellent fielding first baseman, the best
of his era and the first to play the position off the bag.[42]

Rynie Wolters, a native of Schantz, Holland, and a former cricket
bowler, was the pitcher. Wolters, formerly of the Irvingtons of New Jersey,
was erratic and rebellious off the field but — assuming he showed up — was a
cool performer under pressure. He delivered the ball with a sweeping motion that nearly scraped the ground, causing his pitch to rise as it approached
the hitter.[43] Holdovers from the 1870 Mutuals were 20-year-old Dave Eggler, an outstanding fielder and fine hitter, and fiery, strong-armed Johnny
Hatfield, who had set a record by throwing a baseball 132 yards in an 1868
exhibition.[44]

These were the men who took the field for the first major league season.
They reflected the evolution of the game in their makeup. The players were
primarily a middle-class group, as baseball was becoming the common
man's game. The lower class was conspicuously absent.[45] They were all
white, except for Steve Bellan, as the color line was solidly in place. "Colored teams" appeared in towns such as Boston and St. Louis to compete
for their own championship. Patronizing headlines such as "Colored Boys
in the Field"[46] and "Sambo as Ballplayer and Dinah as an Emulator"[47] announced the occurrence of such matches which often took place with
Caucasian opponents. The colored teams generally held their own against
some quality amateur teams composed of whites.

The first known game between Negro teams took place in 1862,[48] the
year before the Emancipation Proclamation. The *New York Times* and
New York Spirit urged the inclusion of Negroes in the old National
Association,[49] but the policy had been set and justified when the organiza-

tion was established in 1857: "If colored clubs were admitted, there would be in all probability some division of feeling; whereas by excluding them, no injury could possibly result to anybody, and the possibility of any rupture being created on political grounds would be avoided."[50]

In 1870 a formal resolution prohibiting colored clubs from joining the NA was presented, discussed at some length and with a degree of animation, then dropped. The press regretted the inconvenience of the unpleasant proposal and rued the fact that the radical papers had taken up the issue "as if some dreadful wrong had been committed."[51] The door was firmly shut in 1884 when Adrian Anson, by then known as "Cap" or "Pop," uttered his famous line, "Get that nigger off the field," in reference to Toledo's Moses Walker.[52] From that date until 1947, major league baseball remained lily-white.

Most of the early professionals were city boys. Roughly 25 percent of those who played in the NA were born in New York City,[53] and many who were born elsewhere received their baseball training in New York. Other urban areas contributed heavily. Philadelphia supplied over 15 percent of the total, while those from Baltimore represented more than 10 percent, for a combined total of more than 50 percent from these 3 cities alone. The cricket influence was reflected in a total of ten players born in England or Ireland while the remainder came from scattered areas, primarily in the Northeast. In the farm country of the Midwest there was rarely the time or the numbers to organize a game. Small-town natives were rare.

Like the game, the players were young. Those who took part in the 1871 season averaged about 24 years of age. Prior to the onset of open professionalism, ball-playing was a precarious way to make a living, and there were few veterans who could afford to take the amateur route. The Athletics had the oldest regulars, averaging more than 26 years, while the 3 teams which brought up the rear of the standings, Cleveland, Fort Wayne and Rockford, had starting lineups averaging between 22 and 23 years of age.

The players were also small by modern standards. Six foot 200-pounders like Adrian Anson were as rare as an errorless game. George Wright, generally considered the premier player of the era, was an unimposing 5'9½" and 150 pounds. Big brother Harry was 7 pounds heavier. Even those who were considered powerful hitters like Boston's Cal McVey (5'9", 170 lbs.) and Troy's Lip Pike (5'8", 158 lbs.) were of modest stature. "Big Jim" Clinton stood 5'8½". Some of the top performers were mighty mites, such as Washington's "Wee Davy" Force (5'4", 130 pounds), Kekiongas hurler Bobby Mathews (5'5½", 145 pounds) and the Mutual's Dicky Pearce, who stood only 5'3½" but weighed in at a muscular 161 pounds. He had an upper body seemingly disproportionate to his lower half, but was a surprisingly agile athlete.

Then, as now, many thought the players were pampered and overpaid. At the end of the 1871 season, Chadwick hoped that fiscal sanity would replace the "preposterous salaries" of the past two years. "Just imagine a ballplayer receiving twenty-five hundred dollars for eight months' service."[54] In January of 1874, the *Clipper* expounded even further,

> In looking at this matter of professional ballplaying in a business point of view, the players lose sight of one or two important facts in regard to their position which are worthy of special attention. They forget, for one thing, that the services for which they are so liberally paid, is one [sic] that hundreds of thousands of people are only too glad to indulge in as relaxation from either mental study or physical labor. They also forget that they are actually paid for doing that which is not only an enjoyable excitement to them, but also a service which in every way works to their physical advantage in giving them sound and healthy bodies. They also forget that for this very service they are receiving a pecuniary return in some instances quadruple that amount which they could earn for ten hours a day of hard toil with the shovel, the pickaxe or the hoe. Under such circumstances, it will not do for professional ballplayers to regard themselves in the light of everyday toilers in the world of industry, as they generally do. The fact is, they may regard their possession of some of these physical attributes which go to make up a skillful ballplayer as the gifts of fortune and their possession of a well-paid field of employment for their particular talents as something to be regarded as an especially fortunate condition of things and one the great majority would be only too glad to enjoy the advantages of at only half the reward the professional ballplayers are now lucky enough to get.[55]

In the context of the time, the point was relevant. In the 1870s those Americans who remained on the farm (an estimated 7 million in 1870) faced a monotonous routine of backbreaking labor rewarded by a subsistence income. Roughly half of those who worked the land claimed ownership of the soil, while the remainder were hired hands. The former were dependent upon the vagaries of weather, pestilence, and human effort for their annual income. The latter generally worked for a fixed income plus room and board. A typical laborer in upstate New York earned $75 in cash for a season which extended from April through November. His workday lasted fourteen to fifteen hours in season but, like most in his line of work, he was fortunate to have any income at all during the winter months.[56]

Beginning just prior to the Civil War, the population migrated to the cities in increasing numbers, drawn by job opportunities in the burgeoning industries and trades. Since most ballplayers grew up in urban areas, the likely alternative to a professional career was employment in the city. For the urban professionals, whose ranks were limited, life was relatively pleasant and remunerative. For the overwhelming majority who toiled in blue collar anonymity, existence was abject misery. The craftsmen and artisans who had painstakingly produced manufactured goods for generations were becoming obsolete, as emerging mass-production techniques resulted in an end product at a fraction of the previous cost. As the unit cost declined, the quality of the employees' worklife deteriorated significantly. Factories were normally uncomfortable, crowded and dangerous. Workers, especially inattentive youngsters, frequently lost digits or limbs to the whirring machinery. The unrelenting pace controlled the speed of the individual's activity and left one drained and exhausted by the end of the day. This was perhaps fortunate, for workers had little money to pay for entertainment in their "leisure" time. Wages for unskilled laborers were set at subsistence levels. A Rhode Island cotton mill paid its workers $4 to $5 for a 69-hour week. Board (valued at $1.25 per week) was an added compensation at a New Haven mill which paid $2.30 for a 66-hour week. Some laborers were paid on a piecework basis that, despite their utmost efforts, generally yielded even less.[57]

Compared to these miserable pittances, the ballplayers' salary, which, for the average regular, approximated $1,000 (for a period of employment beginning in mid–March and ending in mid–November) was a royal reward indeed. Further contrasting the plight of the average factory worker and the athlete was the latter's pleasant working conditions, short hours, and the opportunity to stay in fine hotels and travel from city to city in a style that, if not luxurious, far exceeded the opportunity afforded the aforementioned Rhode Island mill workers.

National Association teams came in two varieties. The first type, which was far more stable, was the stock club, whose capital was raised through the issuance of common stock and contributions from the club members. The capital, plus revenue generated during the season, was used to cover operating expenses, including regular salaries to the players. The second type of ownership, which was more suspect, was the NA's version of socialism, the co-op club. Performers for these organizations received no salary, but relied on a share of the gate receipts for their compensation. Not surprisingly, the teams with poorer attendance prospects chose to take this route, resulting in marginal income for the players involved. Consequently, the co-op teams had a more difficult time attracting the top performers, since there was no promise of a steady income. Generally, they were reduced to picking up the pieces after the stock clubs had filled their rosters. The Kekionga and Rockford nines were the only ones among the 1871 entries in the co-op category, although the Mutuals utilized a hybrid form of salaries and participation in gate proceeds.[58]

A significant problem which arose prior to the start of the season concerned gate receipts, the phenomenon which had grown in importance with the advent of the professionals. The year 1858 marked the first time an admission fee had been charged to view a baseball game, for the Brooklyn-

New York all star series at the Fashion Race Course.[59] When the Union Grounds opened in 1862, William Cammeyer charged a 10 cent admission, which he used for upkeep of the field.[60] At that time all admission fees were retained by the respective proprietors of the grounds. Only later was the gate money split with the competing teams.

The controversy threatened to shelve the NA's first season before it began. The first concern was the admission price. A 50 cent fee was customary in the West, while 25 cents was the going rate in the East, where the competition was more acute.[61] Many, including Harry Wright, argued convincingly that, even at 50 cents, baseball provided much cheaper entertainment than, for example, the theater, where the cost ranged from 75 cents to $1.50.[62] For five years Wright championed the higher fee. He demanded a larger percentage of the gate receipts if a 25 cent entry price was in effect. He cajoled, persuaded and insisted that the teams would profit by raising the price. He cogently observed that a good game was well worth 50 cents and a poor one not worth 25. The answer was to increase the quality of play and assure the integrity of the game, not to lower the price. However, the teams were unable to achieve a consensus. Despite continuing attempts throughout the years to standardize the tariff, the decision was left to the individual teams, and varied by club. Fans were sometimes shocked to arrive at the park to find an unannounced doubling of the usual admission price.

A second question at issue was the division of gate receipts between the home and visiting clubs. The Mutuals and Athletics felt that the home club should keep all receipts.[63] Naturally, this was in their best interests, since games in New York and Philadelphia were likely to draw larger crowds than games in say, Rockford or Fort Wayne. Boston and Washington disagreed and wanted the gate receipts divided between the home and visiting clubs. Chicago sided with the latter contingent. Boston felt so strongly about the matter that they refused to play the Mutuals until the dispute was resolved.[64] The cancellation of the games involving all five teams would have ended the new league's first season then and there.

The primary danger of having the home team retain all receipts was that there was no financial incentive for the visiting team to make the journey to play the final games of the series. The Philadelphia Pearls, in later years, paid for their insistence on the "home team take all" concept when the Mutuals, forever unreliable in keeping engagements, failed to go to Philadelphia after having garnered the receipts from the games played in New York.[65]

The matter was further complicated in Brooklyn since the proprietors

Opposite: **Stock certificate of Ivers Adams, first president of the Boston Red Stockings (courtesy of Transcendental Graphics).**

of the Union and Capitoline Grounds demanded one-third of the take from any contest played on their field. This left a kitty of only two-thirds to be divided among the competing teams. Other teams paid a fixed rent for their playing fields and would have been dividing a higher sum with the visitors, causing inequities in the distribution.

The Boston-Mutual impasse was not resolved until mid–June, when Wright finally persuaded Alex Davidson, secretary of the Mutuals, to accept (at least on an experimental basis) a division of receipts.[66] The entire embroglio was representative of the interteam bickering which was to plague the league throughout its tortured existence. National Association President Kerns was also president of the Athletics, which scarcely made him a disinterested observer. In fact, it placed him in a position where he could not be given the power necessary to run the league's affairs effectively. Each club, unbroken of the independent spirit which characterized its previous activities, was ill-suited to work in harmony with the others. None of the committees so painstakingly assembled in Collier's Rooms had the bite or the inclination to crack down on the powerful teams. Any two teams could seemingly agree to break the rules, amend the rules, or suspend the rules to suit their fancy.

In May 1871, however, the fatal flaw was not yet apparent. The teams were formed, the $10 entry fees had been paid, and the stage was set to *Play ball*!

Chapter 6

Play Ball

There was no Southern spring training for the majority of the 1871 entries. With the exception of the Mutuals' and White Stockings' tour of the South[1] in the early spring, the captains kept their troops at home and waited for the thaw before bringing the players out to loosen the winter kinks. The Red Stockings were all in Boston by March 31, preparing for the season by working out two to four hours each day in the Tremont Gymnasium.[2] Gym work was a staple for most teams during the NA's tenure, and was not always as tame as one might think. In 1873 Tom York of Baltimore toppled from a trapeze and narrowly avoided serious injury.[3] Handball was another training tool. Much of Bob Ferguson's fielding prowess was attributed to his training in that sport.[4]

Spring was also a time for optimism and an attempt to impose discipline upon the traditionally iconoclastic athletes. While waiting for good weather, each manager vowed that his team would be more disciplined than it had been in the previous year. In 1872 all members of the Middletown Mansfields signed an abstinence pledge.[5] Jimmy Wood, managing the Troy Haymakers, claimed to have recognized the error of his lax ways in Chicago the previous season. He warned his charges that 1872 would be different.[6]

Cleveland went beyond empty talk. The board of directors laid down a stiff set of rules for their athletes. All players were required to practice on off-days (Sundays excepted), with any absentees reported to the president. The only excuses accepted were for medical reasons, with a written note from Dr. M. B. Prentice (a director of the club) required under such circumstances. Much to the players' dismay, intoxication did not constitute a valid excuse for missing a practice or a game. In fact, alcohol and late hours were verboten, although setting that rule was much easier than enforcing it. The penalty for inebriation was suspension or expulsion, accompanied by a fine. The acceptance of bribes was also, naturally, proscribed. Other actions which would bring immediate discipline were using improper language (referring to cursing rather than dangling participles) or (much to the relief of the beleaguered volunteer arbiters) disputing an umpire's call without authorization. As a more concrete contribution toward clean living, the players were required to launder their own uniforms.[7]

Other teams followed Cleveland's lead. The Mutuals had expected to do better than their .500 record in 1871 and felt that a lack of discipline had been the main cause of their failure to do so. Management stated that "there will be no more soft things and easy times for the hired men of the professional organizations, at least to the extent of loafing about doing nothing and being well paid for it when there is no match playing going on."[8] Practices were scheduled for all off-days. The Mutuals also instituted rules of conduct similar to those of Cleveland.

The following year Baltimore carried the mania for rules to the extreme. The managers instituted fines ranging from $5 to $50 for offenses such as intoxication, disobeying the captain's orders, and lesser transgressions. The latter personage was given all-encompassing power over his troops, who were required to ask permission to leave the hotel on days the team was traveling. Like their counterparts from Cleveland, the Canaries were responsible for their own uniforms.[9]

Chicago had a natural disadvantage in preseason preparation; the northern snow generally prevented them from taking the field for their first practice game before mid–April. In 1871 they visited New Orleans, but in later years ventured no farther south than St. Louis. A series of practice games against the players from the latter city in 1874 were quite competitive and served notice that baseball in St. Louis would shortly be heard from again.

The Mutuals, always lackadaisical, were usually one of the last teams to start spring practice, slogging through a few exhibition games at the muddy Union Grounds before starting the regular season. Although a fine park in most respects, Union was built on swampland below street level and flooded easily.[10] Adding to the difficulty was the fact that it was used as a skating rink during the winter, as was the neighboring Capitoline Grounds. Proprietor Cammeyer, ever mindful of his investment in the property, refused to allow teams to play when he felt the wet field might be further damaged.[11]

Most 1871 teams went directly to the competitive (loosely speaking) game with a minimum of drills and practices. During the month of April one could count on a number of pathetic mismatches as the professional teams took the field against ragged amateurs or pickup teams brought together merely for the occasion. Chicago took New Orleans by storm, sweeping 6 games while outscoring their opponents by a whopping 142–36 margin. The Mutuals, only 6 years after Lee's surrender, gave the Southerners another drubbing, humiliating Savannah 29–3 and again 23–13.

Up north, Harry Wright's maiden Red Stockings were pounding Lowell 40–1 as Harry himself rapped out 7 hits. The Athletics ran roughshod over the local amateurs, then declined to play for two weeks due to the illness of catcher Fergy Malone.[12] Even the lowly Kekiongas ran up a 20–2 victory over a ragtag collection of amateurs.

Finally, the games began in earnest, initiated by the Fort Wayne–Cleveland opener. Chicago (if one will pardon the expression) started the season like a house on fire (read on). They had a handsome new field named Lake Front Park (which replaced old Dexter Park) on Michigan Avenue with seating for 6,000.[13] In addition to the new ballpark, the White Stockings gathered a salaried stable of imported talent. Most of the players were from the New York City area and many were holdovers from 1870. The *New York Times* referred to "the Chicago branch of the old Eckford club, known as the White Stockings."[14]

Pitcher George "the Charmer" Zettlein was a former member of the famous Atlantic teams of the 1860s. The acquisition of Zettlein filled a gaping hole, as the heavy-hitting 1870 group had been reduced to using infielders Meyerle and Ed Pinkham in the pitcher's box. Zettlein, was tireless, good-humored, ponderous, and slow both afoot and mentally. He had acquired his nickname not from any pitching sleight of hand or any success with the ladies, but from a dancer in Hooley's Minstrels named, coincidentally, George the Charmer.[15] In fact, he was not a pitching strategist of the first degree, and was known for heaving the ball plateward with no idea of location or changing speeds. His dubious claim to fame was an ability to take a physical beating from batted balls without noticeable effect, perhaps the cause of his lack of strategic ability. Tales abounded of Zettlein being cracked on the forehead, neck, and other bodily parts, only to bounce up unperturbed and continue pitching. At the Union Grounds in Brooklyn a line drive ricocheted 60 feet after skulling the indomitable hurler, yet, after a drink of water and a pat on the back, Zettlein was ready to go once more.[16] Photographs of Zettlein hint that the pitcher might have been able to flag down some hot liners with his ears, which protruded noticeably from that resilient forehead.

Captain Jimmy Wood, a fine player but not the strongest disciplinarian, had assembled a team of hired guns to support Zettlein, including fellow New Yorkers Charley Hodes, Ed Pinkham, Joe Simmons, Fred Treacey, and Ed Duffy at catcher, third base, right field, left field and shortstop, respectively. Duffy was a questionable character, having been expelled by the old NA in 1865 for accepting a bribe to throw a game.[17] Stocky first baseman Bub McAtee and curly haired utilityman Mart King arrived from Troy to complete the New York connection. While stocking his team with easterners, Wood had ignored such promising westerners as Spalding and Barnes.

During the 1870 and 1871 seasons, Chicago had a reputation as a group of diverse talents which never seemed to jell as a team. They were chronically contrasted with the Athletics as an example of the futility of assembling an imported team which had no sense of local pride, only a worship of the almighty dollar. They also had a reputation as a team of undisciplined sluggers with no talent for strategy—a dubious call since only the Kekiongas had a lower team batting average among the 1871 entries. However, the White Stockings did their new park justice by winning their first 7 league games and their first 29 overall.[18] Following a loss to the Mutuals in New York in early June, Chicago went into a mild slump while the league lead shifted from one team to another, as none seemed capable of holding down the top spot.

Boston, which had expected to be a top contender for the pennant, was dogged by injuries and unable to poke its collective nose much above the .500 mark. The most serious loss was shortstop George Wright, who suffered a leg injury in Troy when he collided with left fielder Fred Cone while chasing a pop fly.[19] The injury was not believed to be serious initially, but it was the same leg George had seriously injured in 1870 and was slow to heal, causing him to miss 16 (half of his team's total) and would hamper him for the rest of his career. With Wright hors de combat, second baseman Ross Barnes moved to shortstop, while Sam Jackson, a native of England and a veteran of the New York amateur scene, moved in at second base. Jackson finished the season with an average of less than .200, a precipitous decline from George's .409 mark.

Later in the campaign, other regulars fell victim to varying degrees of disability. Cal McVey was injured in a mid-season game at Rockford. Fred Cone and Dave Birdsall limped around with minor nicks. Following a July loss to Troy, Harry Wright decided to cancel some games and take time off to heal the wounded. Boston did not play another league game until August 3, nearly three weeks later. This type of behavior was common among NA entries, since no formal schedule was drawn up prior to the season. An injury to a key player was sufficient reason to refrain from fulfilling previously scheduled engagements or to refuse to make new engagements. The Athletics and Haymakers had previously canceled games due to injuries to Malone and Craver, respectively.[20]

The offensive surprise of the early season was the Troy Haymakers, who had delivered an early one to heavily favored Boston by a 29–14 score. Following that triumph, Troy journeyed to Brooklyn, where they stunned the New York Mutuals 25–10. The following day, upon their return to Troy, they tallied 20 runs against Rockford en route to a 20–15 victory. The Haymakers saved their best offensive display of the season for back to back games on June 27 and July 3. On June 27 they pounded the Athletics for 33 runs and lost, as Philadelphia responded with 49 tallies of their own.

Remarkably, both pitchers hurled complete games and absorbed the onslaught unaided. The contest took four tedious hours to complete and the produced the interesting line score shown below:

Troy	1	2	3	10	4	4	2	4	3–33
Athletics	2	4	3	7	9	8	3	5	8–49

On July 3 the Mutuals journeyed upstate and suffered an attack from the Haymaker bats that produced a 37–16 Troy victory. Mutuals pitcher Rynie Wolters was pounded for 33 hits, including 6 each by shortstop Dick Flowers and left fielder Steve King. No one in the lineup had fewer than two safeties.

Although Troy had many fine veteran ballplayers, there was more than talent behind the tremendous offensive orgies taking place wherever the Haymakers touched down. In the NA there was no standard ball used for the game. Six manufacturers operated in New York alone, any one of which could provide a game ball as long as it met the basic criteria of size.[21] The *New York Times* reported that there were 16 different varieties of baseballs in use, from those used in the NA to those used by children.[22] Not even the color of the ball was standard, with each team free to employ the shade of its choice. At the 1873 convention it was agreed that the Ryan make would be the official league ball for all championship contests. Inadvertently, the provision was excluded from the revised code of rules, and the Mahn, Van Horn, and other balls continued to be employed.[23] While the size of the ball was the same, the quality of the rubber in the Van Horn ball differed significantly from that in the Ryan issue.[24]

Under the rules the game ball was furnished by the visiting team. There were minimum requirements for the dimensions of the ball, but unless the umpire carried a scale and tape measure, there was no way of determining whether a particular ball would pass muster. One ball generally lasted the entire game and, giving evidence to the scarcity of equipment, the winning team got to keep the ball. Foul balls were retrieved from spectators, fished from water, or otherwise rescued and put back into play. The rules committee felt it necessary to limit the amount of time spent looking for a lost ball to five minutes.[25]

Prior to the Haymakers' July 3 game with the Mutuals, captains Craver and Ferguson had an animated discussion over the issue of the game ball. Craver proposed using the Van Horn "dead ball," which was anything but. Ferguson objected and produced a ball of his own choosing. Craver insisted on using the Van Horn model. Each dropped the sphere of his choosing from the same height and each rebounded to the same level. Craver refused to budge, despite the fact that the visitors ostensibly had the choice of ball.[26] The Mutuals, bullied into playing with a ball to which they were not accustomed, had grave difficulty with their fielding. Not only did the elasticized ball produce more and longer base hits, it came off the bat at such frightening speed that the bare-handed fielders were often forced to think of self-defense first and making the play second. Normally sure-handed center fielder Dave Eggler dropped several fly balls.

After the game, even though the Haymakers had won the right to the game ball, Ferguson asked to take it with him as evidence. Craver indignantly refused, but agreed to allow the ball to be dissected and examined. After the sphere had been carved up, Ferguson examined the shreds and realized the futility of it all, since there was nothing with which to compare it. Compounding his distress was the fact that he had now destroyed the evidence and was left with a pile of rubber and yarn. Returning to New York in a sulk, the Mutuals experimented by dropping a Ryan and a Van Horn ball from a table. The Van Horn ball rebounded twice as high. Ferguson had proven his point, but far too late and to no avail.[27]

The Kekiongas were at the center of two controversies regarding the game ball. The first was similar to the incident at Troy. On July 7 in a game at Washington against the Olympics, the Kekiongas supplied the ball, which ricocheted crazily all over the field and resulted in a sloppy 32–12 victory by the Olympics. The capacity of the recently installed 27 by 5 feet scoreboard[28] was strained when Washington ran up 18 tallies in the sixth inning. The lively ball resulted in a long day for the Fort Wayne backstops. After six innings of facing Bobby Mathews's hard stuff, Billy Lennon's hands were beyond salvation. He switched positions with shortstop Wally Goldsmith, who doubted the wisdom of the move when Mathews' first pitch caromed off his thumb. He chased it to the backstop, grimacing with pain. Six passed balls later, Goldsmith, to his immense relief, called it a day.[29]

The second incident was a bit more difficult to understand. The team took the field at Troy on June 16 and, perhaps forewarned of the Haymakers' fondness for the lively ball, supplied a ball of their own. According to some witnesses, it was of dubious quality, had no regulation markings on it, bearing only the stamp "White Stockings."[30] By the seventh inning the Kekiongas had taken a 6–3 lead and the flimsy ball had taken a beating. In that inning it was ripped open. Captain Craver of Troy asked umpire Ed Tighe to put a new ball in play and Tighe agreed. The rules allowed for replacement of a damaged ball, but only at the end of an inning, so that neither team would enjoy an advantage. Craver conveniently had a Ryan "dead ball" handy. The Kekiongas would have no part of it. Captain Lennon insisted that the old ball had gotten them this far and should be kept in play. Craver produced a number of balls and offered Lennon his choice. Fort Wayne remained adamant. They would leave the field unless the old ball was used. Lip Pike stood at home plate for five minutes while Tighe called for the Kekiongas to return to the field. Finally, he declared the game forfeited and it went into the books as a 9–0 Haymaker victory. Lennon, in desperation, appealed to the crowd for their opinion. He got no sympathy from the Troy partisans, and took his case to the Judiciary Committee, where he fared no better.

Rockford had had the guts of its team ripped out by Harry Wright's raid which netted him Spalding and Barnes, the two best players from a strong 1870 combination. Manager Hiram Waldo, a local grocer, responded by going to Marshalltown, Iowa, to sign outfielder/shortstop Sam (Pony) Sager. Sager told Waldo of a young, talented teammate named Adrian Anson who might be able to help the Forest Citys.[31] Anson was a Notre Dame dropout who was a bit rough around the edges, but he was an imposing 6 footer who would eventually fill out to a sturdy 227 pounds. Anson, his father Henry, and brother Sturgis had played on the 1870 Marshalltown team which had put up difficult struggles against Rockford, although losing to them twice.[32] Sager convinced Waldo to offer the 20-year-old youngster a contract for $66 per month which Anson, after some hesitation, agreed to accept. His foremost desire had been to play for Chicago, but manager Tom Foley was not interested, preferring to solicit players with more experience.[33] Spalding was replaced, after an unsuccessful courtship of Zettlein and Mathews,[34] with fireballer Cherokee Fisher of the Troy Haymakers. Fisher was a solid hurler when sober and a good-all-around player. Rockford retained 33-year-old veteran second sacker Bob Addy and re-signed renegade backstop Scott Hastings, who had been playing in New Orleans with the Lone Stars. This move was to cost them dearly.

Rockford had two claims to fame. One was that they rode from town to town in sleeper cars, "two to a berth" as Anson pointed out proudly,[35] rather than in the cheaper day coaches preferred by most of the team managers. The second unique claim was having a home park that was most unusual in its configuration and, in the words of Philip Lowry, "the strangest in major league history."[36] They played their home games at the Agricultural Society Fair Grounds, with the agricultural aspect accentuated by a number of trees behind home plate, in the outfield, and just beyond the foul lines. The terrain was somewhat rolling, with third base on a rise and home plate in a valley. After rounding third, it was literally downhill all the way. The home field advantage did not always work in Rockford's favor. In a mid–July game against Philadelphia, Rockford's Gat Stires powered a long drive to center field that would have been a home run had it not struck a tree. Count Sensenderfer alertly played the carom and held the astonished Stires to a triple.[37]

On June 5 the Forest Citys arrived in Philadelphia to do battle with the veteran Athletics. Knowing that Rockford had stumbled through their tour, Philadelphia was overconfident. By the time they buckled down to business, the Athletics were trailing 11–5 in the ninth inning. They staged a furious five-run rally, but were unable to push across the tying run, and went down to a shocking 11–10 defeat, one of the most surprising upsets of the early season.

The victory was tainted however, as were all of the Rockford successes. It was all due to veteran catcher Scott Hastings. Hastings, born during the Mexican War and named after its greatest hero, Winfield Scott, had journeyed south after the close of the 1870 Rockford season. He caught on with the Lone Star nine of New Orleans and made some extra money playing with them during the winter. On April 16 he was in the Lone Star lineup that faced the White Stockings on their preseason Southern tour. That was his last game for the Lone Stars. He next played for Rockford on May 6 in their opening loss to Cleveland.

In an effort to end wholesale raiding of players while the season was in progress, the NA rules prohibited a member of any club from playing with another club for 60 days. The period from April 16 to May 6 fell clearly short of the 60-day requirement. On May 23 the Kekiongas played their game with the Forest Citys under protest, due to Hastings's presence behind the bat.[38] The Olympics refused to play a championship game for the same reason, consenting only to an exhibition.[39] Despite the fact that Hastings' eligibility was questioned in print[40] and by opposing teams, Rockford Manager Hiram Waldo continued to play him. When the season had ended, Hastings had participated in 25 of the team's 27 games.

The matter of Hastings' eligibility came before the Judiciary Committee on November 3, when the Athletics protested games of June 5 and June 15. Rockford used the argument that, since Hastings had been a member of the Rockford team in 1870, his contract with the Lone Stars was invalid and he was thus never a member of that team. They claimed that the Lone Stars should forfeit their games. This was of little concern to the committee, since the New Orleans club was not a member of the NA. Failing in this argument, the Forest Citys then claimed that they did not forfeit or remove Hastings when the protest was initially made because of the effect an admitted forfeit would have had on attendance at future games. The other clubs were unimpressed. Rockford had never blown the doors off attendancewise, Hastings or no Hastings, forfeits or no forfeits. F. H. Mason of Cleveland moved that Rockford should forfeit all of the games in which Hastings had played illegally. The motion was carried, cleansing the record of four Rockford victories prior to June 16. These included the two victories over the Athletics.[41]

The Olympics also played the season with a cloud over their collective head. Washington's albatross was center fielder George Hall. In a spring organizational meeting, Hall had been elected captain of the Brooklyn Atlantics (according to his claim) in absentia.[42] When others testified that Hall had indeed been present when elected, he countered with the allegation that the meeting was not a legal gathering since the required notice had not been given.[43] Whatever the circumstances of his election, he signed with Washington before playing a game with the Atlantics. It was claimed before the Judiciary Committee that he was a member of the Brooklyn club and therefore ineligible to play with any other team. The case was heard at the November 3 meeting. It was flimsy.

Hall had last played for the Atlantics in the 1870 season, far more than 60 days before his first appearance with the Olympics. He took part in a match in late April as part of a pickup nine, which was outside the scope of the 60 day rule. Since he never played for the Atlantics in 1871 and received not a penny in salary, it is difficult to fault his appearance with the Olympics. The rule covered playing only, not officeholding. The Judiciary Committee agreed with this logic, and declared that all Washington games would count in the standings.[44]

The fleet outfielder seemed an exemplary player. Although accounts written well after the fact refer to Hall's always suspect character, there is no reference to such a stain in contemporary reports. On September 30, 1871, in a game against the Athletics, darkness began to fall as Hall's Olympics faced a slim deficit. Captain Sweasy intentionally dropped an easy popup, delaying the game so that the score would revert to the previous inning, resulting in a Washington victory. George Heubel of the Athletics followed Sweasy's error with a long blast to center field. Hall, "disdaining to win other than honorably" according to the *Clipper*, lit out after the ball and made an outstanding running catch. He thus retired the side and incurred the enmity of his teammates as the Athletics prevailed 22–20.[45]

In 1874 Hall played for Harry Wright, which would never have occurred if his character were suspect in any way. That year the *Boston Advertiser* claimed that he "play[ed] ball with all his heart."[46] The following year, however, while playing with the Athletics, the slick-fielding outfielder discovered betting pools, fell in with an unsavory crowd, and began to acquire a reputation for consorting with known gamblers.[47] Two years later he was expelled from pro ball along with three of his Louisville teammates for throwing games, the first such suspension in major league history.

Chapter 7

The First Pennant Race

By July, the NA was about to lose its first team. T. J. Donnelly and Ed Mincher of the Kekiongas had convinced management to give them advances on their salaries and then jumped the team, leaving the Keks short two players and long two IOUs. Indignantly, the team expelled the deserters, an impotent gesture at best. The *Clipper* duly warned all other teams to refrain from signing either player,[1] apparently not a great temptation, since Mincher had batted .222 and Donnelly an even .200. Indiscretions were quickly forgotten in the NA, however, and Mincher surfaced the following year with the Washington Nationals, the same team with which Donnelly was to appear in 1873.

The Kekiongas replaced the two prodigals and continued on with their schedule, only to face another setback. Captain Billy Lennon began hitting the bottle with greater regularity than he was hitting the baseball (.229). During some games in which Lennon was reported to be ill, one suspects that the words "hung over" might have been a more accurate description. As far back as June 23, during a contest against the nonleague Brooklyn Atlantics, he had deserted the team in mid-game. The following day, at the team's hotel, he "violated all rules of decency."[2]

Lennon was accused of public drunkenness, refusing to obey the orders of the board of directors and refusing to practice.[3] All in all, it was not the type of example to be set by the team captain, falling far short of the ideals exemplified by the estimable Harry Wright. Lennon's atrocious behavior continued, until he abruptly left the team on July 21. True to its earlier policy, the directors gave Lennon his pink slip. For good measure, they also expelled his drinking buddy, Frank Selman, on the same charges. Lennon vehemently denied the accusation, to no avail. Like Donnelly and Mincher, both men returned to their native Baltimore-Washington area, where they would resurface in subsequent years with local clubs.

Management procured Harry Deane, a former Cincinnati Red Stockings reserve, to replace Lennon as captain and restore some prestige to the position.[4] They signed 20-year-old Joe Quinn to take Lennon's place behind the bat. Despite the reinforcements, there was a question regarding the team's ability to legitimately continue its season. The eligibility of some of the newcomers was called into question, since they did not meet the 60-day abstinence requirement.[5] The shortcomings of the rule were clear, as it was quite difficult to sign any player in mid-season who had been unemployed for two months. All hope of carrying on faded when Tom Carey and Bobby Mathews left the team at the end of August. They too were expelled for breaking their contracts. The common wisdom, however, was that it was the management of the Kekiongas which had breached the players' contracts by failing to pay them.[6]

Mathews and several of his teammates returned to their native Baltimore to finish the season with the semipro Pastimes, who played numerous exhibition games against the NA entries. Fort Wayne management continued to put up a brave front, despite the defection of nearly all of their players. They claimed to have raised $12,000 to support a team in 1872, a team consisting of players to be recruited in the East by Deane during the month of October.[7] Deane denied that he was about to do any such thing. He himself had yet to sign a contract, and he had no intention of enlisting recruits for an 1872 Fort Wayne entry.[8]

At the end of the season it was determined that the unplayed Fort Wayne games were to be forfeited. The Eckfords replaced the Kekiongas on August 29, but with the understanding that their games wouldn't count in the official standings.[9] The team that had inaugurated organized baseball's first season with their classic 2–0 victory ended their season and existence with a 7–21 record. Their decline was due to the lack of teamwork springing from the patchwork nature of the team and to an anemic offensive attack. There were only four shutouts pitched during the 1871 season, and all involved Fort Wayne. After Mathews's gem in the opener, the Kekiongas were the victim in the other three games. First baseman Jim Foran led the team with a lusty .344 average, but there was a precipitous drop to Mathews's .281 and an even greater plunge to Tom Carey's .235. Overall, the team posted a .235 average and scored less than five runs a game in that freewheeling era where double digit scores were commonplace.

Rockford, for all intents and purposes, was also out of the race. Their chances were slim to begin with, and were dimmed with the prospect of having to forfeit four early wins. Pitcher Cherokee Fisher could fire the ball with the best of them, but he did not have Spalding's control, strategic ability, or offensive support. The raw-boned youngster Adrian Anson had indeed, as Sam Sager had predicted, proven a valuable addition to the Forest Citys. He played third base, second base, catcher, and the outfield and batted a team-leading .352. There was no one else close among the regulars. Gat Stires had the next highest average at .271. Scott Hastings, whose ineligibility

The 1871 Rockford Forest Citys. This was the rookie season of future Hall of Famer Adrian (Cap) Anson (courtesy of Transcendental Graphics).

had cost Rockford their victories, hit an unimposing .233. Hastings went on to have a solid major league career, but it was Anson who was to prove the gem, winding up his career in 1897 with more than 3,000 hits and an eventual place in the Hall of Fame in 1939. His hit total is remarkable in light of the small number of games that were played in the early years of his career. Despite playing in virtually every contest, he averaged only 49 games per season in his first 5 years and didn't play in more than 100 games until his 14th year. Anson began his climb to the 3,000 hit plateau by maintaining a pace of nearly 2 hits per game from 1871 to 1875. In the 245 games of those years Anson amassed his first 430 hits. Had he played in the era of 154 or 162 game seasons, he would undoubtedly have surpassed Ty Cobb and Pete Rose. Despite his imposing size, Anson was not a wild-swinging power hitter. He used a 52-ounce warclub and choked up generously on the handle.[10] In his long career Anson never struck out more than 30 times in a season.

The young slugger could not carry Rockford alone and catcher Jim White could not lead a mediocre Cleveland entry to the promised land with his undistinguished supporting cast. Other than hard-hitting, strong-armed third baseman Ezra Sutton (.346) and captain Charley Pabor (.310), no one from the 1871 Cleveland team made his mark in pro ball.

As August turned into September, the pennant race came clearly into focus. Fort Wayne was out of the league. Cleveland and Rockford were out of the race. The Mutuals, Olympics, and Haymakers were entrenched in solid mediocrity, and would not challenge for the flag. Troy had proven nearly unbeatable when playing with their beloved lively ball, but were average at best without it; a shortcoming attributed to their lack of "scientific" batting skills. The Mutuals had just finished a disastrous western trip which erased any hope of claiming the pennant. They returned to New York a beaten bunch. Catcher Charley Mills's hands were like raw meat, while Bob Ferguson had a bad arm and was unable to throw. Charlie Smith was "a sick man who [would] not play for some time."[11]

The Mutuals made only one significant contribution to the history of the NA during the final stages of the season. On August 31 Mills was injured in the second inning of a game against Rockford and was replaced by a member of the amateur Flyaways named Frank Fleet.

Although Fleet had played with the Mutuals in exhibition games, this was the first official appearance in a career that would make him the most traveled player in the league's history (among stiff competition). He did this in an era when there were no trades and no waiver lists. He did it on his own.

Before his cameo appearance with the Mutuals, Fleet had played (in 1871) for the Warrens, Atlantics, Union Star, Flyaways, and the Tony Pastor Minstrels—making a shambles of the 60-day rule.[12] He next surfaced with the Eckfords, with whom he played briefly in 1872. Discovering the ferry across the Hudson, the inveterate wanderer was a regular for the 1873 Resolutes of Elizabeth, New Jersey. The following year, it was back to Brooklyn to play for his third New York team, the Atlantics. In 1875 he jumped to St. Louis early in the season, but was released and, despite offers from Louisville, Keokuk, Quincy, and Elizabeth,[13] returned to the Atlantics to finish out that sorry campaign. When he was not playing with an NA team, Fleet was passing his time with any of the number of amateur and semipro teams in the New York area, a journey almost impossible to chronicle with any degree of accuracy.

After the 1873 season the *Clipper* commented that Fleet was "an enthusiast of the game" who, "if he had his choice, would live on a ballfield." He was "always ready to take a hand in a muffin nine, junior team or professional or amateur nine." The only trouble with Fleet, the *Clipper* noted conscientiously, was "his tendency to revolve" (change teams).[14] Revolve indeed. Fleet did not change teams merely from season to season. During the first two weeks of August 1873 he made the rounds. On August 6, he played for the rejuvenated old Irvington team against Easton. The following day he made his way back to the Union Grounds to play for the Resolutes against the Mutuals. On August 11, he played with the Eastons, whom he had opposed only five days earlier, when they challenged the Nassaus in Brooklyn.[15] All of this was illegal, at least as far as the Resolutes were concerned, due to the NA's 60-day rule. In Fleet's case the rule was never enforced, yet the penalty — forfeiture of all of the Resolutes' victories (all two of them) — would have been meaningless.

Not only was Fleet liable to turn up playing for any team, he might be found at any position. During his 5-year NA career, he played a total of only 85 games, averaging but 17 games per team before moving on. He played second base 28 times and he went behind the bat 22 times. Fleet divided time equally between shortstop and third base, appearing at each position 13 times. Need a pitcher? The versatile one happily filled in eight times when a regular hurler was unable to answer the bell, posting a 2–6 record. For good measure, he played two games in the outfield and one at first base. When not playing, he often filled the position of umpire. Although Fleet might have been a psychologist's delight, he was a mediocre, if enthusiastic, ballplayer, compiling a .218 batting average during his travels.

The Red Stockings returned to action and thrust themselves into the thick of the pennant race with five consecutive victories, including key wins over Chicago and Philadelphia on September 5 and 9 respectively. In a 31–10 victory over Cleveland on September 2, Boston unloaded on the tired "Five-Inning Wonder" Al Pratt for 23 runs in the last 2 innings.

In the Chicago game the Red Stockings had been unable to mount any early offense against Zettlein. Meanwhile, Chicago had pecked away at

Spalding for a 3-0 lead entering the Boston fifth. With one out, the score 3-2, and the bases loaded, Charlie Gould stepped to the plate. The original Red Stocking was a native Cincinnatian (the only one on that team) who was one of the least prominent of the famous nine. Tall and lanky, with a neatly trimmed goatee, Gould had been a bookkeeper in his father's butter and egg business before Harry Wright convinced him to cast his lot with the touring Cincinnati professionals.[16] Now he stood at the plate facing Zettlein, with Birdsall, McVey, and Spalding leading away from the bases. Gould connected with a Zettlein fastball and sent a long drive to left field. The crowd rose to its collective feet as Fred Treacey ran toward the fence. Treacey returned empty-handed as Gould rounded the bases with a grand slam home run that was the margin of victory in the 6-3 win.[17]

After a marvelous midsummer homestand, Chicago went east and took two of three games, their only loss the aforementioned 6-3 defeat at Boston on Gould's grand slam. They toppled the Athletics in Philadelphia, as the leaders continued to upend each other.

In Rockford the Athletics suffered a setback to their title hopes. They lost the game, although it was only an exhibition, by an embarrassing 32-12 margin. More important, they lost their center fielder, as Count Sensenderfer tore up his knee in an attempted steal of second. He had to be carried back to the hotel and was finished for the season.[18] In fact, Sensy was never the same player again. Before the injury, he was the regular center fielder and a .300 hitter. Although he stayed with the Athletics for the next 4 years, he was only an occasional performer, appearing in a mere 24 games.

Meanwhile, back in Chicago, the White Stockings leapt into first place on September 29 with a key win over Boston. The Red Stockings nearly overtook the white variety with another ninth-inning rally. Boston had scored two runs to close the gap to 10-8 and had runners on second and third with two out. Ross Barnes, a .378 hitter that year, hit a long drive over the left field fence that hooked foul at the last moment. Zettlein, often maligned for his lack of headwork, refused to pitch around Barnes, daring him to hit the ball. He did, smashing another long foul over the left field fence. Stubbornly, Zettlein again came inside. Badly jammed, Barnes sent a weak popup to Wood, who corralled it to nail down the victory.[19]

It had been an eventful September. Philadelphia had begun the month in the van, only to see Boston overtake them with back-to-back wins over the contenders. Worse yet, the team was decimated by injury. Malone, McBride, Heubel, Reach, Meyerle, and now Sensenderfer were incapacitated to some degree. Chicago, by virtue of their victory over Boston, surpassed the Red Stockings. The manner in which the events of September affected the standings was not universally clear. The demise of the Kekiongas clouded the issue, as did the pseudo-entry of the Eckfords and

The 1871 Chicago White Stockings. They were in first place for much of the season until the disastrous Chicago fire forced them to play their final games on the road (courtesy of Transcendental Graphics).

the Washington Nationals. The ever troublesome exhibition game issue again raised its perplexing head. For some months even the prescient Chadwick was unable to inform his readers of the precise prospects of their favorite team. He followed the race throughout the season with a series of asterisks and disclaimers.

On July 8 the Athletics had moved into first place, sort of. The standings published as of that date by the *Clipper* also included games against the Nationals, who had not paid the $10 entry fee, but were playing a number of games against those teams which had.[20] The Brooklyn Eckfords, a venerable organization in New York circles which had been national champions in 1862 and 1863, were playing an almost regular schedule against the touring pro teams which visited New York. The Eckfords proved difficult competition, as they showed on July 4 when they shut out the Mutuals 7-0. Al "Phoney" Martin was the last of the true "pitchers," lobbing the ball toward the batter rather than snapping in a quick throw. He kept the Mutuals off their stride and held them to only three hits. Four days later the Eckfords toppled Cleveland 4-3 in ten innings behind the legendary slowballer. On July 19 they journeyed to Chicago and pummeled the mighty White Stockings 14-7. Because they had failed to pay the entry fee, none of these games counted in the standings. By the end of the season the Eckfords had taken on the nature of common law wives. Some reports included their contests in the standings even though they, like the Nationals, had not officially entered in the chase for the pennant.

A second cause for confusion was the determination of the champion. At the March convention it was decided that each team was to play a best of five series with every opposing team. This was the simple part. Then came the questions. Would the champion be the winner of the most games or the most series? Or the team that had lost the fewest games? Or the fewest series? Should the teams stop playing each other after one team had clinched the series or should they play on? As the season dragged on other questions arose. Would the use of illegal players cause forfeits? What if a team didn't finish the season? Would any of their games count?

The Championship Committee had considered none of these issues, and shed no light on any of the questions as the season progressed. Fans and press alike were left to speculate upon the identity of the front-runners. This led to an early brand of parity, as virtually any team could claim possession of first place by choosing the method which best suited their circumstances.

As of July 8, the standings were published as follows:[21]

	W	L	Pct.	GB
Philadelphia Athletics	9	4	.692	-
Chicago White Stockings	10	5	.667	-

	W	L	Pct.	GB
New York Mutuals	9	5	.643	½
Washington Olympics	11	9	.550	1½
Boston Red Stockings	8	7	.533	2
Fort Wayne Kekiongas	5	7	.417	3½
Troy Haymakers	5	8	.385	4
Cleveland Forest Citys	5	9	.357	4½
Rockford Forest Citys	5	10	.333	5

As did all published standings, these needed qualification. The records included games played against the Nationals. Further, although rumors of illegal players on the Rockford and Olympic teams were flying fast and furious, no rulings had as yet been made. All their games were counted. If the standings are adjusted to reflect the Rockford forfeits and include only those games counted in the official final standings, the Athletics held a 1½ game lead over the second-place White Stockings.

	Actual Games Played				With Forfeits			
	W	L	Pct.	GB	W	L	Pct.	GB
Philadelphia Athletics	9	4	.692	½	11	2	.846	—
Chicago White Stockings	10	4	.714	—	10	4	.714	1½
New York Mutuals	9	5	.643	1	9	5	.643	2½
Washington Olympics	9	9	.500	2½	10	8	.556	3½
Boston Red Stockings	7	7	.500	2½	7	7	.500	4½
Fort Wayne Kekiongas	4	7	.364	4	5	6	.455	5
Troy Haymakers	5	7	.417	3½	5	7	.417	5½
Cleveland Forest Citys	5	9	.357	4½	5	9	.357	6½
Rockford Forest Citys	4	10	.286	5½	0	14	.000	11½

Other minor problems marred the standings. Chicago refused to play any games with Troy as the dispute over Craver's services lingered. No games between the two teams were scheduled until the final week of the season, preventing the playing of the complete series.

The Mutuals were similarly feuding with the Haymakers, although over a more plausible issue. Following a 9–7 Troy victory in New York on July 13, infielder Dick Higham of the Mutuals delivered a haymaker (lower case "h") to the face of Troy's Clipper Flynn as the teams were leaving the field. The latter, with blood streaming down his face, began running toward the team carriage with two or three husky New York toughs in hot pursuit. Former Mutual President John Wildey then went after Mr. McDonald of the Haymakers' club. The scene threatened to degenerate into a full-scale riot were it not for the fortuitous presence of the Brooklyn police. Captain Waglom and his six stolid troopers were forced to draw their firearms to hold at bay the many fans who had scaled the fences and entered the Union Grounds.[22]

The Haymakers refused to play New York again, despite assurances of additional police protection at any future games. No games took place from mid–July through the end of September. Finally, Alex Davidson was able to patch up the differences and resume the series on October 2.[23]

On September 30, the standings were as follows:

	W	L	Pct.	GB
Philadelphia Athletics	19	7	.731	—
Chicago White Stockings	19	7	.731	—
Boston Red Stockings	19	10	.655	1½
Troy Haymakers	14	12	.538	5
New York Mutuals	17	15	.531	5
Washington Olympics	16	15	.516	5½
Cleveland Forest Citys	10	19	.345	7½
Fort Wayne Kekiongas	7	21	.250	13
Rockford Forest Citys	6	21	.222	13½

Again, explanation is needed. All Rockford forfeits have been taken into account, and all uncompleted series of the disbanded Kekiongas have been awarded to their opponents. For example, Boston had won two games from Fort Wayne, and was thus awarded one additional victory in order to give them the three wins they needed to claim the series. Finally, any games played between two teams after a series had been clinched have been disregarded. The Olympic games, which were still in some doubt due to George Hall's uncertain status, are included.

Another sticky issue was the exhibition game. Although the teams were to play best of five series with each other, they often played more than five games, particularly when the two teams were a good draw. In direct contravention of the rules, the teams would sometimes designate as an exhibition a game that was played before the series had been completed. Often, spectators were informed of this fact after they had paid their admission fee, a circumstance not conducive to good public relations. It was sometimes unclear whether a game had been an exhibition, with the winning team arguing the negative and the losing team the affirmative. Although the NA had prohibited the playing of exhibition games prior to the completion of the full quota of games between the two teams, the rule was neatly skirted. The teams typically swapped batteries making Boston, for example, not Boston. Thus the game could not be construed as a game between Boston and the opponent. Apparently, no one gave any thought to the ramification of the 60-day rule upon such shenanigans. Later, the ten-man, ten-inning game was used to provide the rationale for an exhibition game.

On October 9 the Mutuals and Boston played for the fifth time. The New York press ballyhooed the game as the deciding one of the series and a large crowd made the trip to New England expecting an important battle.[24] Their Boston counterparts knew better. The game was originally to have been played in Brooklyn, but Harry Wright preferred to play in Boston. The Mutuals consented on the condition that Boston agree in writing that the game was an exhibition. They did so and the Boston papers advertised it as such.[25] Fortunately for those New Yorkers who made the trek, it was a well-played, competitive game, even though it didn't count in the standings.

Fortunately, no games had been played prior to May 1. The following season some of the Southern teams began their schedules in mid–April. Did the games count? The rules called for each team to declare its entry for the championship and send in its fee by May 1. Did this mean that the season officially began May 1? Were any games played in April null and void? In the event, the Championship Committee decided that this was not the case. They concluded that once a team had submitted its entry fee, it was free to commence playing championship games at any time.[26]

At this late date in the 1871 season, the *Clipper* indicated that the champion would be decided on the basis of the most series won, with the number of games won to be used as a tiebreaker. For this reason they listed the standings in terms of series.

	Series Won	Series Lost
Chicago White Stockings	5	0
Philadelphia Athletics	4	1
Boston Red Stockings	4	1
New York Mutuals	2	2
Troy Haymakers	1	1

On this basis they declared that the White Stockings were in first place, despite the Athletics' better won-lost record — at least according to their version of the standings. The published series standings also included an elaborate chart indicating the status of the series yet to be decided.[27]

A week later, the *Clipper* published another set of standings.

	W	L	Pct.	GB
Boston Red Stockings	24	12	.667	—
Philadelphia Athletics	24	13	.649	½
Chicago White Stockings	24	14	.632	1
New York Mutuals	21	20	.512	5½
Washington Olympics	19	21	.475	7
Brooklyn Eckfords	15	18	.455	7½

	W	L	Pct.	GB
Troy Haymakers	14	18	.438	8
Rockford Forest Citys	17	22	.436	8½
Fort Wayne Kekiongas	7	14	.333	9½
Cleveland Forest Citys	13	26	.333	12½

This included all games, including exhibitions, and listed the defunct Kekiongas, along with the Eckfords, who had never entered. For some reason, the Nationals were excluded. In contrast to the previous week's standings, one of which favored Philadelphia while the other showed Chicago in the lead, this grouping appeared to put Boston in first place.[28]

Not so, according to Nick Young, manager of the Olympics and a member of the Championship Committee. Chicago was first, Philadelphia second and Boston third, according to Young's estimate. He proposed a new standard of excellence. The championship would be won, he stated, by the team with the best record in games that had been played before a series had been decided, rather than counting all five games.[29] Therefore, each team would have a different number of games played. This was a new twist which, despite all the permutations and combinations put forth by the *Clipper*, had not yet been considered.

For those wishing to cover all the figurative bases, a second set of standings, that of the "legal" games not including, among others, the games of the ill-starred Kekiongas, was available:[30]

	W	L	Pct.	GB
Chicago White Stockings	16	5	.762	—
Philadelphia Athletics	16	7	.696	1
Boston Red Stockings	18	10	.643	1½
New York Mutuals	14	14	.500	5½
Troy Haymakers	11	11	.500	5½
Cleveland Forest Citys	10	13	.435	7
Washington Olympics	4	14	.222	10½
Rockford Forest Citys	3	18	.143	13

And a third set of standings, of those games of which the legality was not open to any question whatsoever.[31]

	W	L	Pct.	GB
Chicago White Stockings	10	5	.667	—
Philadelphia Athletics	10	7	.588	1
Boston Red Stockings	12	9	.571	1
Troy Haymakers	7	8	.467	3
New York Mutuals	8	13	.381	5
Cleveland Forest Citys	7	12	.368	5

The Championship Committee appeared as baffled as the casual reader. Even as astute an observer as Harry Wright carried the impression that the champion would be the team winning the most series.[32] Despite all the confusion, the consensus held that Chicago was the team to beat.

The White Stockings were beaten not only by the rival Boston and Philadelphia clubs. Mrs. O'Leary's famous cow got in a kick as well. As all stadiums were constructed of wood and fire equipment was yet in a primitive state, the danger of destruction by fire was always present. Alarm systems did not come into widespread use until after the disastrous Boston fire of 1872. Several other factors contributed to the probability of a major fire in the larger U.S. cities. Building codes were virtually nonexistent, while the narrow streets often allowed flames to jump across alleys from structure to structure.[33]

In 1874 Chicago and Philadelphia gamely played on despite a fire that raged in the grandstand.[34] The years 1871–73 saw major conflagrations in Chicago, Boston, and Baltimore. Fortunately, the ballparks in the latter two cities were located in areas that remained untouched by the respective blazes. That in the former city was not so lucky. On October 8, as the Rockford Forest Citys approached Chicago for their scheduled game with the White Stockings, they found the city aflame nearly from end to end. The blaze, which likely started in a barn on DeKoven Street, was driven by an untimely breeze, destroyed more than 17,000 buildings, and left more than 150,000 homeless in its wake.[35] When the embers died, beautiful Lake Front Park, which had stood nearly at the center of the blaze, was standing no longer. Not only had the park been burned to the ground, the players had been ruined as well. All but Wood and Foley had been burned out of their homes.[36] The banks in which they had put their savings were destroyed. The players were more concerned with putting their lives back together than with taking to the ball field. The team decided to finish the season, however, accepting free rail passes[37] (the backers of the team had likewise been financially devastated) and traveling east to play their remaining games on the road.

The Athletics and Mutuals made arrangements to play benefit games on the White Stockings' behalf.[38] The two teams had not forgotten their share of the gate money from the huge crowds in Chicago during the summer. Others were not as charitable. Harry Wright wrote to Chicago Secretary Thatcher lamenting the fact that some good late season crowds had been lost by Chicago's inability to visit Boston as scheduled.[39] The sporting goods firm of Peck and Snyder refused to sell the White Stockings new uniforms on credit, demanding cash on the barrelhead.[40] As there was no cash to be had, the team played out the string in borrowed duds of assorted colors and styles.[41]

The grounds had been insured for only $4,000, a mere 10 percent of

**The Chicago White Stockings and Troy Haymakers prior to an October 1871 game.
This picture was taken shortly after the Chicago fire. Note the mismatched uniforms
of the White Stockings (courtesy of Transcendental Graphics).**

the value of the structure,[42] and there was no hope of rebuilding. The financial outlook was gloomy. When the season ended, only $2,000 remained in the treasury, while the club owed $4,800 in back salaries to the players.[43] The financial situation was not helped by the fact that management had signed Mike McGeary of Troy to an 1872 contract and given him an $800 advance on his salary.[44] With 1871 salaries still unpaid, the team resolved to get back McGeary's advance.

Troy, with erstwhile White Stocking McGeary, now became an important element in the pennant race, with games scheduled against all three contenders. With the ire over the Craver situation having run its course, the Troy-Chicago series was ready to commence.

In a plodding game, void of much skill, on October 9, the Athletics beat the Haymakers 15–13. As the teams moved farther into autumn, the lack of extended daylight became a problem. The Troy-Athletic game had to be curtailed after eight innings when darkness moved in.

Although the Haymakers were hopelessly out of the race, they had given the Athletics a scare before succumbing. The Mutuals, on the other hand, inexcusably showed up at Boston on October 16 with only eight players (pitcher Wolters was missing) and forfeited a key game. They moved on to Philadelphia on October 18 for a 21–7 laydown to the Athletics, again minus Wolters. It was incidents like these which added to New York's already shady reputation.

Nine days earlier, Boston had benefited from playing a Troy nine that seemed somewhat less than eager to take the field. The Haymakers had appeared at Boston to play the final game of their series, but were greeted with weather conditions that were far from ideal. Captain Craver assumed that the game would be canceled. Harry Wright insisted that the two teams could play. Craver was unconvinced, but thought he might allow his team to play if the game were considered an exhibition. What he really wanted was to postpone the game until the following day, when he hoped that better weather would bring a larger crowd and more gate receipts. No one was more conscious of gate receipts than Harry Wright, but neither was anyone more honest. He refused to give. Boston wanted to end the series then and there. The Haymakers finally demurred, but their hearts did not seem to be in the game. Boston scored five in the first en route to an easy 12–3 win.[45]

Next, those homeless wonders, the White Stockings, journeyed to upstate New York to play the Haymakers. They arrived without Mart King and Ed Pinkham, probably due to the aftereffects of the fire, which left them one player short. To fill the vacancy they brought along Mike Brannock, who had spent the summer playing for the Chicago Actives. According to NA rules, this made him ineligible to perform for the White Stockings, a fact the Haymakers readily pointed out when Brannock took the field. The White Stockings insisted that their new third baseman would play, since they had no one else.[46] Brannock did not add much to the Chicago attack, managing only 1 hit in 13 at bat, but his appearance cast doubt over the legitimacy of the final 3 games.

The first game was a letdown. Only 500[47] hardy Trojans braved the cold to watch a contest marked by sloppy fielding on the part of the frozen-fingered participants. The White Stockings won 11–5, if it counted. Two days later, the teams met again at Troy with the Haymakers turning the tables 19–12.

These games set the stage for the final and climactic game of the season October 30 at the Union Grounds in Brooklyn. There was little fanfare for the clash between the White Stockings and Athletics. It was nominally Chicago's home game, but drew scant attention on a neutral field. Despite excellent weather for the late date, only 500 or so were in attendance to see the deciding game, a far cry from the crowds at Lake Front Park in midsummer. The press blamed the poor showing on the excitement of the upcoming local elections and the fact that the Athletics were expected to have an easy time with the charred and smoking midwesterners.[48]

Although forfeits had not yet been parceled out, everyone seemed to agree that the game would decide the championship but not what the precise implications were. If Chicago won (according to the *Clipper* and *New York Times*) Boston would be the champions, while the Athletics had control of their destiny and would be the champions with a victory.[49] In actuality, considering the manner in which the forfeits were determined, either of the contesting teams could claim at least a share of the crown with a victory. Prior to the game, the adjusted record of the Athletics was 21–7, while the White Stockings were a game behind at 20–8. Boston, which had finished its season two weeks earlier at 22–10, could not post a higher winning percentage than the winner of the Philadelphia-Chicago game.

Both teams were shorthanded. Chicago continued to use Brannock at third. The Athletics were without Sensenderfer and Reach. Wes Fisler moved from first base to second, where he was equally at home, and George Heubel took his place at first. Bechtel had moved from his usual post in right field to patrol center in place of Sensy. In right field for the championship game was bewhiskered Nate Berkenstock, a 40-year-old geriatric who had been a member of the great Athletic teams of the 1860s. This would be his only appearance in the majors.

The game started at 3:10, with New York veteran Marty Swandell serving as umpire. Ned Cuthbert's leadoff single in the first went to waste but, after setting Chicago down in order, Philadelphia did some damage in the second. They picked up a single run on hits by Fisler and Meyerle. Meyerle's safety was one of three he would get before the day was over. The Athletics padded their lead with a run in the third on errors by Zettlein and shortstop Ed Duffy. In the bottom of the fourth, with Zettlein at first, Berkenstock got his creaky legs under way and made a fine running catch to save a run. He huffed and puffed his way back to his position to great applause. The Athletics continued to peck away, and took a 4–0 lead to the bottom of the ninth. The White Stockings put up a token struggle before succumbing. They avoided a shutout, but were still at the short end of a 4–1 score. In only 1 hour and 35 minutes the championship had been decided.[50]

The first champions had a strong offensive team, and led the league with a .310 team batting average. They averaged nearly 13 runs a game, well over the league average of 9.8, without the help of any gimmicks such as Troy's lively ball. Long Levi Meyerle, making up for his awkward presence in the field, sprayed out hits at a pace that made him the league's leading batter with a .492 average. Al Reach, the veteran left-handed second baseman and thriving sporting goods dealer, wound up second on the team with a .348 mark, followed by the reliable Sensy at .339. Catcher Malone also topped the .300 mark, while the team got unexpected help from their two right fielders, George Heubel and George Bechtel, each of whom batted over .300 in part-time duty.

Chapter 8

The Pernicious Practice

The teams were reluctant to stop playing when the season ended. Chicago nobly attempted to complete their quota of games by playing Troy on November 2. They were now drawing crowds of less than 100, as interest had completely dissipated once the championship had been unofficially decided. The Athletics played an exhibition game in November and amateur teams played well into the month. When weather prevented any more standard games in the North, the games on ice skates began. Southern teams played straight through to spring. However, once the players finally retired from the field, the league officials stepped in to sort out what had happened. President Kerns called a meeting in Philadelphia for November 3.[1]

We have already trespassed upon chronology by relating the story of Scott Hastings's ineligibility and George Hall's legality. These issues took up an interminable amount of committee time and, while a final decision was reached, there was precious little time to discuss other, more pressing matters. The Chicago Club had written to Kerns asking for an extension of time to complete their season, citing extenuating circumstances. The other team presidents said that, fire or no, October 31 was the end of the season for everyone.

As was to become an irksome habit with the NA, minor problems such as Chicago's November games and Hall's status with the Olympics were subjected to agonizing analysis while the key problems which threatened the league's existence were glossed over with mere lip service. Among the foremost of these problems was gambling.

The first mention of an athlete losing intentionally for money dates back to the ancient Greeks, when one of the champion wrestlers took a dive in return for a substantial bribe. When sports migrated to America, the evils of gambling followed, with instances of fraud occurring in horse racing, billiards, rowing, and pigeon shooting.[2]

The advent of baseball was the gamblers' dream come true. The first game in 1846 was followed shortly afterward by the first bet. By 1858, when a team of Brooklyn all-stars opposed a similar contingent from New York, bettors were out in full force. Henry Chadwick overheard a conversation regarding a wager on whether Brooklyn's John Holden would hit a home run. The fan who had bet in favor of Holden strengthened his chances by offering the player a piece of the action to the tune of $25. Sensing a pay-day, Holden muscled up, slammed a ball over the head of young Harry Wright in right center field, and pocketed his share of the winnings.[3]

As baseball expanded into covert professionalism, the interest of gamblers grew even greater. By the late 1860s the betting crowd following the new sport was comparable to that which followed horse racing. The Brooklyn Eagle confided that by 1868 a number of the leading clubs were controlled by gamblers.[4] By that time it was said that the Mutuals had become expert at playing either side of a fix, a useful and rewarding talent.

Fittingly, the Mutuals were right in the center of the first great scandal in baseball history.[5] On September 28, 1865, William Wansley, New York's catcher, was given $100 by a gambler named Kane McLaughlin. In return, Wansley was to enlist two of his teammates as confederates and make certain that the opposing Eckfords won that day's game. Wansley gave $30 each to third baseman Ed Duffy and shortstop Tom Devyr, who agreed to cooperate. When the game started, the Mutuals broke to an early 8–4 lead after the top of the fifth. In the bottom of the fifth Wansley and his fellow blackguards delivered, giving the Eckfords 11 runs. The catcher's play was so noticeably bad that he was moved to right field in the middle of the inning. The Eckfords won the game 23–11, with Wansley's performance registering five at bats without a hit and six passed balls.

John Wildey smelled a rat and confronted his catcher. Nearly one month later the three men confessed and were expelled from the National Association. Eventually all three were readmitted, Wansley at the disastrous convention of 1870.[6]

The advent of open professionalism worried the gamblers and the fixers. With a steady income from ballplaying, players would seemingly be less eager to take money from gamblers and jeopardize their membership in the Association. The fears proved groundless, principally because of lax enforcement of the provisions against gambling.

The one blemish on Cincinnati's 1869 record was a tie with the Troy Haymakers which was, according to most accounts, tainted. It was rumored that someone had offered Cincinnati pitcher Asa Brainard $500 to throw the game at the behest of Troy President John Morrissey. Brainard allegedly earned his money by allowing 13 runs in the first two innings. The Red Stockings fought back and tied the game 17–17, at which point, even with Brainard supposedly in the bag, Morrissey became very worried about the reported $60,000[7] he and his friends had invested on the Haymakers. When an argument ensued over a foul tip by Cal McVey, Morrissey ordered Captain Bill Craver to pull the team off the field, ending the game in a tie and preserving his stake.[8]

The formation of the NA likewise caused no change in the status quo. Liquor was sold at most parks and, at Capitoline, in a saloon adjacent to the field. At the saloon, "the betting sports" were able to drink with the players and establish valuable contacts. Pools (a form of betting similar to that used in horse racing) were sold at most parks and, at Union, at a pool room just outside. The innovation in betting methods coincided with the formation of the NA and made the process much more accessible and efficient. Alex Davidson, the portly bon vivant of the Mutuals, was quite active in pool selling.[9]

As usual in matters of moral rectitude, Harry Wright's Red Stockings led the way. There was no pool selling or sale of liquor on Boston's South End Grounds.[10] At the other end of the spectrum, not surprisingly, were the Union Grounds in Brooklyn, home of the always suspect Mutuals. The Union Grounds were a hotbed for gamblers, with special season tickets available in the covered section for $5. No effort was spared for their comfort. "If ladies were less accommodated than in Chicago, at least the gamblers were well taken care of."[11] In Brooklyn bets on any aspect of the game could be placed within earshot of the players' bench. The participants, therefore, knew how much had been wagered on whether they would get a hit, or score in a certain inning, and also knew who had placed the bet. On one occasion Bob Ferguson, then the league president, charged the pool sellers' stand after a game and accused some of the bettors of "buying up" his men. He threatened physical violence and had to be restrained by the police from mauling one of his companions.[12]

These were probably the most direct threats to gamblers ever made by a league president but, under the loosely formed NA, they were totally ineffective, as were the urgings of Chadwick, Nick Young, and others to curb the sordid influence. Everyone associated with the league was (at least overtly) in fast agreement that gambling was doing immeasurable harm to the NA's reputation and the reputation of baseball in general. League officials were not the only ones alarmed by the alleged fixing of games. Many of the "honorable" gamblers were "tired of having to see Tom, Dick and Harry to learn how the match is to go."[13]

Any upset was cause for suspicion that the fix was on. In 1874 Chicago stunned heavily favored Boston 10-0, putting the Red Stockings' pennant hopes in jeopardy. The players were not the only ones who were shocked. Betting odds had been 100–20 in Boston's favor with no shortage of takers. When the score was telegraphed to Siebert's pool hall in the Bowery, the "betting sports" were incredulous.[14] Some of those mysterious dots and dashes must have been in the wrong position. They wired back asking for confirmation. The score came back again, leaving the Boston backers shaking their heads and reaching for their pockets, certain that the Bostons were on the take.

At the November meeting Mr. Clark, representing Troy, piously stated that he hoped that something would be done about "the pernicious practice of gambling and pool-selling."[15] If so, it would not be done by this august group of handwringers. F. H. Mason of Cleveland suggested that clubs could put pressure on the proprietors of the grounds by refusing to play there if gambling were allowed. There was no mention of the Association itself lending guidance or setting regulations, or of where the teams would play.

Mason next pointed out what any casual fan had noticed; the championship rules were unclear. Harry Wright, a member of the Championship Committee, agreed. It was decided that in the future each team would play five games against every other team and the club with the most wins would be declared champion. In the meantime, the Championship Committee promised to sort out the jumble of the campaign just past and to name a champion by November 15.[16]

The *Clipper* reported that the meeting was "characterized by the utmost good feeling and decorum." Well it should have been, since no substantive decisions were taken. The host Athletic club provided refreshments, and the evening ended amidst a series of pleasant speeches, toasts, and sparkling wit and champagne.

As the Championship Committee manfully struggled with the vagaries of the 1871 season, team managers began to assemble their rosters for 1872.

Chicago had signed their 1872 team before the fire, at a cost of more than $24,000, when they were in first place and emotions were high.[17] With no park, no money, and 1871 salaries in arrears, management now released the players from their obligations.[18] Nearly until opening day, however, Tom Foley, manager of the 1871 entry, had hopes of organizing an 1872 Chicago team.[19] In the end, however, lack of a playing site and an absence of funds decreed that there would be no professional baseball in Chicago until 1874.

The disinherited players scrambled to make arrangements for the coming season. Troy was a large beneficiary of Chicago's misfortune. The Haymakers wooed Jimmy Wood, who brought along Bub McAtee (who had gone from Troy to Chicago earlier), Zettlein, Charlie Hodes and Mart King. The Washington Olympics had encountered financial difficulties, and Troy was able to add catcher Doug Allison and shortstop Davy Force to a team that increasingly took on the appearance of a powerhouse. The roster had been almost completely overhauled, the only holdovers being Steve King, who had led the team with a .396 average in 1871, and Steve Bellan. Newcomer Al (Count) Gedney, an excellent defensive left fielder, was a throwback to the gentleman's era. Gedney was the educated son of wealthy parents[20] who was the post office clerk of the New York State Senate.[21] Troy had a strong New York City connection, as five of the team members had played with the old Brooklyn Eckfords.

The Athletics, despite winning the flag, did not choose to stand pat. Al Reach had been playing ball since 1858, and would have a lessened role in 1872. Sensenderfer was not the same after his injury and likewise saw spot duty. Shortstop Radcliff was allowed to employ his unreliable talents elsewhere, as were part-timers Heubel and Bechtel. As replacements, Philadelphia imported a select group including Adrian Anson, who fit in nicely at third base and in the process increased his salary from $66 per month to $1,250 per year.[22] Denny Mack, his Rockford teammate, took over at first. Wes Fisler moved to second, replacing Reach. Long Levi Meyerle, the 1871 batting champion, went to right field, where there was a better chance to hide his sorry fielding skills. Fred Treacey was plucked from the remnants of the White Stockings to replace Sensy in center and Mike McGeary arrived from Troy to strengthen the team behind the plate and at shortstop.

While the Athletics had apparently assembled a stronger combination, their chief rivals in 1871, the Red Stockings, had added only two players. Andy Leonard joined his former Cincinnati mates from the dying Olympics, while Fraley Rogers arrived from the New York Stars. Harry Wright was convinced that, had it not been for the crippling injuries, especially to brother George, Boston would have won the 1871 pennant. Therefore, he elected to go with basically the same horses in 1872.

The Mutuals added, after much cloak and dagger activity, Candy Cummings (see Chapter 22). John (Lefty) McMullin, Troy's regular pitcher the previous year, joined the New Yorkers in his more natural outfield position. George Bechtel moved over from the Athletics, Chick Fulmer from the defunct Rockford Forest Citys, fiery rifle-armed catcher Nat Hicks from the Eckfords, and good hit-no field Bill Boyd from the Atlantics.

The New York Mutuals lost their captain as the revived Brooklyn Atlantics decided to enter the pro arena. In 1871 the team lost seven of their 1870 starters and had been a mere shell of the powerhouses of the 1860s. Bob Ferguson, unhappy with the Mutuals, now elected to return and assembled a team from the previous year's second-echelon New York teams that was little better than the 1871 entry.

Part of the Atlantics' problem was the increased competition for talent in the New York area. Whereas in 1871 the Mutuals were the only team in the NA, not only the Atlantics but also the Eckfords elected to test the professional waters. The Eckfords had provided stiff exhibition competition for the NA regulars in 1871, defeating Boston, Troy, New York (twice), Cleveland, and Philadelphia, but were less formidable when playing for keeps. Pitcher Al Martin had defected to the Haymakers, and Brooklyn was left with a truly unimpressive cast of characters. The ubiquitous Frank Fleet managed to appear in 13 Eckford contests, batting a robust .190. Dooming themselves to failure before the season started, the Eckfords had signed virtually every malcontent in the New York area. The early season losses exacerbated the on-field bickering which marked the play of most co-op teams.

The Washington Olympics were also affected by increased competition in 1872, as the neighboring Nationals opted to move up to major league competition. The Olympics became a co-op club and the lack of a regular salary caused them to retain but a handful of players from the competitive 1871 team. Only Brainard and Waterman remained from the Cincinnati contingent.

The Nationals had a unique Washington flavor. Vice president of the new team was J. W. Douglas, the honorable Commissioner of Internal Revenue, while William White of the War Department was secretary.[23] Pitcher Bill Stearns, a fastballing right-hander who had pitched and won two games for the Olympics the previous year, became the regular hurler for the Nationals. As his batterymate, the managers procured Bill Lennon, whose drunken escapades had earned him expulsion from the Kekiongas. Ed Mincher, who had also been expelled in disgrace, was the left fielder. Oscar Bielaski (the first major leaguer of Polish extraction[24]), Paul Hines, and Warren White, who would later become important cogs in the formidable Chicago mid-decade teams, honed their talents with the fledgling Nationals. Hines was a particularly noteworthy player. He lasted 20 seasons in the major leagues and retired with a .301 average, having reached the .300 plateau 11 times. The young outfielder became the first triple crown winner in 1878 with Providence, leading the National League with a .358 average, 4 home runs and 58 runs batted in.[25] His budding skills, however, would not be sufficient to make the Nationals a contending, or even a competitive, team.

Three more teams completed the NA lineup for the 1872 season. Cleveland was ready to give it another try, with essentially the same lineup that had served in 1871. They added the renowned Charlie Sweasy, who had been virtually useless to the Olympics, and the erratic Rynie Wolters. It was expected that Wolters would provide some relief for workhorse Al Pratt, who had shown a continuing tendency to wilt in the late innings.

Not all of the entries for the flag were welcomed with open arms. In 1871 the ruling body of the NA had been unable to determine who had won the championship. Now they weren't even sure who was in the league, particularly with regard to new entries.

The Mansfields of Middletown, Connecticut, had been named for the silver-haired Civil War hero General Joseph Mansfield, who had fallen in a cornfield at Antietam. Organized in the fall of 1866 as a junior organization, the Mansfields switched to senior status two years later.[26] They billed themselves the champions of Connecticut and had their sights set on bigger game, although the team had done no better than 15–22 against lackluster competition in 1871.[27]

In early April, Mansfield Secretary Ben Douglas had written to Harry Wright attempting to schedule games for the coming season. Wright had been disappointed with the crowds generated by Middletown in 1871 and doubted that any satisfactory arrangements could be made. He suggested to Douglas that the Mansfields mail in their $10 entry fee, in which case other teams would be obligated to schedule them. The Boston manager was not certain, however, that the application would be accepted by the NA.[28] The officers took Wright's advice, mailed in the fee, and announced their intention to compete for the championship of the United States.

Chadwick was nearly apoplectic. He declared indignantly that the Mansfields were an amateur organization, had always been an amateur organization, and, furthermore, had failed to attend the 1872 professional convention.[29] The thought of the Mansfields competing with the likes of the Athletics and Red Stockings was, in Chadwick's crusty view, a ludicrous proposition. The Nutmeggers thought otherwise. "Tough cheese," they replied; they had sent in their $10 and, according to the rules, were entitled to compete.

They were right. There was no provision for rejecting the application of any organization. The come one, come all philosophy, despite attracting ragtag outfits like the Mansfields, was continued for the duration of the league's existence.

Fortunately, the Mansfields — unlike some of the other marginal teams, as merchants are wont to say — had a convenient central location. Opposing teams could take the 8 A.M. New Haven Railroad train from New York and arrive in Middletown by noon, in plenty of time for an afternoon game. After the game, there was still time to board another train and reach Boston by nightfall.[30] The Mansfields generously offered half the gate money to their opponents, compared to the standard one-third offered by most teams.[31] The proceeds would not include admission fees from ladies, who were given free admittance to games.[32]

The new entry from Middletown was an unknown quantity. None of the players who opened the season had seen major league service in 1871. Secretary Douglas reengaged a number of the 1871 Mansfields and sprinkled in an assortment of newcomers, including some diamonds in the rough. First baseman Tim Murnane went on to a respectable career and later served as president of the New England League and sports editor of the *Boston Globe*. Outfielder Jim Tipper had been with the Middletown team since its inception[33] and was to play an additional two seasons in the NA.

John Clapp, a tough youngster from Ithaca with a powerful throwing arm, was brought to Connecticut to work behind the plate. In January Clapp had written to Harry Wright attempting to secure a position with the Red Stockings but had been rebuffed.[34] He quickly became a standout with the Mansfields and lasted 11 years in the majors, establishing a then record National League consecutive game streak of 212 between 1876 and 1879,[35] no mean feat considering the lack of protection for the man behind the bat. The streak was due not merely to good fortune, but to Clapp's stoic nature as well. He was an ironman in every sense of the word. In an 1872 exhibition against Yale, the catcher was hit in the side with a bat, hit in the head with a ball, and had a finger dislocated, yet he remained in the game.[36] Ironically, he suffered a severe ankle sprain while playing for the Mansfields that season and was forced to miss several games while recuperating at home in Ithaca.[37]

The purest gem on the Mansfield team, however, was 19-year-old short-stop James O'Rourke. O'Rourke had played amateur ball in nearby Bridge-port before being lured to Middletown by Manager Douglas. Allegedly, Douglas was forced to provide the youngster's mother with replacement labor on the farm to make up for the absence of the strapping O'Rourke during the summer months.[38] Although the *Clipper* incorrectly identified the youngster as "Rourke," the paper described him as "one of the best bat-ters in Connecticut."[39] He batted a solid but unspectacular .287 in 1872, but went on to bat .300 or better 14 times in a major league career that spanned 22 full seasons, plus 1 game behind the plate for the New York Giants in 1904. O'Rourke, by then known by the handle "Orator Jim" for his propen-sity for gab and his practice of clubhouse law,[40] caught the entire nine innings at the age of 52. He played regularly in the minors until he was well into his fifties and made his final professional appearance in 1912 at the age of 60. O'Rourke was elected to the Hall of Fame in 1945.

The final new entry, the Lord Baltimores, boasted no future Hall of Famers on the roster, but had a solid core of veteran ballplayers who had been hired away from NA rivals at substantial expense (the average salary was $1,200).[41] Baseball had been introduced to Baltimore in 1858 by wholesale grocer George Beam, who had been invited to New York by Cap-tain Joe Leggett of the famous Excelsiors. Beam was so enthused by the game that he returned to Baltimore and formed his own club, also known as the Excelsiors.[42] The sport continued to grow on an amateur and semipro basis until the city was ready for an out-and-out professional organization. Nick Young had left the Olympics and added his con-siderable organizational talents to the Baltimore cause. The team he assembled was formidable. Slender Bobby Mathews had returned to the Baltimore area after the demise of the Kekiongas and joined the Lord Baltimores, or the Canaries, as they were known for their garish uniforms.

As a backup pitcher and regular at third base and right field, they procured wandering fireballer Cherokee Fisher.

With two hard throwers in the pitcher's box, Baltimore was unwise to acquire Bill Craver for duty behind the plate. Craver was fearless and had the hands to prove it. In order to preserve his hands, the NA backstop needed to bring them back to cradle the pitch, much in the same manner as one would catch a raw egg. Craver held his hands stiff and allowed the ball to strike with full force into his palms.[43] For this reason, he was unsuited to full-time duty behind the plate. The former Troy captain convinced team-mates Lip Pike and Tom York to defect with him. Center fielder George Hall and steady first baseman Ev Mills left the sinking ship of the Olympics. Shortstop Johnny Radcliff of the champion Athletics, jack-of-all-trades Dick Higham of the Mutuals, and infielder Tom Carey of the ill-fated Kekiongas completed a strong team. Other than pitchers Mathews and Fisher, there was not a light hitter in the lot. Moreover, the acquisition of two frontline pitchers marked a radical departure from established tradition. Mathews and Fisher alternated throughout the season, with captain Craver occasionally considering each hurler's record against a prospective opponent before making a decision. Fisher's forte was pure speed, while Mathews, who could throw nearly as hard, employed substantially more guile. Changing pitchers in mid-game could throw opposing hitters off stride. Harry Wright employed this strategy to perfection as he often replaced the hard-throwing Spalding to baffle batsmen with his off-speed junk.

As a supplement to the players' salaries, the Baltimore stockholders adopted the practice of bestowing expensive gifts (principally jewelry) for outstanding performances. For having the most hits in a game against the Mutuals, Radcliff was rewarded with a diamond with a claimed value of $150. Although other clubs rewarded their players in similar fashion, Baltimore did so on a grander scale. Needless to say, the practice did not contribute to effective teamwork, as each player could derive substantial pecuniary gain for accumulating impressive individual statistics. Team achievements were not similarly rewarded. There was no financial reward for winning the pennant nor were there any World Series shares to distribute.

Chapter 9

A Two-Tiered League

The annual prelude to the start of the championship season was the NA convention in early March. The 1872 extravaganza was held at the Kennard House in Cleveland, not the most convenient locale for the eastern delegates.[1] President Kerns felt the meeting to be of such little importance that he could not find the time to attend, placing Vice President Evans in the chair. Evans stated his desire for a harmonious convention. He might have hoped for a productive one. The NA was known for its harmonious, innocuous gatherings, one of the main reasons being that all crucial or controversial issues were glossed over with a few pious observations. A second reason for the NA's lack of effectiveness on this occasion was the lack of enthusiasm. Only six teams were represented. Harry Wright, possibly the most influential man in the NA and certainly the most respected manager, was unable to attend due to illness. Without Kerns and Wright, two vital cogs, the machinery ran slowly and without direction.

The proceedings began with a report from the treasurer who informed the delegates that the Association "[has] received nothing, paid nothing, got nothing." After digesting this bit of intelligence, the delegates decided that there was no further need for a treasurer, and promptly abolished the office. The remaining officers were elected unanimously. Evans suggested that a player should be president and Bob Ferguson was immediately nominated. H. C. Doolittle (an appropriate name for a vice president, particularly in the NA) of Cleveland was nominated for vice president after Hicks Hayhurst of the Athletics declined the honor. The name of Nick Young was put forth for secretary. There was no opposition.

Ferguson, who was present as the representative of the Atlantics, made his way to the chair and thanked his colleagues for the honor they had bestowed upon him. He then added a characteristic wish that the business of the convention would be concluded as quickly as possible. Throughout Ferguson's tenure there is little record of his taking any interest whatsoever in the affairs of the governing body. In 1874 he did not even trouble himself to attend the annual convention.[2] Ferguson was now player, manager, umpire, and league president, though no one seemed concerned about a conflict of interest. His position as president was appropriate, since the NA was run principally by and for the players. Stockholders had yet to discover the thrill of operating their ball clubs as athletic sweatshops, taking instead the position of gentlemen and sportsmen. Making money was a secondary concern.

After the election of officers, the participants began a lengthy squabble over which teams should be represented and whether teams which had not sent a delegate could be represented by proxy. The difficulties of the old Association with the proxy undoubtedly had sensitized the new organization to its dangers. Each member felt it incumbent upon him to add his thoughts on the matter, whether cogent or not, causing the discussion to ramble on interminably. Someone opined that, since Harry Wright was not present, the proposed rule amendments which he had submitted could not be presented or discussed. This would have been particularly unfortunate, since the game of baseball was but 25 years old and needed constant rule revisions. Cricket, which had been played for centuries in England, had reached a static point from which baseball was many years away. During the NA's existence, clever players were always a step or two ahead of the rulemakers. Without an infield fly rule, players allowed routine popups to fall untouched in order to start a double play. Third strikes were likewise dropped by shrewd catchers. Nonetheless, Wright's absence nearly sidetracked any discussion on amendments to the code of rules.

The rules committee went the way of the treasurer, as no further need was seen for it. As its last act, Evans presented the proposed amendments forwarded in absentia by Wright. This was immediately challenged. Evans was allowed to continue only after F. H. Mason provided assurances that the proposals had actually been the work of Henry Chadwick. Chadwick advocated formally legalizing the underhand throw rather than a "true pitch," thereby sanctioning a practice that had been widespread since the early 1860s. No other significant changes were made, although Chadwick attempted to clarify the distinction between the unfair ball and the ball that was not fair. The rules in this instance were so garbled that not even Solomon could have untangled them, much less the unpaid, part-time arbiters who worked NA contests.

Things failed to improve when the other committees made their reports. The Judiciary Committee's Mason informed his colleagues that no other members of the committee were present, no business had been brought before them, and therefore there was no report. After all the disputes that had occurred during the past 12 months, it is difficult to believe that no team or player aired a complaint before the committee. This was most likely a reflection of the perception of the NA's authority or lack thereof. Not only were grievances handled privately, but the Association's rules continued to be brazenly ignored.

Although nothing of any import had been accomplished, the gentlemen once again departed in the glow of goodwill and good cheer, to meet again in March 1873 in Baltimore.

The second year of the NA, 1872, was an election year and the nation's attention was riveted on the presidential contest between incumbent Republican Ulysses S. Grant and Democrat Horace Greeley. It was not much of a choice. Grant was a simple soldier who eschewed anything intellectual or political. The scandals involving his administration would soon be exposed, but not until the election was safely tucked away. Greeley was a crusading intellectual journalist and political neophyte. The *New York Times* endorsed Grant,[3] as did 3.6 million voters on November 5. Greeley finished a distant second with 2.8 million. Before the month ended Greeley, who had coined the phrase "Go west, young man," went west himself, passing away on November 29. His death was possibly due in part to the vicious campaign waged against him, not by Grant himself, but by Grant's supporters in the press. Greeley was caricatured, ridiculed, and lampooned day after day in the *New York Times*, and attacked without quarter in less respectable organs.

A sad event punctuated the opening of the 1872 season. Baseball backers in Cincinnati had finally come to the realization that there would be no team in 1872 and probably no team in the immediate future. On April 13 a large crowd gathered at the Union Grounds in Cincinnati for an auction of most of the Red Stocking memorabilia. Aaron Champion, president of the club during its glory years, was there, as was former secretary Joyce. The highest price was paid for a pitcher and goblet won in an 1867 tournament, which attracted a bid of $40. The championship streamer of the undefeated 1869 team was sold for $7. A number of game balls brought anywhere from $1 to $5.[4] When everything had been disposed of, the crowd departed, not to see professional baseball until 1876.

While the first professional team suffered a symbolic demise, the first amateur team also lost a part of its heritage. For the first time in 28 years, the Knickerbockers would not be playing at the Elysian Fields in Hoboken. The site of the first baseball game was in the process of being converted into a lumber yard, and the Knicks secured one day per week's usage of a cricket field at the foot of 9th Street in Hoboken.[5]

Unbeknownst to anyone, 1871 had provided baseball fans with the most exciting pennant race they were to witness during the NA's existence. The advent of Boston's dominance of the league began in 1872, a superiority that was to become greater with each passing season. Harry Wright had been correct in his assessment that injuries alone had prevented his team from capturing the 1871 crown.

As the NA's second season unfolded, it became evident that the new Baltimore entry posed a serious threat to the returning contenders. Nick Young's decision to employ two top-flight pitchers paid immediate dividends. Bobby Mathews became ill in the first month of the campaign, but Cherokee Fisher filled his small shoes ably, hurling two strong games in succession. The Canaries beat the second-rate local competition (the Nationals and Olympics) handily and upset the Mutuals before a rabid Baltimore crowd. It was a gorgeous spring day, with the sun shining brightly despite a brisk wind, and the stands were packed with approximately 2,000 spectators. Hundreds who were unwilling to pay the admission price stood on the roofs of buildings in the block surrounding the park. The *Clipper* reported that "baseball fever has broken out very badly in Baltimore" and that the overflow crowd was "berserk for the whole game."[6]

The Canaries' early success was not a total surprise since Nick Young, as he was wont to do, had not relied on local talent but had instead imported a crew of Hessians from all points. Every one of the Baltimore hands had been a regular with another NA team in 1871.

A second truth emerging from the early play in the South was the sorry state of the Olympics. In 1871 the team had been competitive, although not a contender at the end. The departure of Young and the decline to co-op status had stripped the team of its nucleus. Brainard and Waterman both batted over .400 in their abbreviated seasons, but it was not enough. Following a 16–0 season-opening debacle at the hands of the Lord Baltimores, the faltering Olympics dropped games by such one-sided scores as 25–5 (to the Mutuals), 18–2 (to Troy), 22–5 (Baltimore again), and 14–2 (Cleveland). They pulled themselves together in a respectable 8–1 loss to Boston and managed their only two victories against their intramural rivals, the Nationals.

Ah, the Nationals. By early May it was obvious that the Nationals had no business being on the field with the other teams in the league. A couple of retread Kekiongas and a mish-mash of local amateurs were no match for the seasoned veterans of Boston and Philadelphia or even for their feeble cousins, the Olympics. In late June, securely moored in last place by virtue of their unblemished 0–11 record, the Nationals quietly gave up the ghost, to the disappointment of no one other than the players, who would no longer be paid. But most of them didn't deserve to be paid. In an era of free swingers, the Nationals had batted a meek .239 and their defense had been found very, very wanting. Pitcher Bill Stearns, who had posted a 2–0 record while filling in for Brainard in 1871, pitched (and lost) every game. Stearns finished his NA career with a batting average (.200) that was higher than his winning percentage (.156) earned by virtue of a career 12–65 mark. His tenure with the 1872 Nationals was a giant leap toward that distinction. The former Kekiongas proved just as inept with the stick in Washington as they had in Fort Wayne. Lennon hit only .231, while Mincher was out of sight at .118, eking out only 6 hits in 51 at bats.

Since there was no set schedule, it was not always evident whether a team had packed it in. After a 15–2 loss to the Athletics on June 3, the Nationals went into hibernation, leaving the baseball world in doubt as to their continued existence. Rumors of their demise, however, proved to be greatly exaggerated as, like the proverbial phoenix, they reappeared in Baltimore on June 26 to absorb a 9–1 setback.

That was the end of the Nationals. They did not self-destruct in a spectacular blaze, but merely expired from inertia. The failure of struggling teams to take the field was not solely their own doing. The stragglers could not draw, either at home or on the road. With teams now agreeing to share gate receipts, Boston and Philadelphia were reluctant to entertain the tailenders and even more disinclined to incur the travel expense inherent in a road encounter. A team such as the Nationals could face difficulty scheduling one of the stock clubs. Their only allure was the prospect of an easy victory.

The city of Washington was without major league baseball, as the Olympics also elected to take an early powder, playing their last game May 24 against the Nationals. The fans had recognized this year's team as impostors and had failed to support the team with any degree of enthusiasm. Attendance was measured in hundreds rather than thousands, and a game against the world champion Athletics on May 21 attracted a gathering of only 500.[7] They witnessed what was perhaps the finest hour of the Olympics' ill-fated campaign, as Asa Brainard and his mates weathered a 25-hit storm before losing a 15–13 squeaker.

The most convincing evidence of the ineptitude of the two Washington clubs surfaced after the teams had folded their tents. Of the players who had appeared with either team, only Brainard, who hooked on briefly as captain of the Mansfields,[8] was picked up by another NA team.

Meanwhile, in the North the snow had melted and some of the other neophytes were getting their feet wet. On April 26 the Middletown Mansfields journeyed to Troy to open their inaugural season against the Haymakers, who were always tough, especially at home. Chadwick could not resist a last dig, stating in his article that the Mansfields were a team that had sent delegates to the amateur convention in March.[9]

The Mansfields got off to a rocky start, hindered by a feeble offense, as did all of the other co-op teams, including the proud old Atlantics. The Atlantics possessed a proud heritage but, other than Captain Ferguson, the players from the glory days were gone. They had a hole at second base that would not be filled all season. By the end of October the Atlantics would use nine different players at the keystone. These were truly the "new" Atlantics, with none of the skill and dash of the old.

The other legendary New York nine, the Eckfords, also stumbled out of the gate. A 16–14 loss to a pickup team on April 27 gave Eckford backers a foreshadowing of the early season disasters that would befall the team. Joe McDermott, who had played such a prominent role in the Cleveland-Kekionga opening game of 1871, resurfaced as the Eckfords' pitcher. He had also quite recently played for the amateur Burnsides, and the *Clipper* took the occasion to caution the club managers about using ineligible players.[10] In the Eckfords' case, it would hardly have mattered, since a 9-0 loss by forfeit was a closer margin than most of their actual defeats.

One of the Brooklyn club's problems was stability, or lack thereof. McDermott was soon cashiered as pitcher, sporting an 0-7 record. The rest of the lineup was in constant flux. Before the season was over, the Eckfords would employ 25 different players. The expansive roster compared poorly with the Red Stockings, who used only ten men. The other contenders got by with 11 or 12. There was a unique reason for some of the turnover, as the reader will presently see, but much of the cause was simply the unreliability of the players and the dearth of skilled performers. In fact, 10 of the 25 played 5 games or less before they were found wanting, indicative of the emergency fill-in or the desperate trial. In what may be a major league record, the Eckfords used three players named Allison, two named Snyder, and two sporting the identical handle of Al Martin. Other than constituting a full house in seven-card stud, this situation represented a scorekeeper's and researcher's nightmare.

Despite the familial ties, or at least ties of nomenclature, the Eckfords were unable to generate any sense of teamwork and exhibited a marked ineptitude at the plate. They struggled to a team batting average of .206 in a year when the rest of the league (including the Nationals, Olympics, Mansfields, and Atlantics) averaged .282. Their fielding, always a key element in that era, was shaky, but really not that bad; however, they had no offense and lacked a reliable pitcher.

The Eckford lineup that faced Boston in a 24–4 debacle was greatly altered from the team that had started the season. Dick Hunt was the second baseman du jour, replacing Al Martin. This was the "other" Al Martin, who sometimes played under the name of May. He was not to be confused with the former and future Eckford pitcher with the identical monniker. Hunt had started the season in right field. Malone was now the pitcher, as McDermott had taken his historic 1871 RBI and 0–7 pitching record into oblivion. Veteran Josh Snyder, who had seen his best days in the 1860s, was an emergency replacement in left. Billy Allison, 23 years old, another new face, was in right, while Bestick had replaced Lentz behind the plate as management struggled to find a winning combination (or any combination that would take the field and generate gate receipts). The new lineup fared no better than the old, as the losing streak continued into July.

Such was their ineptitude that the *Clipper* spoke optimistically after a 15–3 loss to the Haymakers in which the Eckfords committed (to that point) a season-low 13 errors.[11] When considering an embarrassing 20–4 loss to the collegians of Princeton, the positive attitude after the loss to Troy is more understandable.

All in all, there was a marked difference in the competitiveness of the co-op teams and the stock clubs. At the Union Grounds in Brooklyn, a 50 cent admission charge was in effect for games between stock clubs, while only a 25 cent tariff was imposed if the game involved a co-op team.[12] While ostensibly one league, the Association had tacitly split into two clear-cut divisions. In its May 18 issue the *Clipper* published a table showing the one-sided nature of the co-op versus stock club contests:

Team	Runs	Opponents' Runs
Brooklyn Eckfords	11	37
Washington Nationals	24	103
Washington Olympics	13	89
Middletown Mansfields	18	51
Brooklyn Atlantics	9	64
Total	75	344

The same issue listed the records of the stock clubs versus the co-ops:[13]

Team	Record
Boston Red Stockings	4–0
Baltimore	4–0
New York Mutuals	3–0
Troy Haymakers	7–0
Total	18–0

Eventually, the *Clipper* established separate sets of standings for each class, while the *New York Times* didn't rate the records of the co-ops worthy of publication. The *Clipper*, in its fascination with multiple sets of standings, published the records of the stock clubs versus each other and their records versus all competition.

As May turned into June, the co-ops wheezed along, lunging crazily toward the October finish line. Some would wither and die with the daffodils, while others would show unexpected staying power and stagger across the line though beaten and bloodied.

Yes, some would wither and die. Troy (a stock club) had experienced a certain degree of success on the field, although admittedly a good deal of their prosperity had come at the expense of co-ops. When the stockholders closed the doors, the Haymakers had a 15–10 record. Their finest hour had come only 3 days earlier when they upset Boston 17–10 at Boston, putting a sudden and unexpected end to the Red Stockings' 19-game winning streak. Troy played its final game on July 23 at Hampden Park, a horse racing track in Springfield, Massachusetts.[14] They ended the season as they had begun it, shutting out the Mansfields. The Haymakers' next scheduled engagement was an exhibition game with the Mutuals in New York on July 26. They never made it. By July 23 the players were owed one month's back salary, but the till was empty.[15] A contributing cause was the fact that the Haymakers had one of the highest payrolls in the league at $14,100.[16]

The Haymakers had suffered, rightfully so, from a tainted reputation dating back almost to the club's inception. The disputed tie with Cincinnati was the most celebrated incident, but there were many others. During the 1871 season, management had encountered difficulty collecting amounts owing under stock subscriptions.[17] In 1872 a new group of stockholders was assembled, principally in an attempt to shed the former Haymaker image.[18] This new group of stockholders was to be the last. Efforts to raise additional capital went for naught as several of the stockholders were out of town and others were disinclined to throw good money after bad.[19]

The players understandably refused to continue with the season. Unlike the other teams that had disbanded, they refused to go quietly into the night. On July 26 the players petitioned the league for the right to pick up the record of the wobbling Eckfords and finish the season on a co-op basis. At first they were not certain whether the new co-op team would be resurrected as the Eckfords or the Haymakers.[20] On July 30 they played an exhibition game against the Mutuals as the Haymakers. Finally they decided to assume the identity of the Eckfords.

The league hierarchy, rubber stamp operation that it was, approved the move without a hitch. The stockholders were more than happy to acquiesce, since it saved them approximately $5,000 in salary expense through the end of the season. The *Troy Press* reported that total gate receipts for the season had been $4,000, while expenses were accruing at the rate of $500 per week.[21] Even in the pre-calculator era, this added up to a losing proposition.

In early September word emanating from Troy indicated that the Haymakers had been "reorganized" and would visit New York on September 10 to play an exhibition game with the Mutuals. The prospect of these old rivals tangling once again brought a large crowd to the Union Grounds. They were disappointed or enraged, according to their disposition, when the team that appeared on the field was not a reorganized version of the Haymakers, but only the Troy Putnams. Despite all the former Haymakers that had been promised, only Ralph Ham, an obscure journeyman, took part. The Mutuals prevailed easily 31–5.[22] There were no more rumors of a Haymaker revival.

It was a homecoming for most of the new Eckfords, as all except Douglas Allison were former members of the club. Yet a funny thing happened when they became the Eckfords. Perhaps it was the lack of their beloved lively ball, or maybe it was simply the curse that had followed the Eckfords all season. Whatever the reason, the players' averages dropped precipitously after the change in teams, as shown below.

Player	Troy Ave.	Eckford Ave.
D. Allison	.319	.299
A. Gedney	.413	.158
A. Martin	.287	.183
J. Nelson	.368	.235
J. Wood	.322	.176
G. Zettlein	.248	.059

Despite the inexplicable dropoff in production, the Eckfords were a much more competitive team with the new additions. Jimmy Wood immediately assumed the role of captain, and the defense solidified. In Zettlein and Martin they had two bona fide major league pitchers, replacing impostors such as Malone, McDermott, and O'Rourke (not Jim). None of the latter three pitched another game in the big leagues.

Betting on Baltimore in their August 9 encounter with the new Brooklyn team was heavy,[23] despite the fact that the Eckfords were an unknown quantity. Within two hours, they were an unknown quantity no more. Behind the pitching of Zettlein and the fine play of holdover shortstop Jimmy Snyder, the Eckfords crushed their highly regarded rivals 10–1.

Under the capable leadership of Wood, the Eckfords lost to the Athletics by a respectable 12–9 tally. In their first meeting with the Atlantics on August 19, they came away with a 10-inning 4–3 victory. In contrast to the pathetic early season Eckford exhibitions, this was a fine display of baseball. A total of only ten errors were committed in the Atlantic match, a minuscule three by the Eckfords. In their 20–0 season opening loss to Boston, Brooklyn had committed 22 errors. Al Martin pitched the entire ten innings against the Atlantics and added three hits as well.

The Eckfords' run of success was short-lived as they finished with a 3–26 record. The team squandered a chance for a major upset on August 31 versus the Athletics at Philadelphia. With the score tied 5–5 in the ninth inning, Dick McBride reached second base. Al Reach lifted a high fly to center which was corralled by Jack Nelson. McBride lit out for third and arrived at the same time as Nelson's strong peg. Frank Fleet, in the course of his aimless wanderings, now found himself guarding third for the Eckfords, about to become the center of a raging controversy. Nelson's throw was to the inside of the bag, forcing Fleet to catch the ball and make a sweeping tag on the Philadelphia pitcher. "Safe!" cried umpire Tom Pratt and the argument ensued. Jimmy Wood had not accompanied the team, appointing Martin as captain in his stead. Martin sauntered in from his position in right field, claiming to have seen clearly that McBride was out. He calmly asked Pratt to reverse the decision. When he was rebuffed, Martin and the rest of his team carried on the discussion for a full ten minutes. The umpire continued to hold his ground. Martin then coolly pulled his team off the field, packed the bats and left the park. Pratt declared the Athletics 9–0 winners by forfeit.[24]

It was a strange affair. There was no palpably wrong decision and there appeared to be no background of enmity between the two teams. Although Pratt was a former Athletic player, he had made no controversial calls through the first eight innings. Most of all, there was no violent outburst on the part of Martin or any of the Eckford players. They left without apparent malice, with the understanding that they would return on September 14 to play the next game of the series. Perhaps Martin felt that his underdog team had gone as far as it was going to go against the vastly superior Athletics. As always, the possibility of a fix must be considered. Whatever the reason, Philadelphia logged a victory and the Eckfords absorbed one of their 26 defeats.

The Mansfields had shown surprising staying power. Spawned from a small town in central Connecticut, known principally for its location on a major bend in the rambling Connecticut River, the Mansfields were an unknown quantity when the season started. Chadwick, of course, had wanted them to remain an unknown quantity. Once the season was under way, however, Middletown had proved to be the toughest competitor among the co-ops, far superior to Chadwick's beloved Atlantics and Eckfords. As a co-op team, however, the Mansfields had experienced great scheduling difficulties, some of which were of their own making. On June 1 they appeared at the Capitoline Grounds to play the Atlantics, who were not home.[25] They also claimed a forfeit over Baltimore, which failed to consummate a scheduled match.[26] As always, a good payday, which the Mansfields could not provide, outweighed the damage wrought by a forfeit.

On July 4 Middletown was faced with the opposite problem. As the Mansfields and Red Stockings were warming up for their game, the Elizabeth Resolutes were disembarking from their train in anticipation of playing the Mansfields. They had to be sent packing, resulting in a wasted day for the Resolutes and a loss for the Mansfields.[27] Perhaps the Red Stockings should have been sent packing instead.

Nevertheless, in late July the *Middletown Sentinel and Witness* reported that the success of the club as a co-op had led to plans for a stock organization. This would, the *Sentinel* assured its readers, put the club "on a sound financial basis" and consequently launch the team to a standing "among the best in the country." The total amount to be subscribed was a modest $2,500, and it was claimed that half of that total had already been spoken for.[28] On this hopeful note, the Mansfields started on a road trip on July 30.

It was to be their last. On August 13 the announcement was made: the team was ceasing operations due to financial difficulties, finishing the season with a 5–19 log. The *Middletown Constitution* confided that "poor luck for the past few weeks has drawn heavy on the purse strings."[29] No mention was made of the aborted stock offering. Jim O'Rourke, the future Hall of Famer, and Clapp and Murnane, future NA standouts, sat out the rest of the season.

With but six teams remaining, the job market was tight. Only Eddie Booth was able to catch on with another team. The Atlantics, remembering his five hits against them in early August, signed Booth to fill a hole in left field. Local journalists insisted that the problem was not a lack of playing ability, despite the team's unimpressive record.[30] There are strong grounds for agreement. For a small town, undercapitalized entry, the Mansfields provided the league with a disproportionate share of talent, similar to that produced by Rockford in the late 1860s.

Cleveland had survived the entire 1871 season and had finished with a reasonably competitive 10–19 mark. By June 17, 1872, they were a mediocre 5–7, having feasted on the hapless co-op teams, while proving less than a match for the strong stock outfits. After a disastrous whirlwind eastern tour in late May, the team's president ordered Captain Scott Hastings to cancel games against the Eckfords and Mutuals and return to Cleveland straight-away.[31] Struggling back to the shores of Lake Erie, they would never be a factor in the pennant race.

They took to the road again in late June. As the Forest Citys moved down the Atlantic coast, they reached their nadir. They were clobbered 20–1 by the Mutuals, who avenged an earlier loss at Cleveland. The following day brought trouble of a different sort. Right fielder and backup pitcher Rynie Wolters was AWOL in his former stomping grounds for, as the *New York Times* reported, "reasons peculiarly his own."[32] Wolters had pulled a similar disappearing act the previous year, leaving the Mutuals to play with only eight men on several occasions.[33] The pitcher's absence was par-ticularly crippling because the team was on the road with only ten players and unable to procure a substitute. Not only was outfielder Charley Pabor forced to pitch in the exhibition game against the Atlantics on July 5 in place of the injured Pratt, he was supported by a team that lacked a center fielder. Wolters's name appeared in the box score with the designation "ab-sent" in place of his statistics.[34] Also in the box score were the ingredients for a 10–3 Atlantic win. The *Clipper* noted Cleveland's ennui, observing that they had played "like a party of disheartened ball tossers."[35]

In the best Kekiongas "you can't quit, you're fired" spirit, the Cleveland managers dismissed Wolters from the team. They dispatched an all points bulletin for Asa Brainard, late of the Olympics, as a replacement.[36] In the meantime, Wolters's teammates were again forced to take the field with eight men against the Eckfords on July 6. Pabor was again in the pitcher's box.

A crowd of less than 300[37] attended this match between Cleveland, with only 8 players, and the Eckfords, who fielded 9 bodies, not each of which, however, contained a player. Their endless lineup shuffling continued, as out of shape 30-year-old veteran Nat Jewett moved in behind the bat.

Possibly it was a supreme effort under adversity on the part of Cleveland; more likely it was another indication of just how bad the Eckfords really were. Playing with their third string pitcher and without a left fielder, the Forest Citys trounced the Brooklyn team 24–5. The Eckfords' feeble attack managed to dunk just eight hits into the two-man outfield.

Two days later Cleveland continued south to Philadelphia. Pratt had recovered sufficiently from his illness to allow for a full complement of players, even though Brainard had not arrived as anticipated. The addition of a ninth player did not lend sufficient help to the cause as Cleveland played a lackluster game. The Athletics put on a performance that was little better, emerging victorious in a 13–8 affair.

After yet another loss to Baltimore, the Forest Citys returned home to attempt to regroup. While they huddled in Cleveland, licking their wounds, word got out that the team was kaput. Not so, cried the management of the Forest Citys in a defiant *Clipper* article entitled "Cleveland Still Lives."[38] They claimed that the team would be reorganized and would soon be taking the field once again. Due to the torpor that had settled over the professionals during July, it was possible to believe that this was true.

More than a month later the team reappeared on the field in a cooperative guise. They made a poor choice of opponents. On August 17 and 19 they lost consecutive games to Boston. The *New York Times* disgustedly described the two matches as "absolutely the worst ever played anywhere."[39] Perhaps the Cleveland management felt the appearance of the league leaders would draw large enough crowds to make the co-op venture successful, but such was not the case. Wolters returned from his sabbatical to start the first game, but became ill and had to depart.

The two-game experiment came to an end and the team officially ended its season on August 20 with a 6–15 record. Both teams which had participated in the NA's historic opening game were now out of existence. The *Clipper*, lamenting the lack of interest in Cleveland, predicted that "the probability is that Cleveland will never again have a first class baseball club."[40] Those who have faithfully knelt at the altar of the Indians for the past 30 years might commend Chadwick for his foresight.

In Cleveland's wake, they left a pair of budding NA superstars. Catcher-outfielder James White batted .336. Ezra Sutton had a poor season at .282, but handled traffic at the hot corner as well as ever. Scott Hastings was part of a troubled team for the second year in a row, but this time the difficulty was not of his own making. He batted .422 before packing his bags for Baltimore upon the team's demise. Shortstop Jim Holdsworth, brought in to replace fellow New Yorker John Bass, had proved more than a creditable substitute, batting .321. When Armageddon arrived on the shores of Lake Erie, Holdsworth returned to New York and played two games with the Eckfords, who were perpetually in need of short-term fill-ins. He and Hastings were the only two Cleveland players who found employment for the remainder of the season.

Chapter 10

The Tournament

The Athletics had gotten off to a flying start, winning their first six games, including an early victory over the Red Stockings. Their first loss came on June 1 to the unpredictable Mutuals. The defeat dropped the Athletics into second place, for after beating the Red Stockings in early May, Philadelphia had been unable to shake them. While the Athletics had not lost, Boston was playing as though it would never lose again. Not only could they outhit any team in the league, but their defense, anchored by George Wright in the infield and Harry in the outfield, was second to none. They turned a remarkable three double plays in a single game against Troy.[1]

Boston also had Al Spalding. While other pitchers such as Zettlein, McBride, Cummings, and Mathews threw hard and had good control, it was Spalding who was the dominant pitcher of the era. He won 207 games in 5 years, leaving McBride a distant second with 151. In the 1870s a pitcher's record was primarily a function of his team's strength, since a pitcher would generally pitch a complete game in every game his team played. However, it could also be argued that a team's success was highly dependent upon its pitcher's ability to overpower or baffle opposing hitters. Spalding could do both. When the big Boston bats failed to produce enough thunder, Spalding and a tight defense did the job many times.

Despite strong performances by Troy, Baltimore, and New York, the race was developing into a two-team affair. None of the co-op teams had more than three wins. On June 3, the standings read as follows:

	W	L	Pct.	GB
Boston Red Stockings	9	1	.900	—
Philadelphia Athletics	6	1	.857	1½
Troy Haymakers	11	4	.733	½
Lord Baltimores	10	5	.667	1½
New York Mutuals	8	4	.667	2

	W	L	Pct.	GB
Cleveland Forest Citys	4	7	.364	5½
Middletown Mansfields	3	6	.333	5½
Washington Olympics	2	7	.222	6½
Brooklyn Eckfords	0	4	.000	6
Brooklyn Atlantics	0	5	.000	6½
Washington Nationals	0	9	.000	8½

On June 12, in a battle of the first and second place teams, the Red Stockings defeated Philadelphia easily 13–4. This game was the turning point of the season. It put some breathing room between first place Boston and second place Philadelphia, and the ease of Boston's victory established the confidence of the Red Stockings. They were now definitely the team to beat. By June 24, Boston had compiled an 18–1 record, capped by 15 wins in a row. The lofty record was no surprise since, according to the unofficial statistics published by the *Clipper*, six regulars were batting over .300, with Cal McVey a shade below at .299. The team batting average was .314. Harry Wright, on the down side of his brilliant career, and Fraley Rogers were the only two slackers below McVey.[2]

By late August the only teams left in this battle of attrition were Boston, Philadelphia, Baltimore, the Mutuals, Atlantics, and Eckfords. Evidencing the New York origins of the game, half of the remaining teams were based in that metropolis.

On July 27 Boston and Philadelphia met for the third time, prior to Boston's departure on an exhibition tour of Canada. It was a do-or-die situation for the Athletics, as a defeat would not only drop them farther back into the pack, but would establish Boston's superiority beyond a doubt. The Athletics would be, in modern parlance, "psyched out" in future encounters.

On the eve of the big game Philadelphia shook up its lineup. Mike McGeary, the former Haymaker who had been playing shortstop, was now asked to catch. Fergy Malone, due in part to his weak arm, was moved to first and Denny Mack was shifted to shortstop, where he had never before appeared in a pro game. This was a bold move but if ever there was a time for bold moves, this was it. The Athletics had their collective back to the wall.

Again, the clash was a tremendous draw, attracting nearly 5,000 Philadelphia fans who prayed that the home team could spring an upset. The timing was good. Boston had just returned from a summer idyll and had been shocked by the Haymakers, ending their long winning streak. Dick McBride was magnificent. He had played with the Athletics since their inception in 1860 and was not about to let the championship slip away without putting up a struggle. McBride allowed the heavy hitting Boston club only four hits, with hardly a sharply stroked out. For good measure, he reached Spalding for two hits of his own. McBride took to McGeary well, and the battery worked together splendidly. Mack did not make a single error in his maiden appearance at short.[3]

The Red Stockings took out their frustrations on the poor Atlantics, routing them three times within the space of a week. The Athletics kept pace, and by August 18 Boston's lead hovered at six games. The standings stood as follows:

	W	L	Pct.	GB
Boston Red Stockings	29	3	.906	—
Philadelphia Athletics	19	5	.792	6
New York Mutuals	20	12	.625	9
Lord Baltimores	21	13	.618	9
Brooklyn Atlantics	4	15	.211	18½
Brooklyn Eckfords	1	13	.071	19

Although both Brooklyn teams were winless through June, captains Ferguson and Clinton did not conceive of the idea of playing each other, guaranteeing a win for one of the teams. Perhaps they feared the game would end in a scoreless tie. More likely, they were concerned that not a single spectator would show up.

Despite playing in the same city, the two teams were unable to complete their full quota of games before the November 1 deadline. They scrupulously avoided each other until August 19, when they met for the first time.

In the meantime, the Atlantics had come to life and broken into the win column. Only 300 partisans braved a New York heat wave that had sent temperatures soaring in excess of 100 degrees on July 2 to watch the struggling Atlantics take on the heavily favored Mutuals.[4] The Mutuals were so confident of victory that they gave shortstop Dicky Pearce the day off, replacing him with former Rockford infielder Chick Fulmer. No one was surprised when the Mutuals led 6–0 after three innings. The Atlantics refused to wilt, and tied the game 8–8 with a six-run rally in the sixth that was greatly assisted by their opponents' misplays. In the eighth the Mutuals again failed on defense, handing the Atlantics three runs and an 11–10 victory. Captain Ferguson was jubilant[5] after vanquishing the team whose managers had criticized his management style the previous season. The first win was a long time coming, but it could not have been sweeter. For the Mutuals, it was just another suspicious loss.

The Atlantics became more competitive in the latter stages of the season, recovering from their winless start to finish 8–27. The *Clipper* charitably described the Atlantics and Eckfords as "the top two contestants for the co-op championship."[6] To substitute "only" for "top" would make the statement more accurate. The two Brooklyn teams played out the string, drawing increasingly smaller crowds as the weather grew colder and the insignificance of the battles more apparent.

On August 28 the Atlantics were overwhelmed by the Athletics 26–12. Left fielder Albert Thake of the Atlantics scored a one run, had one hit and four putouts.[7] In the course of a 38-run slugfest, these statistics might seem insignificant. Thake was not one of the more noted Atlantics, even though he batted a solid .274, second highest on the team. Thake's performance against the Athletics was more significant than he or anyone else realized at the time, for it was the last game that the left fielder would play.

On September 1, while fishing from a boat in New York Harbor, near Fort Hamilton, 23-year-old Thake lost his balance and toppled into the water. Although he was within swimming distance of shore, Thake was not a swimmer and sank directly to the bottom.[8]

As a sign of respect for his death, the September 2 game with the Eckfords was postponed. Flags at the Union and Capitoline Grounds were lowered to half mast.[9] On October 23 Bob Ferguson organized an exhibition game between the old Cincinnati Red Stockings and the old Atlantics, with the proceeds earmarked for Thake's unfortunate widowed mother, who had been deprived of her only means of support. Despite the cooperation of the players from these legendary teams, threatening weather kept attendance to a minimum. A disappointed Ferguson was able to turn over only $200 to Mrs. Thake.[10]

Meanwhile, the Athletics' pursuit of Boston continued. On September 4 the fourth game between the two teams dashed any hopes Philadelphia might have cherished of repeating their championship performance of 1871. In front of a delirious home crowd, Boston batters knocked McBride's pitches all over South Boston. They reached the usually reliable hurler for 23 hits en route to a 16–4 win.

During the prior season, the Athletics, with the exception of the Bechtel/Heubel right field platoon, had played a set lineup. In 1872 the players were shifted from position to position throughout the season. Mack played an almost equal number of games at first base and shortstop, while McGeary divided time between shortstop and catcher and Malone did the same between first base and the catcher's position. Although the team would finish a strong second, it never jelled to the extent necessary to overtake Boston.

Despite two Boston losses to the Mutuals within a five-day period, the race was over. On September 9 the Athletics and the Red Stockings played a 5–5 tie in a game that was called because of a rainstorm in the ninth inning. The standings reflected the same margin that had existed for several weeks.

	W	L	Pct.	GB
Boston Red Stockings	32	4	.889	—
Philadelphia Athletics	24	9	.727	6½
Lord Baltimores	29	13	.690	6
New York Mutuals	25	17	.595	10

Baltimore had caught fire, winning seven games in a row since adding Davy Force from the defunct Haymakers, and were challenging the Athletics for second place. On September 12 Mathews brought them closer with a seven-inning one-hit gem against the Eckfords. Unlike the 1871 race, however, there would be no photo finish for first place.

This posed a serious problem. There were only six teams remaining in the league, only four of which were competitive. The repetitive presence of the same teams was beginning to wear thin with the fans, whose numbers showed an alarming decrease. A mere 100 watched the Atlantics play the Mutuals on September 16.[11] Five years earlier, this rivalry was drawing several thousand. Some teams were playing the always suspect exhibitions after completing their series. Including the exhibitions, Baltimore and New York met 13 times during the season.

Despite the dearth of competitive alternatives, not all quotas were completed. The top teams could command a much more satisfying draw by playing exhibitions among themselves than by playing championship games with the Atlantics or Eckfords. While New York and Baltimore met 13 times, the Mutuals failed to complete their quota with either tailender. They got a late start with the Eckfords, meeting them for the first time on August 24.

Harry Wright laid out a tale of woe in his year-end report to the Championship Committee.[12] Baltimore had refused to play the final two games of their series, leaving Boston short one home game. The final game with the Atlantics was rained out and never made up. The Red Stockings managed to play a full nine game series with the Athletics; however, the makeup game for the September 9 tie was postponed by rain and Philadelphia declined to reschedule. The Eckfords, Haymakers, Mansfields, Nationals, and Olympics had no hope of completing their quota with the Red Stockings.

Problems other than overexposure hindered attendance. As the seasons changed, the weather grew colder and spectators grew fewer in the absence of a hotly contested pennant race. Ferguson, as president of the NA, might be expected to address the problem, but he was first and foremost a ballplayer, with no use for administrative duties. He refused to acknowledge the matter and, indeed, no one was pressing him to do so. The Championship Committee had taken it upon themselves (without proper authority, claimed the *Clipper*) to increase the required series between each set of teams from five to nine games.[13] While this eliminated the necessity for the dreaded exhibition game, it did nothing about the lack of excitement occasioned by Boston's firm grip on the pennant.

As early as July a Philadelphia gentleman had proposed a tournament in that city in late September. He offered to put up $4,000 in prize money if the top five contenders would appear and play one game against every other team. The team with the most victories would be declared the winner. First prize was set at $1,800, second prize at $1,200 and third prize at $1,000.[14]

By the time October rolled around, attendance for most games was measured in hundreds rather than thousands. Boston continued to draw well, but attendance in other cities suffered. A Baltimore-Atlantic clash at the Capitoline Grounds in Brooklyn attracted only 100 diehards.[15] They were rewarded for their devotion as they were treated to a 35-14 slugfest, with the victorious Lord Baltimores slashing 42 hits with the lively ball they had brought north.

The sickly attendance figures led to a revival of the tournament proposition. This time the offer was made by William Cammeyer. He contributed a purse of $4,000, with a distribution identical to that offered in Philadelphia.[16] The Athletics, Mutuals, and Red Stockings accepted the invitation.

The tournament began on a high note on October 8, with an exciting 7–7 tie between the Mutuals and Red Stockings which was called due to darkness and an injury to Boston's Dave Birdsall after 10 innings.[17] The following day the competition was even better, as the Athletics needed 12 innings to defeat the Mutuals 9–7. Despite the excitement of the two extra-inning games, there was a disquieting note to the proceedings. The fans had shown a decided lack of interest in the contrived affair, and Cammeyer was beginning to doubt the wisdom of his $4,000 investment. It was beginning to look as though he might not recoup the sum from the gate proceeds. Attendance at the Union Grounds was not helped by the fact that Boston, the odd team out on October 9, moseyed over to the Capitoline Grounds to take on the Atlantics in a game that competed for the attention of the Brooklyn fans. The small gathering at Capitoline saw their Atlantics upset the mighty Red Stockings 5–3.

Meanwhile, back at Union, the tournament continued with an Athletic victory over a crippled Boston team and a Red Stocking triumph over the Mutuals. Under the round robin format, an Athletic victory over the Mutuals set up a confrontation between the Athletics and Boston for the championship. On October 14 the 2 teams played to a 10–10 standoff that was called due to darkness after 12 innings.

The Mutuals were allowed to reenter the extended competition, splitting a pair of games with Boston. Cammeyer was showing signs of

desperation, and the tournament was beginning to take on a carnival atmosphere. He put up $50 in prize money for a throwing contest. With
selected players from the 3 teams heaving the ball from center field to home
plate, Johnny Hatfield broke his own record with a toss of more than 133
yards. Andy Leonard of Boston picked up the second prize, while George
Wright won $10 with a throw of 117 yards.[18]

On October 17 Boston beat the Athletics to set up a second championship match (under the jumbled format) the following day. The next day
brought rain, however, and the game was postponed indefinitely. Boston,
with a number of injured players, begged off from further competition.
After ten days of play and nine games, there was no champion. The two
teams supposedly agreed to accept $1,500 each, a settlement rumored to
have been made well in advance.[19]

Another reason Boston and Philadelphia were unable to reschedule
their rained out affair was that they had to hustle down to the latter city to
compete in yet another tournament. They were joined once again by the
Mutuals, returning from Baltimore.[20] New York and Baltimore had been
scheduled to play a championship game on October 18, but New York had
begged off due to an injury to Cummings. The 18 players randomly chose
teams among themselves and played a practice game. The league's credibility
was rapidly disintegrating as the season ground to a merciful finish.

The Philadelphia tournament did nothing to restore the NA's prestige.
Attendance was slim for the three-game affair, which the Athletics captured
with victories over their two rivals.

There seemed no end to the troubles that plagued the league in the
season's final month. On October 29, the Mutuals and Baltimore met for
the twelfth time. Baltimore prevailed 4–1, but the big story broke the
following day. The betting had been so strongly in favor of the visiting
Baltimore team at heavy odds that suspicions arose regarding the integrity
of the Mutuals' effort. The word went out that some of the Mutuals had
been bought. The *New York World* deplored the "...ancient and very fish-
like smell which surrounded the affair." The *New York Sun* reporter
observed a gentleman who was very anxious to wager on Baltimore. So
transparent was his eagerness that he was unable to find any takers, even
at long odds. Other publications made similar claims and the *Clipper* urged
a thorough investigation.[21]

Of course, nothing of the sort was ever done. A telling statistic which
darkened the cloud of suspicion hanging over the New York team was their
poor record in exhibition games. While they posted a fine 34–20 record during the regular season, the Mutuals stumbled (intentionally?) to a 4–8–1
record in exhibition matches against the same teams.

The season officially ended on October 31, to the dismay of no one,
although the teams continued to play exhibition games versus amateur

clubs until the mid–November cold drove them to cover. The final standings reflected Boston's dominance and the significant attrition factor.

	W	L	Pct.	GB
Boston Red Stockings	39	8	.830	—
Philadelphia Athletics	30	14	.682	7½
Lord Baltimores	34	19	.642	8
New York Mutuals	34	20	.630	8½
Troy Haymakers	15	10	.600	13
Cleveland Forest Citys	6	15	.286	20
Brooklyn Atlantics	8	27	.229	25
Washington Olympics	2	7	.222	18
Middletown Mansfields	5	19	.208	22½
Brooklyn Eckfords	3	26	.103	27
Washington Nationals	0	11	.000	21

Chapter 11

Financial Troubles

When examining the 1872 standings, one is struck by the gap between fifth place Troy's .600 winning percentage and sixth place Cleveland's .286. In 1871 even teams such as Rockford and Fort Wayne had provided a difficult test. The success of the maiden season had attracted too many charlatan combinations. The stock club/co-op dichotomy perceived by the press was acute and a source of ragged mismatches.

By any standard, it had been a miserable season. Eleven teams had started, and only six had answered the final bell. In the preceding year, only the Kekiongas had proved incapable of weathering the campaign.

To make matters worse, there was little drama in the pennant race after Boston's initial winning streak. The Athletics were never able to get within striking distance, making the late-season, head-to-head confrontations anticlimactic. After the exciting if confusing finish of 1871, the pennant race, or lack thereof, was a definite disappointment.

In an effort to combat these problems, team managers succeeded only in compounding them. Not only was the tournament scheme a financial loser, the New York extravaganza was an artistic failure as well, as the event fizzled out without siring a champion. The attempt to generate contrived excitement was not well received by the fans or the sporting press. Exhibition games, as always, created the opportunity for "upsets" and odd happenings. The integrity of the professional game was coming under intense scrutiny; the suspicions heightened by the amount of gambling that took place on the grounds.

The "pernicious practice" continued to be deplored, but not discontinued. The prospect of winning or losing a large sum of cash made for ugly fans. The most notorious umpire baiters were drawn from the gambling crowd, which also heaped abuse upon any player whose performance or lack thereof was detrimental to the heckler's pecuniary interest.

At the 1873 convention in Baltimore the issue was addressed by Bob Ferguson, who had been reelected President.[1] While deploring the presence of gambling and its possible undue influence on players, the Atlantic captain abdicated any position of responsibility for its abolition. He stated that any legislation passed by the NA would be ineffectual, although he did not say why. The first line of defense against gambling, Ferguson declared, was club management. If only they enforced their club rules stringently, it would be unnecessary for the league to take any action. Having his hands full with his multiple responsibilities, Ferguson was in favor of any resolution which eliminated the need for action on his part.

All of the league's problems led to a final, overiding problem. The teams were losing money. It was not surprising that second-rate teams such as Cleveland, the Mansfields, or Olympics would come upon hard times. In addition to these tailenders, however, championship teams were having difficulty making ends meet.

The Athletics concluded their 1871 championship season with a deficit of more than $2,000.[2] The *Clipper* commented that a few more successes like that would leave the Athletics rather weak.[3] Another strong season in 1872 brought the team out of debt and left them with a handsome surplus of $8.45. The fiscal results for the 1872 season[4] can be seen below:

Revenue

Dues from Members	$ 3,825.00
Gate Receipts	21,457.23
Rent of Grounds	440.00
Credited to Treasurer	300.00
Other	25.00
Total	$26,047.23

Expenses

Salaries (inc. 1871 arrears)	$15,860.25
Traveling Expenses	3,899.68
Repayment of 1871 Loan	3,060.00
Administrative and Incidental	2,310.00
Groundskeeper's Salary	535.00
Uniforms and Equipment	373.85
Total	$26,038.78
Balance on Hand	$8.45

Since nearly $4,000 in revenue was derived from dues paid by club members, the operating results of the team were even more dismal than depicted above.

Boston, successor to Philadelphia as league champions, also succeeded them in the poor house, accumulating unpaid debts of more than $5,000, including accrued salaries.[5] During the winter of 1872–73, there were serious doubts regarding the ability of the Red Stockings to place a team in the field to defend their title.[6] The catastrophic fire which swept the city in October did nothing to alleviate the financial distress of the team or its backers. Harry Wright was forced to use all of his considerable persuasiveness to convince the incumbent Boston players to return for the following season. He assured them that the unpaid 1872 salaries would be made up and told them that he himself would not have stayed if he was not confident of this fact.[7]

During the winter of Boston's discontent, the citizens of Cincinnati engaged in a bit of gratuitous grave dancing. They made it known that, if the Boston team were disbanded, they had all intentions of bringing back the Wright brothers as the nucleus of a revived Cincinnati nine.[8]

These discussions became moot shortly after they were initiated. Unlike the 1871 White Stockings, the Red Stockings were able to rise from the ashes of their conflagration. On December 11 more than 150 supporters met in Brackett's Hall in Boston to effect the salvation of their beloved champions. It was decided that the Boston Association, which had operated the team in 1872, would be effectively dissolved. In its place would be the Boston Base Ball Club, which would assume the debts of the Boston Association and sell new stock to raise funds for the 1873 season. All parties agreed to make concessions. The Boston Association stockholders relinquished majority control with the issuance of the new stock. The players were asked to accept their accrued salary in installments during the 1873 season. In return for their patience, it was proposed that the players receive a share of the profits (if any) at the end of the season.[9]

The team survived the crisis, as an early season Southern trip replenished the barren treasury and enabled the new stockholders to begin making good on the salary arrears. Much to the chagrin of their NA opponents, the 1873 team was even stronger than the 1872 edition. Slugging Cal McVey elected to sign with Baltimore as team captain and Charley Gould retired, but all other key players returned to the fold. In addition, Harry Wright was able to do some grave dancing of his own, scooping up James White and Jim O'Rourke from the defunct Cleveland and Middletown clubs, respectively. Pitcher-outfielder Jack Manning, 19 years old, who had batted a robust .517 for the Boston Juniors,[10] moved up to the big team, replacing Fraley Rogers, who retired from the game. Al Pratt of Cleveland was offered a contract, but declined, feeling the company was "too fast."[11]

The 11 teams which had left the starting gate in 1872 had been whittled by attrition to 6, leaving jobs hard to come by. After the end of the season, the venerable Eckfords closed shop. Many well-known players were out of work as the 1873 season began, and the team managers, now dealing from a position of strength based upon supply and demand, held the line on salaries. The stiff competition for roster spots had undoubtedly played a part in the concessions made by the Boston players.

Three new teams threw their skimmers into the ring, the most formidable of which was the Philadelphia White Stockings. The White Stockings raided the crosstown Athletics and stripped the cupboard bare. When the Athletics took inventory, they were missing hard-hitting Levi Meyerle, left fielder Ned Cuthbert, center fielder Fred Treacey, catcher Fergy Malone and first baseman Denny Mack. The Athletics were so embittered by the brazen pirating of their players that they at first refused to let the upstart White Stockings (or Philadelphias, as they were commonly known) share their Jefferson Street Grounds.[12] Finally, the Athletics relented (for a rental fee, of course)[13] and vowed to vent their anger on the playing field whenever the two teams met.

While the White Stockings presented a strong stock club that would be a bona fide contender, the other two new entries were mere pretenders, in the best tradition of the Nationals and Eckfords. The Elizabeth Resolutes, who had played competitively against pro teams in 1872, beating the co-op Atlantics and Eckfords, decided to take the $10 plunge in 1873. They kept their 1872 team virtually intact, making very little attempt to lure established performers from their competitors. They could have used some.

The Resolutes took the field as a co-operative venture, as did the third new entry, the Marylands. Based in Baltimore, the Maryland team had a storied past, having captured the mythical championship of the South in 1868 and 1869 behind Bobby Mathews.[14] The team had disbanded after a series of defeats in 1870,[15] causing a number of the players to move to the Kekiongas. Now the Marylands were reorganizing, minus Mathews, who was rumored to be joining the team,[16] but had the good sense to move on to the Mutuals instead. A handful of former Kekiongas supplemented by a ragtag assortment of local amateurs comprised the 1873 edition of the Marylands.

The revival was to be short-lived. By the time the Marylands realized the futility of their mission, they were 0–6 and finished for the season, or any other season. There was no formal announcement of the Marylands' dissolution. As late as June Harry Wright was still attempting to arrange games with the nonexistent team. "Are they a club?" he had written to Nick Young in frustration after receiving no answer to three letters.[17]

In the 6 losses, the Marylands employed 17 different players, including 4 former Kekiongas. The offense was feeble, with the team batting average resting at a pathetic .147. The team produced only five earned runs all season.[18] Of the 17 players, 7 failed to get a single hit, registering a combined zero for 42. The batting star of the team, fittingly, was an anonymous creature with the surname of Jones, whose first name has been lost in history. Jones played one game (a characteristic 26–5 drubbing by Baltimore), going three for five. He resurfaced in 1874 and 1875, playing a total of three NA games before disappearing without a trace, as did the Marylands.

Despite stirrings and rumblings from Chicago and Cincinnati, neither city was able to raise a sufficient combination of capital and talent. Thus, nine teams, including the revived Nationals, stood restlessly in the starting gate in late April.

As usual, there was a shuffling of rosters. Candy Cummings and Bobby Mathews, the two mighty-mite pitchers, swapped teams as Cummings signed with Baltimore and Mathews moved to New York. Baltimore also added Cal McVey, who proved a valuable utility man, playing six different positions.

As in 1872, Baltimore was a heavy hitting team, with five regulars bettering the .300 mark. Only one nonpitcher (Scott Hastings) failed to bat at least .280 on a team which compiled an outstanding .301 percentage. McVey proved an invaluable acquisition, although limited to 35 games by injury. He caught, played every infield position and the outfield, and batted a powerful .369. A muscular, sturdy fellow, he combined with Lip Pike to give the team extra base power. Although home run totals are hard to come by, Pike was known to wallop one now and then. McVey was more apt to let loose a flurry of doubles and triples. Center fielder George Hall, who also had home run power (he led the National League with five in 1876), third baseman Davy Force, and second baseman and captain Tom Carey were defensive stalwarts who provided stability in the field behind curveballer Cummings. Although the Athletics were left with only four starters, they filled the holes well with players stranded by the flood of disbanded teams. John Clapp and future sportswriter Tim Murnane were plucked from the wreckage of the Mansfields, while pitcher-outfielder Cherokee Fisher arrived from Baltimore and Ezra Sutton from Cleveland to complete the team.

The Mutuals, who had hitherto put a salaried stock club in the field, now tried a questionable experiment. Hicks, Mathews, Hatfield, and Eggler received salaries while the remainder of the players shared in the gate proceeds on a co-op basis.[19] On a team with a chemistry as fragile as that of the Mutuals, this new arrangement could hardly help matters. For the rest of the team, New York picked at the remains of the Haymaker/Eckford carcass and signed outfielder Count Gedney, pitcher Al Martin, and infielders Jim Holdsworth and Jack Nelson. Nelson merged perfectly with the bickering Mutuals, as he had a well-deserved reputation for "growling" on the field.[20] Another natural returned to the fold in the person of Dick Higham, who had first appeared in the NA in 1871 as a substitute for the injured Charlie Smith.

The *Clipper* made no attempt to mask its contempt for the young hothead Higham. There were repeated references to his "erratic play" and "uneven play" which, to those who followed Chadwick's drift, hinted that the erratic and uneven nature of Higham's play was no accident. Like the Mutuals, his performances were always cloaked with suspicion. The *Clipper* opined that "Hatfield and Higham ought to be brothers for their mutual fondness of growling and fault-finding."[21] Although a .300 hitter during the league's first three years, he bounced from team to team, returning to New York like the swallows to Capistrano on three different occasions. He later performed for the minor league Syracuse Stars[22] before earning his infamous niche in baseball history. To this day, Higham remains the only umpire expelled from the major leagues for dishonesty.[23]

The Atlantics improved their chances by adding veteran shortstop Dicky Pearce, who was reunited once more with Captain Ferguson. The two had been part of the old Atlantic dynasty and had formed the left side of the Mutual infield in 1871. Pearce and the Mutuals had become disenchanted with each other late in the 1872 season. Dicky had relinquished his role as captain when he realized that his charges were incorrigible and that he had absolutely no support from management in his attempt to enforce discipline on this unruly bunch.[24] Management, in turn, replaced him at shortstop with Chick Fulmer, depriving the team of Pearce's leadership in their pique. Former Mutual Bill Boyd tagged along with Pearce to play right field. Charley Pabor became his counterpart in left and led the team in hitting, whaling away at a lusty .346 clip.

The Nationals had petered out in 1872, but found new life during the off-season under the leadership of newly married[25] Nick Young, fronting his third team in three years. They returned with essentially the same cast of characters, although not even their mothers would recognize the team from the box score. In center field was John Hollingshead, who played under the name of Holly. At second base was Tommy Beals, who used the *nom de beis bol* Thomas. Warren White appeared alternatively as "Warren" or "White." Mrs. Waterman would not realize that her son Fred was playing shortstop unless she knew that he sometimes used the pseudonym "Waters." Unfortunately Frank (Williams) Selman had moved on to the Marylands. Had he stayed, the Nationals would have been well on their way to fielding an all-alias team. Selman's entry in the *Macmillan Baseball Encyclopedia* reads like a wanted poster.

Selman, Frank C.
Played as Frank Williams 1871–73, part of 1874
Also known as Frank C. Williams.

Adding to the confusion was the fact that he was commonly misidentified as "Selliman." Selman/Williams moved around like a man on the shady

THE DAILY GRAPHIC, NEW YORK, MONDAY, SEPTEMBER 15, 1873.

CHAS. PABOR, R.F.

J. BURDOCK, 2ND B.

JAS. BRITT, P.

Wm. BOYD, A.F.

CAPT. R. FERGUSON, 3RD B.

H. DEHLMAN, 1ST B.

THOS. BARLOW, C.

J. J. REMSEN, C.F.

R. J. PEARCE, S.S.

THE ATLANTIC BASE-BALL CLUB, OF BROOKLYN.

THE NATIONAL GAME.

side of the law, playing for the Kekiongas, Olympics, Marylands and Lord Baltimores over his 4-year career and batting an unimposing .250 in just 35 games. Even the usually reliable *Clipper* became confused by the multiple identities of the Washington team. On March 22 it reported that Thomas would replace Beals at second base.[26] The replacement would certainly be adequate, for Thomas was indeed Beals!

Under Young's magic wand, the Nationals had gone from horrible to merely bad. They were no longer steamrolled by every team which came to town. Washington was capable of beating the Marylands (as could any respectable amateur combine) and, of greater relevance, could stand toe to toe with the NA contenders, although they generally went down to defeat.

The Resolutes emerged with a number of faces familiar to New York fans. In addition, they imported the Allison brothers, their only major acquisition. Douglas would catch and brother Art would play right field. The team was hampered from the start by its inadequate playing facilities at the Waverly, New Jersey, Fairgrounds.

The metropolis of Waverly is no longer in existence, the fairgrounds site now resting on the Newark-Elizabeth border. The fields over which the brothers Allison and their teammates romped is now B'nai Jeshuran Cemetery.[27] If the current residents had taken the place of the Resolutes in 1873, they would have won only two fewer games. In addition to having a poorly maintained field, the team had no regular practice site,[28] and seemed incapable of adequately publicizing their games. On several occasions, sparse crowds were attributable to the fact that most fans were unaware that a game was to be played.[29] They were also attributable to the miserable play of the home team.

The Resolutes demonstrated the need for great improvement in the field, and for a stronger PR effort. The team treated its schedule like a state secret. The Resolutes needed to draw from the New York market in order to be successful, yet for some unknown reason they never communicated their schedule to the New York papers. After a July 16 game at Waverly, the *Clipper* reported that the "Mutuals returned home as victors and with about two dollars each as their share of the gate receipts."[30]

Prior to the start of the season, the *Clipper* spotted trouble across the river in the form of "growling."[31] It warily observed the number of hard-core complainers on the Resolute roster and predicted trouble if things went badly for the team. Mike Campbell, the first baseman, and brother Hugh, a pitcher, were renowned grumblers. Doug Allison was moody to the point of sometimes allowing his pitcher to chase his own wild pitches while Allison stood disgustedly at the plate.[32] His batterymate, Rynie Wolters,

Opposite: **The 1873 Brooklyn Atlantics (courtesy of Transcendental Graphics).**

had already worn out his welcome with New York and Cleveland. Elizabeth tired of him even more quickly, and Wolters lasted only one game.

Once again, the league presented an unbalanced lineup. Boston, Baltimore, New York, the Athletics, and the new Philadelphia entry promised to be competitive. For the princely sum of $10 each, however, the league had burdened itself with the Atlantics, Nationals, Resolutes, and Marylands, who promised only a stream of dreadful mismatches.

Chapter 12

The Umpire

During the existence of the NA, there was but one umpire. Prior to 1858, each team had provided an umpire, with a referee named to decide any calls upon which the two umpires could not agree. In most cases, each sided with his own team and the referee was required to make all close calls. Thus, the system was abandoned and that of a lone umpire adopted.[1]

In baseball's first years, the umpire was accorded the respect initially anticipated with the establishment of the function. Players were expected to acquiesce in the decisions of the arbiter and any verbal, let alone physical, abuse was considered quite ungentlemanly. Any member of the Knicker-bockers who dared to dispute an umpire's decision was subject to a fine of 25 cents.[2] In 1866 the *New York Times* was shocked by a string of epithets unleashed by an Eckford player to express his displeasure with an umpire's ruling. "We never witnessed a like occurrence on a ball field and we trust we never shall witness another."[3]

They were to be disappointed, as the spread of professionalism eased gentlemen from the game and opened it up to the middle and lower classes. By 1871 rhubarbs were commonplace and respect for the umpire's position had declined precipitously, due in no small part to their deficient knowledge of the rules and sometimes faulty or biased judgment.

These men were not operating under conditions that led to optimum performance. They were prohibited from entering the field of play, and were forced to make their calls from foul territory,[4] rarely the best vantage point. The umpires were neither professional nor full-time operatives and were chosen by mutual consent of the competing teams. The visiting team sent a list of five prospects to the home team. The local club was to select from that list. If none of the five were acceptable, two additional names were to be provided by the visitors. Umpires, particularly in the first years of the NA, were usually players from nonparticipating teams or, on many occasions, from one of the teams involved. Nick Young was a frequent ar-biter (even when a team he was managing was a contestant) and ex-players such as Theodore Bomeisler and quick-tempered former prize fighter[5] William McLean gained considerable reputations for their fairness and knowledge of the rules.

Fairness and a knowledge of the rules, however, were not a prerequisite for selection as an umpire. Many, including the players, were ignorant of the rules or flagrantly disregarded them. Pressure from the home crowd, often far from an empty threat, clouded the judgment of even those with the most honorable intent. On occasion it was necessary to replace an umpire in mid-game, and games were delayed or even canceled when the teams could not reach a consensus on the selection of an umpire. The press did not take the difficult working conditions of the umpire into consideration, nor did they endear them to the home crowd. They often vilified the poor devils with headlines such as, "The Umpire Gives the Game to the Bostons 14–13" which blared from the pages of the Hartford Courant in June 1874.[6]

The officiating problem did not take long to surface, beginning with the gala opening day game between the Red Stockings and Olympics on May 5, 1871. For that encounter, Hicks Hayhurst, manager and former player of the Athletics, had been engaged to act as arbiter, but failed to put in an appearance.[7] H. A. Dobson, a reporter for the *Clipper*,[8] was drafted into service. While mention has already been made of the handicaps under which NA umpires operated, Dobson suffered from an additional hindrance. The reporter had lost a leg in the Civil War, and was forced to hop awkwardly about on crutches in order to position himself to make calls. In the eighth inning, he took a nasty shot on his only leg, which sent him sprawling. Gamely, Dobson was able to raise himself up on his crutches and continue his duties.[9]

During the course of the game, Dobson made several gaffes, the most notable of which was calling a ball for every ball that was not fair, rather than every third one, as decreed in the rules.[10] This resulted in an astounding 30 walks divided between pitchers Spalding and Brainard. Harry Wright took full advantage of the situation, urging his batters to wait Brainard out.[11] Thie latter's 18 free passes played no small part in the Boston triumph.

The *Clipper*, not mentioning the affiliation, praised the "great umpiring job."[12] Other opinion was not as laudatory, as Dobson was accused in print of partiality toward the Red Stockings. The *Boston Herald* added a bipartisan denunciation, concluding, "we sincerely hope that he may never fill the position in any first class match again."[13]

Six days later at Cleveland, in a game against the White Stockings, the enraged Forest Citys stalked off the field in disgust at what they considered to be the palpably biased calls of umpire J. L. Haynie.[14] When left fielder Charley Pabor was called out at third, the Forest Citys decided to take an early powder. The irate Cleveland newspapers charged that Haynie had been the arbiter on a similar day in 1870 when the Athletics had left the field in anger over his Chicago bias.[15] This allegation was not corroborated and would have been strange if it were true since, under the rules, Cleveland had consented to Haynie's selection as umpire. In any event, Cleveland forfeited the game, a minor point since they were trailing 18–10 at the time of their departure. The matter was referred to the Judiciary Committee, where it died a lingering death.

In mid-season Chicago was again involved in an officiating fiasco, this time on their home field. On July 14 an estimated 8,000 fans showed up for a battle with the front-running Athletics. Prior to the game, the two teams could not reach agreement on an umpire. After much hemming and hawing, the Athletics agreed to the placement of Mr. Bonse in that delicate position. They yielded against the wishes of some of their partisans, who had heard that Bonse (like Haynie) had officiated a Chicago-Cleveland game in 1870 in which Cleveland had removed its team from the field in protest over Bonse's partial decisions. The arbiter claimed to be a member of a baseball club with the ponderous handle of the Railway Union Club of Leland. Knowledgeable observers claimed that no such club existed.

By the midway point of the game, the Athletics wished that Bonse was not in existence. He had called a Philadelphia batsman out after the player had been hit by a pitch and had called another out when a third strike had eluded the catcher and hit the fence in front of the grandstand. Fortunately, in the latter case, Chicago captain Jimmy Wood humanely intervened and read the rule to the ignorant arbiter, who reversed his decision. However, aided immeasurably by their ally Bonse, the White Stockings upset Philadelphia 11–9, toppling the Athletics from the upper rung.[16]

In mid–September, the two teams met again in the heat of a close pennant race. Although the weather was chilly and very windy, the conditions for play were much better than when the two teams met in July. At last, they had found an umpire who could give both teams a fighting chance. In place of the incompetent and partial Bonse, the teams enlisted Sam Holly, from the Niagaras of Buffalo. Holly was "impartial and fearless, much to the disgust of a party of toughs from Chicago who tried to intimidate him and threatened violence."[17] His moment of truth came in the fifth inning, with the bases loaded with White Stockings and the Athletics clinging to a tenuous 5–2 lead. Charley Hodes hit a weak tap in front of the plate. Joe Simmons charged in from third as McBride hustled over to field the ball. Dick had his back to Simmons as the base runner, under full steam, separated McBride from the ball and nearly from his senses. Holly, correctly interpreting the interference rule, ruled that Simmons was the third out. An argument ensued and the Chicago partisans, especially those with money on the table, threatened to see to it that Holly never made the return trip to Buffalo. Nevertheless, he courageously stood his ground and held to his proper decision.

The Athletics then scored three times in the bottom of the fifth and coasted to an 11–6 victory. Holly had to be escorted from the field by Chicago captain Jimmy Wood and a cordon of police.

The incidents which occurred during the first season were unfortunate and inexcusable, but none created the turmoil engendered by the Baltimore-Athletics feud of the following year. The two teams were right in the thick of the pennant race when they squared off in Baltimore on May 20.[18] At the close of the seventh inning the undefeated Athletics were trailing 7–4. Leading off the top of the eighth, Fred Treacey of Philadelphia hit a grounder to Lip Pike at second base. Pike's errant throw pulled Ev Mills off the bag, but the umpire called Treacey out nonetheless. Adrian Anson followed with a walk and went to second on an opposite field single by Mike McGeary. From this point, the narrative becomes a bit cloudy, as partisan journalism on both sides muddied the issue.

The most plausible account of the ensuing action is that Denny Mack, following McGeary in the lineup, worked Mathews for a walk. After the third and final ball was delivered, catcher Craver fired to Pike at second. Pike tagged Anson, who was starting for third, having been forced along by the base on balls. The umpire called Anson out! The Athletics, incensed by this obvious violation of the rules, charged onto the field en masse and surrounded the arbiter, demanding that he reverse his palpably incorrect decision. McGeary, who was forced to second by the walk, wandered off his base and joined in the argument. Pike, who had started the trouble by tagging Anson, now tagged McGeary. The umpire called him out! Despite the fact that both teams were swarming all over the field, the umpire ruled that time had not been called and McGeary was not entitled to any protection when he abandoned his base.

At this point, captain McBride and the rest of the team were all over the poor umpire, who now agreed that Anson could proceed safely to third, but that McGeary was definitely out. This weak compromise was unsatisfactory to the Athletics, who continued to press the argument. Anson, McGeary, and Mack refused to vacate the bases and Ned Cuthbert, the next batter, refused to approach the plate. The umpire ordered Mathews to pitch. Bobby threw three pitches, and Cuthbert was called out on strikes.

The scene then disintegrated into complete mayhem. The capacity crowd began to encroach upon the field and the Athletics, sensing the danger posed by the hostile gathering, packed their bags and fought their way out of the park, putting an end to the game. The umpire stood at home plate and declared that Baltimore was victorious by a 7–4 score. This was inconsistent since, if a forfeit had been declared due to the Athletics' disappearing act, the score should have been 9–0.

The Athletics were obviously unhappy with the decision and claimed that it was the swarming crowd, not their leaving, which had caused the game to end. The team intended to bring its case before the Judiciary Committee, but may have been barking up the wrong tree, given that august body's proclivity for inactivity. The opinion of the *Clipper* was that the outcome of all bets placed on the game should be held in suspense until the Judiciary Committee made its decision.[19]

A further development of the dispute was the cancellation of games between the two teams scheduled for May 23 and May 25. There was bad blood between the Athletics and Baltimore to the extent that there was a very real possibility that no more games would be played for the remainder of the season. Under NA rules, this would have resulted in the ineligibility of the two contenders for the championship, which would have forced the committee to make some difficult decisions.

In the days that followed the erroneous calls, local newspapers attempted to apply a revisionist touch to the fiasco. Readers of the *Baltimore Gazette*[20] were told that, in the course of play, Mathews picked McGeary off second, and that the Athletics had become so infuriated by this that, after failing to intimidate the courageous umpire, "they packed up their bats, refusing to play." The Philadelphians, according to the paper, then stormed off the field with their bag of bats, putting an abrupt and inexplicable end to the contest.

Subscribers to the *Baltimore Gazette* might have been confused if they discussed the matter with their neighbors who had read the competing *Baltimore Dispatch*.[21] The sportswriter who had covered the game for that paper had seen things in a somewhat different light. He stated that Anson was attempting to steal third. Since the intent was to steal, and since Anson had started before the third ball was called, he was not protected by the base on balls, having clearly cast his fate upon his feet, as it were. According to the writer, any "doubt was instantly dispelled" when the circumstances were carefully analyzed. Not only, however, was this interpretation of the rules somewhat wishful, but the facts differed from all other accounts. Straining his credibility even further, the writer stated that Captain Craver had indicated his willingness to concede every questionable point to the Athletics in order to allow the game to continue. The Athletics' refusal to accept the generously proffered terms caused the umpire to reach the limit of his patience. He "was justly incensed at their irate misbehavior." Unlike other reporters however, the *Baltimore Dispatch*'s man on the spot knew, or at least suspected, the cause of the Athletics' boorish display. The source of the trouble, the scribe confided to his audience, was the fact that the Athletics could not face the inevitability of their defeat at the hands of the home team. His own words describe it best. "A few minutes before the rupture occurred, one of [the Athletics'] backers was seen to leave the pool seller's stand and, mingling with the players was observed in close confabulation with McBride. Whether or not this had anything to do with the events is not known, but that it had is shrewdly suspected."

The *Philadelphia City Item*[22] presented the visitors' side of the story, referring to the "barefaced swindle" to which McBride and the others objected. According to their version, the Baltimore players recognized the absurdity of the decision and urged the umpire to reverse it. All the players, that is, except Craver. Given Craver's contrary temperament and subsequent escapades, this version is not without credibility. The *City Item* reported that when Craver refused to allow play to continue, the crowd charged onto the field and the Athletics had to be escorted off by the police.

The matter was deposited squarely into the lap of the impotent Judiciary Committee which, as was its wont, acted with due deliberation. The *Clipper* suggested that the clubs renew the contest in the top of the eighth with the bases loaded and Cuthbert at bat. It opined that, should this advice be followed, the final innings might be watched by the largest crowd in baseball history.[23]

On July 27 the Judiciary Committee was finally roused to action. In a meeting at New York the committee heard testimony from Joseph Allen, a former director of the Athletics, and from Nick Young of Baltimore. Allen convinced the judges that the unruliness of the crowd had been the sole reason for the stoppage of play. Alex Davidson moved that the game be declared null and void. His cohorts were in agreement, and the matter was settled, only two months and one week after it had arisen.[24]

Although the incident has been described in virtually agonizing detail, it serves to illustrate so many of the shortcomings of the NA in a single still picture. First, the original call indicts either the competence or integrity of the league's umpires. The NA was still dependent upon unpaid volunteers, many of whom had either an imperfect knowledge of the rules or an ax to grind. As seen by the compromises and reversals after the original decision, the umpire was wide open to intimidation by the players. The rules, in fact, allowed an umpire to take testimony from players on a play he had not seen clearly. The bad feeling between the two teams threatened to disrupt the entire league schedule (such as it was) and throw the championship question into a state of confusion. If the two teams did not complete their series, there was some doubt whether the games that Baltimore and Philadelphia had played with other teams would count in the records of those teams.

Another significant dilemma and cause of much public debate was the disposition of the bets placed on the game. The open nature of the discussion, the magnitude of the dollar amount involved, and the obvious implications of the committee's decision pointed out an ongoing league problem with embarrassing clarity.

Finally, there is the sorry performance of the Judiciary Committee. By the time its members finally arrived at a decision, the matter had virtually resolved itself. In a league where the Judiciary Committee could have operated on a full-time basis — given the number of disputes, problems, and clouded issues — it chose to abdicate responsibility in as many cases as possible and procrastinate in those matters where action could not be avoided.

By mid–June Baltimore and Philadelphia had buried the hatchet and decided to play each other after all. On June 17 they squared off in Philadelphia. Despite apprehension on the part of many, there was no trouble, as Billy Lennon's umpiring was competent and beyond reproach.[25] The Athletics atoned for their rude treatment in Baltimore by administering a 14-3 thrashing which pleased the home folks immensely. Craver, the chief villain in the fracas at Baltimore, suffered the added discomfort of being struck in the face with a foul ball, which forced him to leave the game. The Athletics played a superb game in the field while Cuthbert, left standing at home plate in the previous game, exacted revenge by cracking four hits.

On June 28 the two teams returned to the scene of the great altercation, Newington Park, where the homestanding Lord Baltimores prevailed by a 17-10 score. Fearful of another riot by the fans, the Baltimore police force was well represented.[26] Whether it was their ominous presence or the fact that the prior incident had been virtually forgotten, there were no disturbances of the peace.

Those who said the umpires didn't know the score could point to a distressingly concrete example, which occurred at Washington on June 20, 1873. The Nationals staged a furious eight-run, ninth-inning rally that fell one run short of catching the Atlantics. Or did it? The Atlantics left the field claiming a 19-18 victory. The Nationals insisted that the score was tied and the game should continue to the tenth inning. Umpire Mike Hooper of the Marylands was not sure. He looked for help from the scorers, but neither team had brought a scorer with them. In desperation, he began to poll the reporters. No one was certain whether he was looking for a plurality, a majority, or a consensus. Fortunately, all of the scribes agreed that the final score was 19-18 in favor of the Atlantics, and Hooper declared the game ended.[27]

The level of competence aside, the existence of multiple roles was bound to create conflicts. No one wore more hats than Bob Ferguson, who was player, manager, umpire, and league president. As president, Ferguson often set a poor example. In a June 2, 1873, home game against Boston, he became incensed over a call by Umpire Theodore Bomeisler, generally considered one of the league's better arbiters. Ferguson complained, argued the point, and then appealed to the crowd, insinuating that Bomeisler had placed a wager on Boston. He kept up a steady stream of abuse until the indignant umpire stalked off the field, refusing to tolerate any more of Ferguson's arrogance. He was replaced by Dick Higham, hardly a paragon of integrity.[28]

The *Clipper* was mortified at such insolence on the part of the league president. It pointed out smugly that Ferguson had made more errors than anyone else during the game and had failed to get a base hit. Perhaps, they intimated, he should master his role as player and captain before he tried to act simultaneously as umpire.[29]

Bob Ferguson did act as an umpire, of course, and it was in that role later in 1873 that he committed perhaps his most serious indiscretion.[30] Ferguson was one of the best player-umpires, whose only flaw, as expected, was his hair-trigger temper. On July 24 he was officiating a game between the Mutuals, for whom he had no great love, and Baltimore. Johnny Hatfield, who was playing third for the Mutuals, had been scattering the fans behind first base with his wild throws all day. Despite this, the Mutuals carried an 8–5 lead into the ninth inning. New York shortstop Jim Holdsworth started the Baltimore half of the ninth with a throwing error, allowing Davy Force to reach base. Force went to second on a passed ball by catcher Nat Hicks. Bobby Mathews, recognizing the need to take things into his own hands, struck out Bill Craver. A pair of singles drove in a run before Mathews was able to get the second out. At that point, his defense collapsed completely. Cal McVey struck out, but Hicks dropped the ball. He had plenty of time to throw McVey out, but for some reason, elected to try for the force at third. Hatfield, as surprised as everyone else in the park, failed to cover and the bases were loaded. The next batter, Lip Pike, fouled off a pitch which Hicks had in his hands but dropped. Pike then hit a hard grounder which caromed off Hatfield, hit base runner Ev Mills, and rebounded into Hatfield's hands. Johnny, again for reasons unknown, tried for the force play at home. His throw eluded Hicks and before the ball could be retrieved, three runs had been scored and Baltimore had a 9–8 lead. Holdsworth supplied the coup de grace with another error, boosting the score to 10–8. When the Mutuals dragged off the field, they were jawing feverishly, accompanied by much finger pointing. Hicks and Hatfield, in particular, exchanged harsh words, each accusing the other of indifferent play.

Ferguson, who, as an umpire, should have been far removed from all this, injected himself into the middle of the fracas. He made a gratuitous remark concerning Hicks's integrity and insinuated, as he had done with Bomeisler, that Hicks had dumped the game. The Mutuals' catcher naturally took offense, and snarled back at Ferguson, calling him a damned liar. Bob, in an action many league presidents would like to take, grabbed a bat and took a wild swing at Hicks, catching him squarely across the arm. The crowd, noting Ferguson's unexpected deep involvement, accused the umpire of having a pecuniary interest in the contest and charged the field as if to attack him. Someone handed the umpire a club with which to protect himself and the police escorted him safely to the clubhouse. Once inside, Hicks and Ferguson exchanged apologies and settled the matter amicably, at least on the surface.[31] In the event, Hicks wound up with his arm in a sling,[32] while Ferguson, by any standard, should have had his posterior in one.

No action was taken by the league against its president, although Hicks missed the remainder of the season due to his injury. The incident served only to underscore the unstable nature of the high-strung Ferguson and the lack of leadership from the Association.

Another form of conflict of interest arose when a reserve from one of the competing teams filled the role of umpire. On July 13, 1874, Boston defeated the Athletics 7-6. The Athletics' loss, claimed the Boston press, was not from any want of assistance on the part of umpire Tim Murnane, a reserve for the Philadelphia team.[33] Murnane had been a compromise choice reluctantly accepted by Boston. The Athletics had not been willing to accept anyone from Boston, and had brought George Bechtel, the former player, with them. Bechtel's reputation had been tainted for years, and he was later banned from pro ball; therefore, Wright took a strong stand against the proposal that he officiate. Finally, he agreed upon Murnane, who was also a member of the Athletics but whose reputation was spotless.

Unfortunately, there were a number of close calls during the game and, equally unfortunate, Murnane decided in each instance in favor of the Athletics. At the end of the game he was pushed and jostled about by irate Boston fans and reached the Athletics' coach only with the aid of the Boston police.

The *Clipper* commented on the obvious, which unfortunately was not so obvious in the NA. The use of a player from one of the competing teams was bound to raise eyebrows when a close call went in favor of the umpire's team. Although Murnane's alleged bias was not enough to swing the game in the Athletics' favor, the part-time umpire, like pool selling at the park, was a factor that always led fans and the press to question the legitimacy of NA contests. Although many of the important games were now officiated by the capable William McLean, the ill-informed and partial umpire was still an integral part of the NA scene.

Chapter 13

A New Powerhouse

The year 1873 was marked by an uprising of the Modoc Indians in the Western United States. They terrorized the white man until their leader, who had taken the name Captain Jack, was captured and imprisoned. The marauding red men spread fear throughout the settlers in the outlying regions and monopolized the front page of the *New York Times* for the greater part of the summer.

An unnoticed event with long-term implications occurred in December. Chester Greenwood, 15 years old, of Farmington, Maine, was cursed with a set of very sensitive ears. In Maine this was a serious inconvenience, as the cold winter winds often caused his ears to become frostbitten. Employing classic Yankee ingenuity, he fiddled around with some cloth and baling wire, and the earmuff was born. Although Greenwood's accomplishment was little noted in 1873, he was a local hero by the 1980s. He became the subject of a poem entitled "Necessity Is the Mother of Invention, or Chester Had Colder Ears Than Most of His Peers," and is honored by a Farmington celebration each year.[1]

Against this background of significant and trivial happenings, the NA prepared for its third season. The Philadelphia White Stockings, intent on making a strong showing in their maiden season, were particularly vigilant in training. The Athletics, with their veteran players and secure reputation, were less likely to be found at the gym.[2]

The predictable denouement in fact occurred as the new team displayed a shocking mastery over the old, winning nine of the ten games played, including the first eight. The Philadelphia fans took to the new rivalry instantly, as the presence of former Athletic players on the new White Stocking entry heightened the interest. An estimated 8,000 to 10,000 fans turned out for the third game of the series on June 11. Johnny Hatfield and Dave Eggler of the Mutuals sat in the stands, perhaps to see how the game should be played. Fans spilled out onto the field, despite the efforts of the police to contain them. Right fielders Cherokee Fisher and George

Bechtel shared space with several of the spectators who encroached upon their territory. The White Stockings' stockholders were happy to have them, for the take for the day exceeded $5,000. Larger amounts were wagered on the contest, with more than $100,000 rumored to have changed hands. Former Haymaker President Morrissey was said to have won $5,000 by backing the White Stockings.[3]

The large crowd was due in part to the result of the second game, an exciting 13-inning affair in which the White Stockings emerged the victor by a 5–4 margin. Due to the high scores run up in the 1870s, extra-inning games were rare, the last 13-inning encounter between major teams having taken place in 1865 between the Gothams of New York City and the Enterprises of Brooklyn.[4] The stockholders tried to milk the rivalry a bit too much, as the fourth game was played only 10 days after the third before a crowd of 5,000.[5] An inartistic 17–5 White Stockings win reduced the attendance on June 30 to 3,000.[6]

The Athletics were not the only team to fall victim to the White Stockings. Philadelphia, with its seasoned veterans, made short work of the other established teams, winning 27 of their first 30 games and surging to an 8½ game lead over Boston, its closest pursuer, by mid–July. The Red Stockings had stumbled early, including two losses to the Atlantics, and had been unable to attain the consistency to challenge the leaders.

The Boston club turned uncharacteristically apologist after their early losses, stating that George Wright had been suffering from rheumatism and should not have played. Jim O'Rourke had been a late signee and therefore had arrived in Boston only in mid–April. James White was not yet in fighting trim, having reported late after wrestling with his conscience and religious scruples before resuming his ballplaying career.[7]

White was devoutly religious, earning the nickname "Deacon." He neither drank, smoked, nor played poker, a rarity in the gambling, boozing NA. By mid–April White had overcome his reservations and decided to report to Boston, concluding, according to the *Clipper*, "that a man can play ball in a reputable professional nine despite the fact of a recent conversion to religion."[8]

After a resounding loss to the sorry Mutuals in mid–July, the fans and press gave Harry Wright and his troops up for dead. The *Clipper* confidently declared that "it is evident that [Boston] will not be the champions this year. Indeed, if they do not show improvement in September, they will hardly reach second place."[9] They were not alone in their sentiment, for all the smart money was now on the White Stockings.

At this point, the teams took stock and a couple of them decided to make changes. The White Stockings released second baseman Bob Addy at his request and signed Jimmy Wood, the former captain of the Chicago, Troy, and Eckford teams. Wood had announced his retirement during the winter, but made it known that he would be available to play with Philadelphia in "important" games.[10] The White Stockings now decided they needed him on a full time basis.

Addy, temporarily unemployed, returned to Rockford, where he had played prior to 1872, and knocked around. Exactly what he did while knocking around became a matter of great importance, as will be seen later.

The annual August torpor overtook the teams and they scattered for points far and wide. On August 9 Boston left on their western tour, with plans to visit Allegheny, St.Louis, Keokuk, Chicago, Rockford, Detroit, Guelph, Ottawa, Toronto, and Ogdensburgh.[11] The Athletics were in the midst of their hiatus, but the White Stockings were following in Boston's tracks, heading north to Canada. The two teams also planned to hook up in Chicago to play a pair of important games.

Baltimore was relatively inactive during this period, emerging from its hibernation only to post a decisive victory over the Atlantics. Once again, the league was handicapped by its catch-as-catch-can schedule. Teams embarked on long tours of exhibition games or vanished entirely, as they saw fit. Baltimore, which should have been in the heat of a pennant race, had played much more frequently than the others in April and May, due to their favorable climate, and was now standing idly by as the competition knocked each other off.

As the weather heated up, the pennant race generally cooled off. Due to the reluctance of the fans to brave the intense heat, most teams planned a light schedule for the month of July. In 1872 the *Clipper* informed its readers of the Red Stockings' midsummer hiatus, stating that on July 6 the team "went to camp on the island in Boston Harbor to shoot, fish, bathe and recuperate generally for the fall campaign."[12] Thus rejuvenated, Boston intended to take a tour of Canada, with the purpose of making short work of the Canadian amateurs and filling the till before returning to the NA wars.

Baltimore had preceded their rivals north of the border that year, falling to the Maple Leafs of Guelph 10–9 on Dominion Day, July 1. Ecstatic at beating an American professional nine, the officers of the Maple Leafs threw an elaborate banquet at the Royal Hotel for both teams. The Baltimore players proved to be good sports, joining the conquering heroes in toasts to President Grant and Queen Victoria.[13]

Guelph, a small town located on the outskirts of Toronto, fielded a strong team for a number of years, playing competitively with NA teams whenever they passed through. Despite the known ability of the Guelph team, the Americans did not play with the same seriousness that marked regular season games. Nick Young inserted himself into the lineup during the Canaries' loss and acquitted himself well, banging out three hits.

The Canadian teams did not have much luck against the Red Stockings, whose tour did not take place until August. Boston swept through the countryside, outscoring their opponents by a whopping 524–48 while emerging unscathed with a 14–0 record. Included in the total were victories by such convincing scores as 68–0, 64–0 and 66–1. Five members of the team batted over .500, led by Ross Barnes at .544. The only player to bat less than .438 was an embarrassed Harry Schafer, who trailed the field at .370. Harry Wright, not generally a major cog in the Boston offense, weighed in at .447, in addition to proving a superb relief pitcher for Spalding. In 32 innings, Harry posted an ERA of 0.56.[14] Unfortunately for the stockholders, the financial results did not approach those achieved on the field, as gate receipts barely covered traveling expenses.[15]

In 1873, flushed with victory, the Philadelphia White Stockings departed en masse for the resort town of Cape May, New Jersey for an extended period of rest and recreation. According to all accounts, the boys had a lively time celebrating the success of the first half of the season.[16] While Philadelphia was lounging on the Jersey shore, the Athletics were likewise taking a three-week hiatus. Championship games were few and far between as the teams braced themselves for the September-October stretch run. The last two months did not promise much excitement, other than the three-way battle for second place. After all, no less an authority than Chadwick himself had declared that Boston was finished. The Philadelphia White Stockings, in their first season, were about to dethrone the Red Stockings after a one-year reign. "The king is dead, long live the king," cried the Philadelphians. Harry Wright wrote to Athletics manager Hayhurst, "Let us get our and your second wind, then look out Philadelphias."[17]

The second half of the season began on a negative note, with the demise of the two tailenders. While negative for those directly involved, the development was positive for purists who had suffered through the miserable displays of the Resolutes and Marylands. The latter were the first to fall. After three early thrashings, the Marylands had crawled into a protective cocoon and had not emerged for two months. Everyone connected with the NA assumed that the club was defunct, and the *Clipper* had removed their games from the standings, muddling them as in prior years. In late June manager William J. Smith dashed off a defiant letter indicating that the team was alive and well, and would soon be taking the field again.[18] They did just that on June 27 and managed only one hit against Candy Cummings. Baltimore collected 20 hits and 20 runs off Ed Stratton. It was apparent that the rest had not helped the Marylands. After a second hiatus, the hapless team had returned to absorb another shellacking by Baltimore on July 11 by a 20–10 score. With an 0–6 record, they disappeared once more, this time for good. Although there was no formal announcement of the team's passing, few were disappointed when they failed to make an appearance for the rest of the season. The Marylands had barely ventured outside of Baltimore, had been outscored by an average of 25–4 and had served no apparent purpose other than to fatten the won-lost records of Baltimore and Washington.

The Resolutes had played on a more consistent basis than the Marylands, completing 23 games, but had met with little more success, even suffering the ignominy of losing to the collegiate team from Princeton in May. Guaranteed $50 for their appearance, the team had played with little enthusiasm.[19] When the Resolutes did come to play, fate sometimes conspired against them. A third-inning 8–0 lead over the Atlantics was washed away in the early season. Generally the team's level of play was the principal culprit. After suffering some frightful losses, however, they not only beat the Atlantics, but scored a stunning upset in Boston on July 4.

Harry Wright, pondering how to reap a decent payday from a meeting with the miserable New Jersey team, suggested that the teams play two games, one in the morning and one in the afternoon. There were boat races scheduled for the afternoon and a morning game would give some Bostonians an opportunity to see both boating and baseball in the same day; thus the first major league doubleheader. Wright, of course, charged a separate admission fee for each game.[20] In the first game, the Resolutes emerged as 11–2 victors behind a fine pitching performance by Hugh Campbell. The shocked Red Stockings took revenge in the nightcap, administering a 32–3 lesson, not resting until they had scored 21 runs in the ninth inning.

The win over Boston was to be the high point of the Resolutes' season. They disappeared in late July, only to reappear unexpectedly for an August 4 loss to the Atlantics, much to the dismay of the *New York Times*, which had described the team's earlier efforts as "pathetic" and "wretched" and hoped to have seen the last of their miserable exhibitions.[21] The Resolutes had a patchwork lineup on the field to face the Atlantics. Some of their best players had departed to join a rejuvenated Irvington team. Irvington had been a force to be reckoned with in the mid-1860s, surfacing with a shocking victory over the champion Atlantics in 1866, the latter's first defeat in over two years. The team had lasted only briefly and was but a fond memory until August 1873. The present incarnation lured the Resolutes' battery of Hugh Campbell and John Farrow, along with Art Allison, away from the Jerseyites.

The Irvington revival was short-lived, but it was the straw that broke the Resolutes' back. After the initial defections, the rats began to desert the sinking Resolute vessel in droves. The team's last gasp was, fittingly, a 20–3 loss to the Mutuals on August 7. The remaining players scattered – Doug Allison to the Mutuals, Eddie Booth to the Atlantics, Frank Fleet to a number of semipro teams. This raised an interesting question. Were members of a disbanded team bound by the 60-day rule? While the rule was intended to prevent players from jumping from team to team, a literal interpretation would prevent any members of a defunct organization from earning a living playing professional baseball for at least 60 days. Interested parties received no guidance on the subject from the Judiciary Committee, which remained mute. The *Clipper* made the assumption that a rule was a rule and declared that all of the Mutual games in which Doug Allison participated should be forfeited.[22]

The issue had seemingly been settled in 1872, after Cleveland and the Mansfields ceased operations. The Mutuals had protested Baltimore's use of Hastings, who had been a member of the Cleveland team; however, the prior treatment of the Troy players who had been allowed to join the Eckfords had set a precedent in regard to players cut adrift by failing organizations.[23] This decision should certainly have carried over into the next season. An 1873 meeting of the Judiciary Committee which could have shed light upon the subject was canceled, leading the *Clipper* to lament that "confusion continues and no one knows how the championship record stands."[24] Eventually, all players would be declared eligible.

For the Mutuals and the Atlantics, both far removed from pennant contention, the issue was academic. For Fleet, it was old hat. For Boston, however, the question of eligibility would prove to be of grave importance. While on their western tour in early August, the Red Stockings signed Bob Addy to replace Jack Manning in the lineup. Jim O'Rourke was moved to first base while Addy was stationed in right field. Captain Wright had fervently pursued his new outfielder, who had been a solid veteran for Rockford for a number of years. Wright, who possessed a very entertaining dry wit, had written to Addy, "Telegraph you will join us in St. Louis and we will go for them all, raising the standard of the mighty Reds higher and higher until we ... just say you will come, that's all."[25]

Charm and wit were indeed required, since Boston's salary offer was a mere $75 per month. Wright pointed out that signing in mid-season would provide Addy with a leg up on obtaining an engagement for 1874, although he was careful not to make a firm offer himself.

Cap Anson later described the talkative Addy as a good ballplayer and "an odd sort of genius."[26] The latter tag was at least partially attributable to the fact that, according to Anson, Addy permanently terminated his baseball career to journey to the Oregon wilderness to run a tin shop.[27] To Anson, whose only passions in life were baseball and billiards (and possibly Mrs. Anson) this was indeed odd behavior. Eccentric or not, Addy was a loquacious sort who kept up a steady chatter on the field designed to un-nerve his opponents.[28]

There was no question that it had been more than 60 days since Addy had last played with Philadelphia. In any event, he had obtained a legal release from the White Stockings, which entitled him to play with any other team. While lingering in Rockford awaiting another opportunity, it was alleged that he had played with a local group that had challenged a Chicago team to a July encounter.[29] If this constituted a legitimate game within the parameters of the rule, Addy's participation would make him ineligible until September. Nevertheless, he was in right field for Boston for the remainder of the season.

Chapter 14

The Mutuals

The Mutuals got off to a rocky start, the worst in their history, losing six of their first seven games. This was enough to commence the ugly rumors about "hippodroming" and the more plausible analysis that the Mutuals lacked cohesion and leadership. Both Ferguson and Pearce had departed to the Atlantics, leaving the team without a true captain. Johnny Hatfield, filling the role, was a longtime team member, but moody, erratic, and generally unsuited for the position.

After respectable losses to strong Philadelphia and Baltimore teams, the Mutuals suffered an embarrassing 12–0 blanking at the hands of the Athletics. They were able to nick McBride for only two hits. A back-to-back, two game series with Washington produced the Mutuals' only victory, but also resulted in an upset win for the Nationals the following day. The defeat was the result, the *Clipper* confided, of the team, "not tak[ing] the slightest care of themselves regarding sanitary rules."[1] One can assume this means excessive imbibing. After the strong 34–20 finish of the previous year, New Yorkers had high hopes for the 1873 season. The rudderless Mutuals, however, drifted through May, leading only the hapless Marylands and Resolutes.

The Mutuals had always been an unpredictable, mysterious combination. Closely aligned with the Tammany Hall crowd,[2] the team had been subject to the same type of sordid accusations that had dogged William Tweed, Oakey Hall, and their henchmen. The green-stockinged team had also been the simultaneous perpetrator and victim in the game's first public scandal, the disgraceful Wansley affair of 1865.[3] The entire team was reported to be controlled by gamblers as early as 1868.[4] Throughout their five years in the National Association, they seemed to have a propensity for losing to inferior foes under unusual circumstances. Was it a case of not "playing in harmony," as was often claimed, or were the New Yorkers doing less than their level best to win?

As a charter member of the NA, the team had aroused suspicion in its first season with its erratic play. After handing Chicago its first defeat of the season, they beat Cleveland and the Philadelphia Athletics to vault into first place. After defeating two of the most powerful teams in the league, New York fell from first place by falling victim to the lowly Kekiongas on the Mutuals' home field. Not only was Fort Wayne several rungs below the Mutuals in terms of talent, they arrived in New York battered and bruised. The Kekiongas were minus one starter due to injury and catcher Lennon's hands were suffering badly from the effects of Bobby Mathews's fast ball. The crowd put their money heavily on the home team, which was strongly favored in the apparent mismatch. The Kekiongas, behind the plucky Mathews, jumped to a 4–0 lead and withstood a ninth-inning New York rally for a 5–3 triumph.[5]

Given the disparity of talent and records, the Kekionga victory was viewed as a great upset. Unfortunately, many of the disgruntled betting men felt that the supposed overachievers from Fort Wayne had had no small assistance from the favored Mutuals. With open betting both at the park and in pool halls throughout the city, there were any number of "betting sports" with ample reason to attempt to buy a key error here and there. The temptation was present not only for the bettors to offer the occasional payoff, but also for the players to accept, given the lax enforcement of any Association sanctions and the irregular compensation offered by the co-op teams.

The following season the Mutuals again displayed shocking inconsistency in the midst of a pennant race. On June 8 New York traveled to Philadelphia, where a crowd of 6,000–7,000 cheered heartily as the home team began its first inning with 3 straight singles. By the time Mutual pitcher Cummings retired the side, the Mutuals had thrown the ball aimlessly around the infield and the Athletics had crossed home plate five times. In the third Cummings was knocked out of the box[6] and the Mutuals were on their way to a 19–0 humiliation. This was the same team that had pinned a 3–2 defeat on the 1871 champions just a week earlier.[7] The real(?) Mutuals reappeared two days later in Brooklyn to face Boston. Playing in an intermittent drizzle, the two teams put on an excellent display. At the end of nine innings, the game was tied at 2–2. Cummings and Spalding dueled into extra innings until Harry Schafer's double in the bottom of the eleventh allowed the Red Stockings to escape with a 3–2 victory.

In 1873 the team finally achieved consistency. Unfortunately, they were consistently bad. One of the reasons for the horrendous break from the gate was a problem at third base. Since they entered the league in 1871, the Mutuals had had a gaping hole at third. Charlie Smith, Bob Ferguson, Bill Boyd, Chick Fulmer, Jack Nelson, and Johnny Hatfield had all seen regular duty at the hot corner and all but Ferguson had been found wanting. Hatfield had an erratic, if legendary strong arm, and his wild throws to first had drawn the ire of first sacker Joe Start. In late May New York signed former Haymaker Steve Bellan as the new incumbent.

Bellan made his debut at the Union Grounds on May 24 versus the Athletics, and proved a worthy successor to Hatfield. The trouble began in the very first inning. With one out, Dick McBride hit a soft tapper to third. Bellan fielded the ball cleanly. So far, so good. Then he uncorked a throw that sailed well over Start's head, allowing the Athletics pitcher to reach safety. Two batters later, Start saved a second error as he made a fine grab of an errant throw from third. From that point through the top of the third, Bellan not only stayed out of trouble, but atoned for his earlier miscue by driving in the tying run with a base hit. In the bottom of the third, the Mutual third sacker was charged with his second error on another wild throw, but erased the runner by starting a double play. Thus far, he was even. In the fourth inning he began to lose ground, making another bad throw. By the seventh inning the Athletics knew where to hit the ball. McGeary tried Bellan again. Register another throwing error, and yet another in the eighth. At this point Hatfield decided he could do better and switched positions with poor Steve, sending him to second base. In the ninth inning Anson, perhaps forgetting that Bellan had moved, slapped a grounder to third, now guarded by Hatfield. Johnny, of course, unleashed another wild throw, sending the fuming Start off in hot pursuit once more.[8]

The Mutuals lost the game 11–7, with the sieve at third base playing a major contribution. Obviously, Bellan was not the answer to the problem. After seven games he was dismissed, along with his .189 batting average. His fielding average was not much higher. The search continued.[9]

Two weeks later, New York put forth its worst performance of a dismal season, committing 26 fielding errors. The Philadelphia White Stockings were less than perfect themselves, with 14 miscues, but they hung on for a dreadful 12–10 win. Included among the Mutuals errors were ten fly balls or popups that were dropped.[10] There was no mistaking it. The Mutuals really were as bad as they appeared to be. By mid–June they were completely out of the race, and management was so disgusted with the team's loose play that it was considering a return of the team to amateur status.[11]

Throughout the season, Mutual watching remained an entertaining pastime. Then, as now, playing in the New York area gave the team added attention, and every shortcoming was pointed out in excruciating and embarrassing detail. In 1873 critics had a field day, since so much had gone wrong.

On July 4 they had another incident to recount with glee. Before a large holiday crowd of 8,000, the Mutuals took a commanding 6–0 lead against the rival Atlantics, having taken liberties with Atlantic pitcher Jim Britt's deliveries. Britt led off the fourth with a grounder to Hatfield, who was guarding (in a loose manner of speaking) third. He scooped the ball cleanly and sent it "like lightning" over Start's head. By the time Start had chased the ball into the crowd, Britt was perched on third. Joe glared across the diamond but kept his own counsel. Harmon Dehlman, following Britt in the batting order and recognizing an opportunity when it stared him in the face, slapped another grounder at the Mutual captain. True to form, Hatfield reared back, let fly, and once more Start was off in hot pursuit. Dehlman streaked around the bases and beat Start's belated throw to the plate.

Later in the inning Jack Burdock tried Hatfield again. Equal to the task, he first booted the ball, then threw it low to first base. By now Start had reached his boiling point. He had been run ragged chasing Hatfield's errant heaves and, as one of the steadfast, honorable Mutuals, he was suspicious of the intentions of some of his shady colleagues. Joe marched across the diamond and confronted Hatfield, lecturing the erring infielder in a strident tone in front of the large crowd. Johnny pacified the irate first baseman by banishing himself to right field, switching positions with Jack Nelson. At that time, a fortuitous rain shower caused a short delay, allowing tempers to cool somewhat. When the weather cleared, the Mutuals settled down and held on for a 10-6 victory. Their fielding was substantially improved, thanks in no small part to Hatfield's removal from the infield.[12]

Notwithstanding his wretched infielding, Hatfield was a more than capable picket man. The Mutual managers and captains, himself included, insisted on using him to plug holes in the infield, where he was prone to displays such as that described above. Playing men out of position and frantically juggling the lineup were Mutual trademarks, and helped to explain their less than impressive 5-16 record at the end of June.

Their lack of organizational skill was monumental. On July 2 the New Yorkers were to travel across the Hudson to Waverly with the expectation of notching an easy win at the expense of the hapless Resolutes. Arriving at the train station, they discovered that two or three of their number were AWOL. While Cleveland had played with eight men in 1872 and the Mutuals would do so in 1874, six or seven would not do, even against the Resolutes. Undaunted, the team repaired to the Union Grounds to watch the game between the Atlantics and Washington, leaving the Resolutes standing at the altar in Waverly.[13]

At the same Union Grounds five days later, the Mutuals hit a new low, something which seemed impossible after their sorry May and June performances. Against the league-leading Philadelphia White Stockings, New York built a solid 7-0 lead after two innings. Significantly, the *Clipper* reported that "the knowing ones did not hedge in their betting, keeping their confidence on Philadelphia."[14] Whether the fix was on or not, the New York defense suffered a total collapse. Philadelphia, on the other hand, was not exactly putting on a fielding exhibition in their own right. Perhaps both teams were attempting to throw the game. When the totals were tallied, they would show 35 errors, 20 of which lay at the hands of the bumbling Mutuals. Hatfield was again especially guilty, his misplays allowing six unearned tallies and carrying the White Stockings to a 13–10 victory.

Although 1873 represented the nadir of the team's NA existence, the Mutuals continued to have their share of embarrassing and inexplicable snafus. On July 10, 1874, the New Yorkers could muster only eight of the lads (Joe Start being unable to play) for a game against Hartford and were forced to leave center field unguarded. The box score listed eight players and a ninth position labeled "absent." Absent had no hits but, on the other hand, committed no errors. This was more than could be said for the team-mates of said Absent, who combined for 12 miscues en route to a 13–4 set-back. The *Hartford Courant* felt that the lack of a center fielder had directly contributed to four of the home team's tallies.[15]

The league's final season brought more of the same, as New York continued to sign many of the NA's shadiest characters. From one game to the next, the fans had no clue as to how the Mutuals would perform. They played like champions one day and tailenders the next. Despite their moral lapses, they were accepted as a charter member of the National League in 1876. The Mutuals did not seem aware that the rules had changed. They refused to make their final road trip of the 1876 season, an act that would have been, if not sanctioned, as least tolerated in the loosely managed NA. The new league had no patience for such shenanigans, however, and promptly expelled the surprised Mutuals, putting an end to their major league existence.

Chapter 15

Boston Makes a Run

Something had happened to the Philadelphia White Stockings team in Cape May, something very beneficial to Harry Wright, Bob Addy, and the rest of the Red Stockings. The White Stockings had lost their early season momentum and now they had lost their first baseman. While in Chicago for a neutral site game, Denny Mack had been run down by a horse and injured so seriously that it was feared his career might be over.[1]

The White Stockings lost their first five post–Cape May games, then righted themselves to capture eight of the next ten. Their slump, however, brought them back to the pack and into a Red Stocking buzz saw. Boston commenced a tear that would enable them to capture 26 of their final 31 and keep relentless pressure on Philadelphia all the way to the wire. Whether intentionally or not, Wright had saved the lion's share of Boston's quota of games with the struggling Nationals for the stretch run. During a six-week period in September and October the Red Stockings had defeated Washington a like number of times.

Boston's late charge set the stage for the most important game of the season to date, a September 15 clash between Boston and Philadelphia at the Jefferson Street Grounds. Boston had momentum, while Philadelphia was exhausted after a 14-inning marathon with the Atlantics. Their fatigue was evident in a loss to the Mutuals, which was followed by a train ride to Philadelphia and a game against the defending champions.

Mack's injury was not as serious as had been feared and he returned to the lineup at first. George the Charmer, however, was not feeling well.[2] When reports of poor health were set forth in contemporary accounts, it is difficult to determine whether the player was suffering from disease or merely the aftereffects of the previous night's libations. In either case, Zettlein's indisposition resulted in a subpar performance. He was wild and when he delivered the ball over the dish, Boston batted with authority, resulting in 15 hits. Andy Leonard's double, his fourth hit of the game, keyed a two-run ninth-inning rally which propelled the Red Stockings to a 7–5 victory.

By virtue of their win, Boston slipped ahead of Baltimore into second place and began to close in on Philadelphia.

	W	L	Pct.	GB
Philadelphia White Stockings	32	10	.762	—
Boston Red Stockings	27	13	.675	4
Lord Baltimores	29	14	.674	3½
Philadelphia Athletics	20	16	.556	9
New York Mutuals	21	20	.512	10½
Brooklyn Atlantics	15	27	.357	17
Washington Nationals	6	25	.194	20½
Elizabeth Resolutes	2	21	.087	20½
Marylands	0	6	.000	14

At this point, the published standings became somewhat murky as the *Clipper*, the most reliable source of baseball news (among weak competition) could resist no longer their passion for obfuscation. What if the Resolute and Maryland games were removed from the standings? Wasn't Addy an ineligible player, causing several Boston forfeits? And what about the other players whose eligibility was in question, like Washington's T. J. Donnelly and Doug Allison of the Mutuals? Should the Mutual and National games be considered forfeits or disregarded altogether?[3] If one considers all the possible combinations and permutations, it is relatively easy to see how the true standings might become clouded as the *Clipper* speculated as to what the Championship and Judiciary committees might decide.

Boston would allow the White Stockings no respite, staying fast on their heels with wins over the Atlantics and Mutuals. The Mutuals, playing an important (if vicarious) role in the pennant race, helped the Red Stocking cause by upending Philadelphia on September 25. The 8–4 loss seemed to rattle the nerves of the White Stockings, as they played very poorly in the field. Five Mutual second-inning runs were unearned due to four Philadelphia errors. In the fourth inning Zettlein departed and George Bechtel, who had done some hurling for the 1871 Athletics, took over the pitching chores. Dave Eggler touched Bechtel for a hit to left field which Ned Cuthbert misplayed badly. Fergy Malone, never known for sangfroid, became incensed at what he felt was lackadaisical play on Cuthbert's part. He engaged in a shouting match with the left fielder, which broached the possibility that the Phillies were beginning to come unraveled (or possibly that Malone felt some of his teammates had been "bought").[4]

The *Clipper* maintained its faith. It still felt that "Philadelphia will almost certainly win unless they fall flat on their faces in the next four weeks."[5] This was a cavalier statement which would not stand the test of hindsight, although the conditional phrase might be sufficient to bail out its author. Only four days after falling to New York, the White Stockings lost to the Athletics for the first time in nine games. Dapper Count Sensenderfer, making one of his mere 19 appearances for the season, stroked 4 hits to back the 8 hit pitching of Cherokee Fisher, resulting in a 7–6 win. Dick McBride, who had suffered all seven prior losses, spent the day in right field.

Bechtel pitched for Philadelphia the following day (September 30) when they faced the Lord Baltimores. Apparently, management lacked confidence in Zettlein's ability, or his commitment to the cause, for he was pulled from the lineup for this crucial series of games.

With the autumnal equinox having passed, the early onset of darkness was beginning to be a problem. Most games were scheduled to start at 3 P.M. or 3:30 P.M., in order to accommodate businessmen leaving the workplace. Daylight savings time was more than 50 years away, stealing an additional hour of precious sunlight. If started promptly and played briskly, a game could still be completed well before the sun sank below the horizon. Promptness, however, was not one of the virtues of the NA. Delays in arrival, delays or disputes in the selection of an umpire, and innumerable other protractions often resulted in late starts and a subsequent race against the receding daylight. The race was lost on September 30, as Baltimore's 10–6 win had to be called because of darkness after only five innings. Umpire Frank Selman (aka Frank Williams, aka Frank C. Williams) was forced to bring the teams off the field in the midst of a crucial game that had been little more than half played.

On the following day the White Stockings, now reeling badly, stopped in the District of Columbia to beat up the Nationals. They treated the game lightly, pitching second-liner Bechtel once more and moving shortstop Chick Fulmer behind the bat. Lumbering 31-year-old catcher Fergy Malone played short, with first baseman Denny Mack in right field. The Nationals were perhaps insulted by the casual attitude of the Phillies. Before Philadelphia began to play in earnest, Washington held a 14–2 lead. A key error by Malone, playing out of position, contributed heavily to a six-run fourth-inning rally. Jimmy Wood realized that he had a battle on his hands and returned Fulmer and Malone to their normal positions. Fulmer proved no better than Malone at shortstop, his wild throw to the plate allowing another run to score. After they bore down, the White Stockings made a valiant effort to salvage the game. They battered poor Bill Stearns for six hits and six runs in the eighth and appeared to be on the verge of tying the score in the ninth. Levi Meyerle led off with a sharp single to left and promptly stole second. With one out, Fulmer singled, with Meyerle proceeding cautiously to third. Fred Treacey lifted a fly ball to right field that should have been the second out, but Oscar Bielaski fumbled the ball and allowed Meyerle to score the Phillies' tenth run. By this time Stearns had visions of yet another loss about to be added to his already staggering career total. Overthrowing, he uncorked a wild pitch which allowed Fulmer to score. Treacey dashed across the plate on yet another wild heave. Mack waited out a walk, as Stearns had totally lost the plate. A double by Jim Devlin made the score 14–13 and placed the tying run at second. Cuthbert legged out an infield hit to short, but Devlin, with the play unfolding in front of him, made a belated break to third and was gunned down by first baseman John Glenn. This broke the back of the rally, as Jimmy Wood grounded out to end the game. Philadelphia came up 1 run short despite 18 hits and 19 Washington errors.[6]

The loss was costly. Not only had Philadelphia lost a game they should have won easily, but they had done so on a day that the Red Stockings were defeating the Atlantics in Brooklyn. The Boston win and Philadelphia loss edged the Red Stockings to within percentage points of the Phillies, setting the stage for a head to head confrontation on the following day.

More than 4,000 fans at the Jefferson Street Grounds cheered heartily as the locals scored 4 times in the top of the first, due to some sloppy Boston fielding. This was the high water mark for Philadelphia, as their own sloppy play gave Boston four runs in the bottom half of the inning. The Red Stockings took a 7–5 lead into the fourth inning, at which time their counterparts in white became completely unglued. With two runners on base, Al Spalding lifted a lazy fly ball to short center. Treacey came in, Wood went out, and the two shadowboxed with each other as the ball dropped between them. While the players stood screaming at each other in center field, George Wright and Ross Barnes scampered around the bases and scored. All this time, the ball was lying harmlessly on the outfield grass.

Later in the inning Wood dropped a throw from shortstop Fulmer, allowing a runner to arrive safely at second. The captain fired the ball to the ground in disgust, allowing yet another run to cross the plate. Wood was hardly exhibiting leadership qualities, demonstrating why, although a fiery, likable player, he was considered lacking as a field general. Erratic captains like Wood and Johnny Hatfield led teams which mirrored their own tendencies toward self-destruction and uneven play.

In the fifth inning Wood made wholesale lineup changes which were the product of disgust, resignation, or panic. Chick Fulmer, with virtually no pitching experience, was thrown into the pitcher's box, while Zettlein moved to first base. Devlin moved across the diamond to third and Meyerle switched to shortstop. By that point, the game was out of hand. When darkness interceded, Boston had achieved a demoralizing 18–7 triumph.[7]

Although the two teams were virtually tied, they had merely intersected while traveling in opposite directions. Boston had made a furious charge from nine games back and had not tasted defeat since a loss to the

Mutuals on September 9. Ten consecutive victories had been registered in the interim. Philadelphia, at the other end of the spectrum, had lost five in a row and had blown a substantial lead in embarrassing fashion. The petulant displays of Jimmy Wood during the Boston game were the mark of a team in an advanced state of disintegration. The White Stockings had the look of a loser. Their failure to use Zettlein in some of the most crucial games of the season was clouded with suspicion. There was some mention of an illness, but it did not appear to have been anything acute. From time to time there were rumors that the Charmer's efforts to win were sometimes less than total. There was no solid evidence that Jimmy Wood or any of the club managers felt that Zettlein might have been dumping games, but his absence from the lineup at such a pivotal point makes one curious.

Boston officially moved into first place with the win over Philadelphia on October 2. Two days later the Red Stockings broke a 3–3 tie with five seventh-inning runs and held off the Athletics 8–7.

On the same day Philadelphia lost its sixth straight. The Mutuals, behind a Johnny Hatfield first-inning homer, sent the White Stockings reeling to a 5–4 setback. A reporter hinted that Philadelphia did not hit Mathews well because they didn't try very hard.[8] Devlin, whose baserunning blunder had proven so costly in the Washington game, pulled another rock in the ninth inning. His fly ball was dropped by left fielder Al Gedney, allowing Fulmer to score the Phillies' fourth run. Devlin, trying to carry the tying run into scoring position, was thrown out by catcher Dick Higham, who had taken Gedney's belated throw to the plate. The tag applied by second baseman Jack Nelson ended the game and knocked Philadelphia out of the race for good. The remainder of the season was anticlimactic. After taking the lead, Boston pulled away like a locomotive under full steam. Following a loss to the Athletics on October 6, Boston won eight more games in a row before losing a pair to the Athletics on October 24 and 25. Harry Wright, in his final season as a regular, belted two home runs in a key victory over the Atlantics. In a remarkable stretch run, Boston had rung up records of 12–1 during September and 11–3 in October.[9]

Philadelphia, moving like wildfire in the opposite direction, seemed to lose interest after descending into second place. They played only three games in the last four weeks of the season, closing out the campaign on a typically sour note by absorbing a 12–1 shellacking at the hands of the Atlantics. After starting the season at a 27–3 clip, the White Stockings had compiled a horrendous 9–14 mark after returning from their infamous dalliance at Cape May.

Harry Wright had led his Red Stockings to the championship for the second consecutive season, finishing four lengths ahead of the faltering White Stockings.

	W	L	Pct.	GB
Boston Red Stockings	43	16	.729	—
Philadelphia White Stockings	36	17	.679	4
Lord Baltimores	33	22	.600	8
Philadelphia Athletics	28	23	.549	11
New York Mutuals	29	24	.547	11
Brooklyn Atlantics	17	37	.315	23½
Washington Nationals	8	31	.205	25
Elizabeth Resolutes	2	21	.087	23
Marylands	0	6	.000	16½

Following the close of the championship season, the Philadelphia White Stockings and Athletics continued to attempt to exploit their rivalry. They played 2 exhibition games in November, making 12 matches in total. The final game, on November 6, drew only 500[10] hardy souls, who witnessed a lackluster 10-man game played with numerous substitutes.

Chapter 16

The Return of
the White Stockings

Philadelphia, which had conceded the pennant so easily on the field, now attempted to wrest it away from the Red Stockings before the Judiciary Committee. The crux of their contention was that Bob Addy had been ineligible to play for Boston. If this was so, Boston would be obliged to forfeit all games in which Addy had participated prior to September 4, giving Philadelphia a pennant they should have been embarrassed to claim.

The question was whether a game in which Addy played on July 4 was a "regular" game as defined in the NA rules. All indications pointed toward answering this question in the negative. Addy himself offered a sworn affidavit stating that the game had been a mere pickup affair.[1] A. N. Nicholds, former secretary of the defunct Forest Citys club of Rockford, sent along a statement pointing out that it would have been impossible to have a regular game in Rockford since there was no team in Rockford. The contest in which Addy had taken part was played by a group of youngsters who had banded together to have some fun and play a little ball.[2] The idea that this chance encounter should render Addy ineligible was preposterous.

Yet the issue officially kept the championship banner away from Boston until well into the winter. Finishing the season in first place was not enough, in itself, to earn the coveted streamer. The award could not be made until the Championship Committee had put its seal of approval on the entire process, ostensibly to be certain that the i's had been dotted and the t's had been crossed. In this muddled case, however, the committee simply failed to do anything. Although charged by the rules to make a decision by November 15, the deadline came and went with nary a peep from the three estimable gentlemen. Those of a less charitable nature might have attributed the inaction to partisanship, as the committee was composed of two Philadelphians, Hicks Hayhurst of the Athletics and Frank McBride of the White Stockings, and one Bostonian, Harry Wright.

130

Early in 1874 McBride claimed he had not signed the resolution which would have declared Boston the champion because he was waiting for the Judiciary Committee to act upon Philadelphia's charges against the Red Stockings.[3] President Reid of the White Stockings continued to pester the members of the Judiciary Committee with communications expressing the need for them to convene.[4] The committee members countered with lame excuses concerning the difficulties of time and distance and indicating that there were no matters worthy of their solemn pontifications.[5]

Oh, yes there were, replied Reid hotly. Philadelphia had charges to make upon which hinged the awarding of the championship banner. The prudent action for the committee would have been to meet, expose the charges as groundless, and clear the path for the declaration of Boston as the league champions. Prudence and action, however, had never been the long suit of any NA committee. They continued to dawdle, providing McBride and Hayhurst with the excuse they needed for continued procrastination. Finally, Harry Wright, in desperation, convinced Hayhurst to sign the championship resolution, creating a 2–1 majority and, at long last, a decision. McBride, oblivious to his own ridiculous posturing, pouted that Harry had coerced Hayhurst into agreement.[6] Nevertheless, the decision held.

Now that their ruling was no longer needed, the Judiciary Committee sprang into action. Nick Young announced that a meeting would be held at the St. Claire Hotel in Baltimore on January 20. Philadelphia presented its case and Boston replied with what was essentially a demurrer. Since the Championship Committee had already acted, even an adverse decision would have no practical effect. Hall, Young, and Smith of the committee, anxious as ever to avoid the slightest hint of responsibility, eagerly agreed.[7]

Next on the agenda was the case of Baltimore versus Candy Cummings. Cummings, who had signed up with everyone but the U.S. Marines in 1872 (see Chapter 22), was on the carpet once more. Baltimore claimed he had walked out on his contract, abandoning the team late in the 1873 season. The club's subsequent expulsion of the wandering curveballer would have rendered him ineligible to play for any team in 1874.

An affidavit from Cummings stated that he left the team because his pay was in arrears to the extent of $82.73. The team countered with its bookkeeping records which indicated, on the contrary, the pitcher owed the team $39.40 in advances. Evidence against Cummings included his previous history of dishonored contracts with the Haymakers and Athletics. The amount of $82.73 seems a trifling sum, even in 1873, over which to jump ship. On the other side of the ledger was the sorry state of the Baltimore club's finances. They finished the season between $5,000 and $7,000 in debt, including a host of salary payments.[8]

The committee members took the position of compromising parents.

They would forgive the recalcitrant this time, but should he tread afoul of the law again, they would not hesitate to take harsh action. Thus, Cummings once again escaped scot-free and signed with Philadelphia for the 1874 season.[9]

With the championship finally decided, the teams again examined their financial standing. Unlike the NA's first two years, the champion did not bathe in red ink. At their December 3 meeting, Treasurer Fred Long of the Red Stockings proudly reported that the treasury showed a surplus of more than $700, even after paying over $4,000 in 1872 expenses and salaries.[10] Approximately $3,700 in stock subscriptions and stockholders' tickets were entered as revenue, certainly a departure from accepted accounting principles. By most standards, however, Boston had had a profitable season.

Philadelphia, despite its late season collapse, had proven that there was room for two teams at Twenty-fifth and Jefferson. They ended the season with a surplus of almost $6,000, and a net profit of roughly $4,000 ($1,500 after deducting amounts contributed by shareholders).[11] The rivalry with the Athletics had played no small part in the financial success of the White Stockings.

With the exception of the woeful Baltimore results, the financial picture around the league was better than in the past two years. Even Nick Young reported that he had brought the dismal Nationals home without registering a loss (a financial one, that is).[12] The Atlantics were so encouraged by the results of the season that they were planning to step up from co-op status to that of a stock organization.[13] Baltimore, on the other hand, was hoping at best to send a second line co-op team into the field in the spring of 1874. The players were to receive a small salary, with the bulk of their income accruing from the division of gate receipts.[14] The stock team's debts had made it impossible to continue the operation of the corporation, and management was unable to wring concessions from its players, as had the Red Stockings after the 1872 campaign. All of the players were released from their contracts with several later suing (and losing) for the balances due. Litigation continued well into the following year, with the team officially declared defunct in March 1875.[15]

As usual, there were a number of cities threatening to place organizations in the field the following spring. St. Louis talked about gathering the finest from among its local talent to compete in the NA arena.[16] Warren White was trying to drum up support for yet another Washington team, despite the artistic failures of 1872 and 1873.[17] Neither St. Louis nor Washington was able to gather the resources to field an entry, but there were rumblings of a more serious nature from New England and the Midwest.

Following the collapse of the Middletown Mansfields in 1872, G. B. Hubbell, a gentleman from Hartford who had been an officer in the old Association in 1870, had declared that there would never again be a professional team in Connecticut.[18] Two years later, he was proving his statement premature. With Hubbell as president and Benjamin Douglas, Jr., formerly of the Mansfields, as treasurer, a stock offering of $5,000 was subscribed with relative ease.[19] Unlike the 1990s, when municipalities construct stadiums costing tens of millions of dollars in the hope of later attracting a major league team, Hartford entered the league and then endeavored to find a park. As late as March, the team was still searching for a place to play. After a feint to the north,[20] the Hartfords wound up in the South Meadows section, with a fine park near Colt's Rifle Works within easy walking distance of downtown.[21]

Hartford's location (approximately halfway between New York and Boston) was advantageous, as touring teams could make the stop easily and without great expense. Hubbell took the stock proceeds and scoured New York, Baltimore, and Philadelphia, returning with a satchel filled with signed contracts and much of the stock proceeds gone.[22] The players procured by Hartford were for the most part established journeymen, a number of whom had at one time or another played with the old Brooklyn Atlantics.

Power hitting Lip Pike, released from his contract with the bankrupt Baltimore organization, signed on as captain and center fielder. He was joined by former teammate Ev Mills. Bob Addy would play second base (no doubt after Hubbell had assured himself that Addy had played in no regular games within the last 60 days). Tommy Barlow, renowned for his bunting, and Bill Boyd, known for his hitting, deserted the Atlantics. The remainder of the team consisted of well-traveled mediocrities like Cherokee Fisher (Rockford, Baltimore, and the Athletics), Scott Hastings (Rockford, Cleveland and Baltimore), Bill Stearns (Olympics and Nationals) and slick fielding, weak hitting Jim Tipper (Mansfields). The *Hartford Courant* noted with satisfaction that six of the ten men secured by the home team were married "which is of course in their favor or ought to be."[23] In a send-off which added new dimensions to the phrase "cautious optimism," the *New York Times* opined that, "this is a very hard team to beat and if managed properly will not be last in the race."[24] They were right. Hartford nosed out tailend Baltimore for seventh place.

On the shores of Lake Michigan, Norman T. Gassette was resurrecting professional baseball in Chicago more than two years after the disastrous fire. The ubiquitous Nick Young was to live out his next incarnation as Gassette's business manager, while Jimmy Wood had been engaged as playing captain, despite his well-publicized failures of the past two years.

A new stockholder joined Gassette to assist in the reincarnation of the White Stockings. William Hulbert, a graduate of Belard College, was a driving, energetic proprietor of a grocery and coal business who had proudly and repeatedly declared that he would rather be a lamppost in Chicago than a millionaire in any other city. Hulbert was of a different breed than the club executives who composed the ruling board of the NA. He had never played baseball and viewed the professional version of the sport as a vehicle for making money, rather than as a source of recreation or civic pride.[25]

The White Stocking roster had been well known since the previous August, when a number of supposedly secret signings had become public knowledge.[26] Wood, Zettlein, Malone, Devlin, Meyerle, Cuthbert, and Treacey had all been spirited away from the Philadelphia White Stockings. The massive defection, planned well in advance of the prior season's conclusion, put the precipitous collapse of the 1873 White Stockings in a most unfavorable light. The absence of Zettlein from key games, Devlin's ninth-inning baserunning blunders, and Wood's erratic lineup changes took on a new meaning in this context.

With the "look the other way" attitude of the NA, wholesale roster changes were not without precedent. The managers of the White Stockings (Philadelphia variety) had been victimized in a classic illustration of the saying "what goes around comes around," following Philadelphia's raid of the Athletics' roster the previous year.

Philadelphia President George Young now claimed that many of the deserters had come around asking for conditional contracts to become operative in the event that the Chicago enterprise failed to materialize. Young reported that, contrary to Gassette's pious claims, he had replied firmly in the negative and had no intention of tampering with Chicago's signees. They were on their own, he declared, and should Chicago fail to honor the players' contracts, they would have to scramble as best they could.[27]

The new Chicago club, however, showed every indication of succeeding. The remainder of the team comprised solid veterans John Glenn, Davy Force, and Paul Hines, plus promising 24-year-old second baseman Johnny Peters. A new park (Lake Front II or Twenty-Third Street Grounds) had been constructed following the fire along what is now Cermack Road. As recounted earlier, the park had been the site of several neutral field battles, including two key Boston-Philadelphia matchups of the previous season. By the time May rolled around, the park was occupied by the White Stockings II, who played their first home game against the Athletics on May 13.[28]

They took the field without captain Jimmy Wood. Wood's track record as a field general was not an enviable one. His 1871 White Stockings and 1873 Phillies had both blown late season leads, the former with good excuses and the latter in embarrassing fashion. His 1872 Haymakers had folded, and the resulting Haymaker/Eckford combination had won only three games. A common denominator of all of these teams had been a discernible lack of cohesion. Wood's own on-field tantrums did little to build teamwork and camaraderie.

Wood's luck in his second tenure in Chicago was even worse than in the first. When the White Stockings took the field in the spring, Jimmy was sometimes on the sidelines, sometimes absent altogether. During the winter, Wood had developed an abscess on his left thigh. In this era, long before the advent of trainers and team physicians, players often took the healing process into their own hands — literally in Wood's case. According to the tale set forth by the *Chicago InterOcean*, Wood lanced the abscess with a pocket knife. The usually sure-handed second sacker fumbled the knife, the blade slipping from his hands. With the infected fluid from the left leg still on it, the blade imbedded itself in his right leg just below the knee. An infection now lodged itself in his right leg, causing it to stiffen unnaturally. As spring ended, the knee showed some improvement, and Jimmy continued to sustain hope that he would soon be back on the ball field. By summer, however, he still could not straighten the leg.

On July 10 a team of three doctors went to Wood's home to make a last effort to effect a cure. After putting him under the effects of ether, the doctors attempted to straighten Wood's leg and place it in a splint to keep it straight. Before the doctors had finished positioning the leg, the bone snapped, cutting into an artery. After stopping the flow of blood, the doctors were able to thoroughly examine the limb. They found an advanced state of decay and realized that amputation was the only way to prevent the infection from permeating Wood's entire body.[29] Minus his right leg, Jimmy gradually regained his health and served as nonplaying manager of the White Stockings for the remainder of their tenure in the NA. When the league folded, Wood disappeared from the major league scene.

Chapter 17

A Trip to Europe

The Boston winter produced news of a much more cheerful variety. Buoyant after back-to-back pennants, the Red Stockings could not seem to get enough baseball, playing pickup games on Thanksgiving and Christmas.[1] Sliding around on the ice and kicking up the snow, the Wright brothers, Spalding, and the rest of the crew could not wait for the 1874 season to start. On Thanksgiving, a holiday originated in Massachusetts, the Boston management presented turkeys to each of the married players. As Spalding said, "No wife, no turk."[2] The pitcher, along with George and Harry Wright, were passing the winter months as clerks in the office of Foster and Cole, agents for the Royal Liverpool Insurance Company, to supplement the $1,800 salary each earned during the baseball season.[3]

Spalding's main occupation during the winter of 1873–74 would have far greater ramifications than his clerking in an insurance company. He was about to become an international ambassador.

In that era of manifest destiny for Americans, nationalistic currents ran strong. The country was less than 100 years removed from the Revolution, and less than a decade from Britain's tacit support of the Confederacy. The *Clipper* erroneously stated of Irish native Fergy Malone, "we are glad to hear that Malone is an American. We had heard he was an Englishman."[4] Spalding's credentials as an Anglophobe were impeccable. He later wrote that "cricket is a splendid game, for Britons," and went on to characterize the sport condescendingly as "genteel."[5] Baseball, by contrast, was action packed and manly. Several of the top British cricketers had visited the United States during the 1860s and early 1870s, and the Red Stockings and Baltimore had swept through Canada in 1872 and 1873.

As early as the 1860s, there had been talk of bringing the game of baseball across the ocean for a tour of Great Britain.[6] Now Harry Wright was determined to bring the idea to fruition and selected young Spalding as his emissary. Prior to taking any action, Wright approached the Athletics and proposed that they join the Red Stockings in their undertaking, offering

136

to divide the revenue. Boston President Appolonio, along with Spalding, met with Athletics' President James Ferguson in New York[7] and reached preliminary accord, pending Spalding's visit to Europe.

The stockholders of the two teams were not so unanimous in their approval of the venture. Many felt the trip would be a financial failure[8] and one went so far as to accuse the players (who had nothing to do with the planning) of wanting nothing more than a free vacation.[9] Others were concerned about the effect of the lengthy absence of the two teams upon the pennant race.

The first question was unanswerable. The second was not as pressing as many thought. During the month of August, championship activity was habitually sporadic. Boston had typically toured Canada and the Midwest during the late summer. By canceling the Canadian trip for 1874, Wright was able to make up for lost time in Europe. The only venture north of the border was a side trip to Guelph on the way to Chicago.

On January 17, 1874, Spalding set sail for England, arriving in Queenstown, January 29. The pitcher seemed an unlikely emissary, primarily because of his youth, having just turned 23 the previous September. For such an important mission, it would have seemed that Harry Wright or perhaps one of the officers of the NA was a more likely candidate.

Young Spalding was mature beyond his meager years, however, so reliable that he acted as captain of the Red Stockings whenever Wright was absent. Born in 1850 in Byron, Illinois, he moved to nearby Rockford in 1862, three years after the death of his father.[10]

His introduction to the game of baseball is the subject of some confusion. The common story states that he learned the rudiments of the sport from a disabled Civil War veteran in Rockford.[11] Spalding himself spun a much more interesting, if possibly apocryphal, tale of his baptism. According to Al, the shy youngster was sitting deep beyond center field watching a group of boys play when a long blast headed straight toward him. He snagged it like a veteran and uncorked a powerful throw that reached home plate on the fly. The boys immediately surrounded him, not in anger over his interjecting himself into the middle of the action, but to insist that he join the game.[12]

Whether Spalding's childhood fantasy actually occurred is irrelevant. In any event, he began playing first base, then discovered a natural talent for pitching. He possessed good velocity (or "pace" as it was then described) a knack for changing speeds, excellent control, and a sneaky "quick pitch." His first team was called the Pioneers, and was composed of a group of local youths under the age of 16, including talented Ross Barnes. Spalding's innate leadership abilities propelled him to the position of team president. When the Pioneers showed the capability of occasionally upsetting a team of adults, the Forest Citys club — Rockford's crack collection of surreptitious semipros — began to take notice. They plucked both Spalding and Barnes from the Pioneers and added them to the Forest Citys roster.[13]

Spalding played for the Forest Citys from late 1865 through the 1870 season. In the wake of the stunning victory over the touring Nationals in 1867, the young pitcher received an offer to journey to Chicago to play for the ostensibly amateur Excelsiors. While he would not be paid directly for playing ball, Spalding stood to be perhaps the best paid grocery clerk in the city of Chicago, and perhaps the entire United States. In Rockford, Al was earning $3 per week, and was docked whenever a baseball game prevented his appearance on the job. While playing for the Excelsiors, Spalding would be paid $40 per week for his clerking, and would have free rein to work as his baseball schedule would permit. After heart-to-heart consultations with his mother and Rockford manager Waldo, Spalding decided to accept the offer and move to Chicago.[14]

Perhaps in retribution for violating the spirit of the amateur code, and quite possibly in direct consequence of an overabundance of $40 per week clerks, the proprietor of the grocery store went bankrupt before the 1868 season, leaving Spalding stranded high and dry in Chicago. He sold insurance for a brief spell before returning to Rockford to play with his old teammates.[15] The Forest Citys were a major force in 1868–70, showing surprising strength despite their small town backing. In 1871 they joined the fledgling NA. But they joined without their star pitcher, who had been wooed by Harry Wright for the new Boston team Harry was assembling. Spalding received a princely salary[16] which he justified by becoming the finest pitcher in the new league. In 5 years he compiled a spectacular 207–56 mark for a glittering .787 winning percentage, averaging more than 40 wins per year. Even in the era of the ironman pitcher, this was an awesome feat. While Spalding's talented teammates doubtless had something to do with his success, he also had a great deal to do with theirs.

A poised, cool customer on the field, Spalding was a gentleman away from the diamond. Unlike most of his peers, he was a moderate drinker who avoided gamblers as he would the plague. His business acumen would soon be evidenced by the formation of a small sporting goods firm which was operated quite successfully by his brother Walter. By the age of 23, Spalding was well on his way to a distinguished career.

While with the Red Stockings, the young pitcher was known as a sterling performer on the field, but was dwarfed by Harry Wright in league circles. Escaping Wright's awesome shadow in 1876 by jumping to Chicago, Spalding emerged as a force in his own right. He retired from the playing field prematurely in 1877 at the age of 26. In his final season, being a strong batter, he played first base regularly and took to the pitcher's box infrequently. With the advent of sidearm pitching for the 1877 season, the curveball and other trick pitches assumed increasing importance. While he undoubtedly could have adapted to the new rules, Spalding felt he could no longer be a dominant hurler.[17] Therefore, he turned his talented attention to the business aspects of the game.

In 1878, his first season away from the playing field, Spalding continued in the active management of the White Stockings as secretary and right hand man to President William Hulbert. He and brother Walter continued to expand the sporting goods business, publishing the *Spalding Guide* and works on archery, tennis, cricket, football, boxing, fishing, and virtually every other sport known to man.[18]

In April 1882 Hulbert died suddenly and Spalding ascended to the presidency of the Chicago club at the tender age of 31. With Cap Anson as captain and field manager, the White Stockings dominated the 1880s, winning pennants in 1880–82 and 1885–86.

While Chicago's prowess was evident on the field, Spalding's influence in National League affairs grew steadily. He was a general in the war with the rival American Association, Union Association, and Players' League.[19] By the end of the century the by then portly Chicago president was the most influential man in the game. A. G. Spalding and Brothers, with A. G. unconcerned about a potential conflict of interest, was a major supplier of baseball equipment and had made vast inroads in other sports. No less a personage than the venerable Henry Chadwick was employed to edit the annual *Spalding Guide*, having been warned to go light on his beloved statistics.[20]

In 1891, with both the American Association and the Players' League destroyed, the 40-year-old Spalding shocked the baseball world with his sudden resignation as president of the White Stockings.[21] The early exit paralleled his premature retirement as a player.

In his later years the former pitcher held no official post in the national game (other than a brief quasilegal reign as president of the National League after a bitter 1901 election)[22] but, as always, wielded tremendous influence behind the scenes. His energies were devoted principally to his diverse business ventures, which had branched out from the sporting goods field. Unlike his early mentor Harry Wright, Spalding applied his keen business acumen to a number of non-baseball pursuits, including an unsuccessful race for the U.S. Senate in 1912.[23] Spalding died on September 9, 1915, at the age of 64. He was elected to the Hall of Fame in 1939.

Arriving in England in the winter of 1874, Spalding began to make arrangements for a grand tour by his champion Red Stockings and their perennial rivals, the Athletics. He won the support of the venerable Marylebone Cricket Club, after a somewhat awkward audience,[24] and selected Charles W. Allcock to coordinate affairs in Britain. Allcock was the secretary of the Surrey Cricket Club and cricket editor of the *London Sportsman*.[25] In both capacities he had excellent contacts within the British sporting community.

A series of games was tentatively scheduled for the end of July and the month of August, including an interlude in Paris, to which Spalding had repaired in mid–February. On February 27, he organized the first game of baseball played on English soil. He pitched for one nine while Allcock hurled for the opposition. Each was backed by eight cricketers in the six-inning affair which resulted in Allcock's achieving that which eluded most NA pitchers, a victory over Albert Spalding.[26]

Spalding returned to the United States, after an arduous sea journey, in mid–March. In hand was an ambitious schedule calling for the two teams to crisscross England, Scotland, and Ireland, in addition to the aforementioned jaunt to Paris. The Red Stockings and Athletics were scheduled to give the Englishmen a taste of baseball by playing among themselves, but would also combine to play cricket against their hosts. At this point it was felt that the baseball games should count in the league standings, but wiser heads later prevailed. They would be exhibitions.

When he returned to the United States, Spalding presented the cricket matches almost as an afterthought.[27] The cricketers across the sea, however, considered their sport to be the main attraction, with baseball a curiosity to be introduced as an exhibition.[28] The only common link between the British and Americans was Spalding, who neatly straddled the fence. Realizing the wishes of the English, he touted the Americans as expert cricketers, the best in their country.[29] To Harry Wright, he spoke of the Europeans' thirst for baseball.[30]

Throughout the spring Wright sent Allcock clippings from the newspaper accounts of the Boston games, profiles of the Boston players, and other pertinent information on the teams Allcock was supposed to be promoting.[31] On the other side of the Atlantic, the Englishman was less diligent. A serious injury suffered while playing soccer slowed him somewhat[32] and, all in all, he was quite dilatory in his duties. Harry was somewhat uneasy with the lack of progress,[33] but was confident that the British would be quite curious to see the new game and that the trip would prove both an artistic and financial success.

The other major development of the off-season was the endorsement of a ten-man, ten-inning game by Henry Chadwick.[34] Chadwick was much more than a mere reporter of the game. Born in England in 1824, he had come to New York with his family in 1837. Ten years later the young immigrant witnessed his first baseball game, a Knickerbocker match at the Elysian Fields. That same season he played shortstop for an amateur team in Hoboken, which constituted the extent of his playing career.[35]

It was his journalistic career which contributed so much to the game of baseball. He turned to reporting in 1848, and by 1857 he was covering the sport regularly and, at various times, contributed material to the *Clipper,* the *Baseball Chronicle, New York Mercury, New York Messenger,*

Veteran baseball reporter Henry Chadwick, (circa 1885) known as the Father of the Game (courtesy National Baseball Library, Cooperstown, New York).

New York Herald, New York Times, and *Brooklyn Eagle.* Chadwick was the driving force behind the Rules Committee until after the 1874 convention and exercised an influence upon the sport that entitled him to the honor of being known as the "Father of the Game."

The press played a necessary part in the growth of the new sport, representing, in this preelectronic era, the only source of information available to the public. The 1869 tour of the Cincinnati Red Stockings was reported faithfully to the anxious residents of Porkopolis by Henry Millar of the *Cincinnati Commercial*, who traveled with the team. Millar owed his job, at least in part, to Cincinnati President Aaron Champion, and spared no opportunity to praise the home team and its exploits. Champion and Harry Wright recognized the value of the free publicity in the columns of the *Commercial* and, in return, treated Millar quite well.[36]

The 1874 transatlantic journey of the Athletics and Bostons was likewise covered by H. S. Kempton of the *Boston Herald*, who cabled his daily dispatches, dripping with minutiae, to the eager fans at home.[37]

Chadwick, however, remained the pioneer of sports journalism and was for many years the undisputed giant in the field. His fussy style was readily recognizable, and was liable to appear anywhere. He scolded those who did not play the game in the preferred style (preferred by him, that is) and was instrumental in the transformation of the game from mere sport to business. Unlike many of the early proponents of the game, he took baseball and the quality of play seriously. Unconventional or comical play was no laughing matter. He was a prolific writer and a man of almost puritan integrity, an unfortunate trait in anyone associated with the NA. He expected all others to achieve similar levels of rectitude. Chadwick's constant carping about dishonest play led many to suspect treachery where in fact there was none and eventually even Harry Wright felt that the constant negative journalism had done at least as much harm as good.[38]

Lesser known journalists attempted to parody Chadwick's style, but none had his extensive knowledge of the New York game. By today's standards, the contemporary style was dry and uninteresting, often consisting of a recitation of the number of runs scored in each inning and a description of the basic facts, including the weather and the attendance. The local professional team often rated a complete play-by-play description. Chadwick's incisive editorial comments were the exception rather than the rule.

The rule was hyperbole and florid language as well, as scribes competed to produce the wittiest, wordiest phraseology. A shutout was known, in contemporary parlance, as a "Chicago."[39] The term enabled sportswriters to wax poetic about each whitewash. After an 1873 shutout of Baltimore by the Mutual's Bobby Mathews, the headline trumpeted that Bobby had "sent (Baltimore) safe to the whitewashers' city by special express. Canaries all aboard for Chicago."[40]

Chicago itself was the home of hyperbole, in the form of the local *Chicago Tribune*. Its reporters, since the advent of pro ball in 1870, had seen the local team either as worthy of beatification or damnation depending on the outcome of the most recent game, and suffered perhaps more than anyone from the absence of major league ball in 1872 and 1873. When Troy visited the city for a neutral site game in 1872, the *Tribune* unleashed an attack which dripped with sarcasm and was aimed at the former White

Stockings who played with the Haymakers.[41] Their New York counterparts hinted uncharitably that the vituperative nature of the press accounts could be ascribed to the betting losses of the reporters.[42]

After an 1875 upset of the first place Boston Red Stockings, the shameless *Chicago Tribune* declared that the White Stockings had "throttled (the Red Stockings) until they were black in the face and ready to cry 'enough.' St. Louis started the rivets in their armor, but it was ordered by the destinies of the ball field that the Chicago White Stockings should give them a home thrust. Harry Wright is stabbed to the heart and the Bostons lie wounded on the plain, kicking their red legs in agony."[43]

First prize for overwriting, however, rests with the reporter from the *Cleveland Leader*, who was able to report optimistically on the preseason preparations of the 1872 Forest Citys. "The pitcher for the summer of 1872 has been practicing for several weeks outside of the city limits, and although not feeling well, can now throw a regulation ball with such swiftness that it cannot be seen unless covered with phosphorous and often the friction occasioned by its passing through the air causes heat so great as to burn the ball to ashes before it reaches the catcher." And in case the stalwart hurler should tire, "The reserve pitcher has been practicing only a few weeks but he can throw a ball through 18 inches of oak plank now."

Other members of the team were in equally fine condition. The second baseman, for example "can stand on his head, catch the ball with his feet, reverse his position and knock a grasshopper off a mulling stock at eight rods nine times out of ten. There will be no use for the runner trying to dodge him, for he has globe sights on his nose and can plumb a man in the brig or rigging just as he chooses." The outfielders completed a strong team and "can move on all fours faster than many professionals can on two and they arc so limber that circus men die off like sheep after seeing them perform once."[44]

The fans, or at least the writers, were not interested in the players' thoughts or opinions, as no interviews were conducted. Gender equality prevailed in the clubhouse, with neither sex entering the hallowed sanctum.

While the less urbane writers used blunt adjectives such as "putrid" and "wretched" to describe the home team's play, sophisticates like Chadwick hinted obliquely at the shortcomings of the athletes, employing such phrases as "paying no attention to sanitary rules" and "overindulgence in the flowing bowl" to describe chronic alcoholism.[45]

In the winter of 1873–74 Chadwick had a fresh cause to espouse the ten-man, ten-inning rule. Using the pages of the *Clipper* generously, Chadwick sowed propaganda for his proposal. Teams were no longer designated as "nines" in print, but as "tens," as in "The Connecticut Club Ten," a headline appearing in the January 31 issue.[46]

Chadwick had long been an enthusiast of the low-scoring game, and probably would have preferred placing 20 men in the field. Each year he wrote rapturously of 2–0, 3–2 and 3–0 games, looking disdainfully at the 15–14 slugfests which so often occurred. The point was valid. In an era when fielding was crucial, skillful work in the field was the primary cause of low-scoring affairs. Conversely, lack of fielding ability was usually the cause of a 25–15 margin. Few will argue with the thesis that good fielding is preferable to sloppy fielding, with the result that a low-scoring game represented a higher degree of skill. Even so, Chadwick took the rationale to the extreme, declaring that ties in the standings should be resolved by determining the number of low-scoring games that each team had played.[47]

The tenth man was expected to assume a shortstop position between first and second base, the better to cut off singles bounding through the in-field. An alternative was to slide the entire infield to the batter's left, posi-tioning the third baseman in foul territory to reduce the number of fair-foul hits chopped down the line.[48] It would have seemed less radical to eliminate the fair-foul hit by mandate, but Chadwick shivered at the thought, repeat-edly praising the skill of the successful fair-foul practitioners. He decried "a rather silly effort" to rule foul all balls going foul before first and third bases.[49] With the failure to outlaw the fair-foul, third basemen were forced to endanger life and limb by creeping to within 40–50 feet of the batter.

The fair-foul was not the only potential victim of the ten-man game. Wild pitches, passed balls, and missed foul tips could be largely eliminated if the extra fielder was stationed behind the catcher, another of Chadwick's suggestions.[50] Ten men, ten innings was the battle cry of the *Clipper* and was pounded into the readers' heads all winter long. There was no doubt in Chadwick's mind that his proposal would be rubber stamped at the March convention.

The delegates thought otherwise. There had been considerable opposi-tion to the proposal in Philadelphia[51] and, as it turned out, in other cities as well. Alex Davidson of the Mutuals was the only representative to vote in favor of the ten-man rule, his six colleagues feeling that nine was quite enough.[52] Chadwick proved to be a very poor loser. In late March he used the *Clipper* to alleviate the confusion over whether nine or ten players con-stituted a regulation team. "What if one team has nine and the other ten?" a puzzled reader wondered. For 1874, Chadwick replied, the sorrow crying through each word, every pro team would field nine athletes.[53] Left unsaid was the hope that the delegates might see the light in 1875. As far as the amateur game was concerned, the door was still open. The editor was hopeful that the amateurs would see fit to adopt the ten-man rule at their spring convention.[54] In the weeks that followed, the *Clipper* continued to trumpet the advantages of the ten-man game and insisted that the rule's passage was but a matter of time, comparing it to the elimination of the one bounce fly ball out as a positive step in the game's evolution.[55]

The Boston convention installed a new president of the NA, Charles Porter of Boston, with the popular President Hubbell of Hartford being enthusiastically elected vice president. These men, along with the rest of the delegates, instigated various rule changes. The batter's box was established for the first time. The sorry lot of the umpire was improved somewhat with the allowance of compensation for the arduous task. Half of the umpire's pay was to come from each team,[56] with the league itself totally removed from the umpiring process. Taking a step in the opposite direction, the convention voted to allow umpires to take testimony from spectators when a decision was in doubt.[57] It also provided for an arbiter to be dismissed without pay in mid-game upon the agreement of both captains.[58] The league's attitude toward its beleaguered umpires was best described by Chadwick's summary which accompanied the new rules: "In revising the code for umpires, the idea has been to remove as much responsibility from them as possible."[59]

Two efforts were made to correct the off-field deficiencies that had plagued the league since inception.[60] Unfortunately, neither dictum had any teeth. The first proclaimed that any player signing for a subsequent season before the end of the prior season could be expelled or, at the option of the Judiciary Committee, forfeit his salary under the illicitly executed contract. Passed in the aftermath of the sorry Philadelphia collapse, this well-intentioned rule was conveniently ignored the following year when the heart of Boston's team defected to Chicago.

In a seemingly superfluous ruling, the delegates banned gambling by the players. The penalty for placing a wager on a game in which the culprit was involved was expulsion from the NA, while gambling on any other game could result in suspension. While the intent was unassailable, the impotent NA committees proved unwilling or unable to impose any of the threatened sanctions.

Unlike prior years, the league was not deluged with applications from fledgling organizations wanting a taste of big-time baseball. The failure of the Kekiongas, Eckfords, Nationals, and their ilk had shown that $10 could not buy success. Only Hartford and Chicago chose to join the six holdover teams from 1873. Baltimore, although representing the same city, was far from the same team. Operating primarily on a co-op basis, they were unable to retain the high salaried players who had made them contenders the previous two seasons.

The convention behind them, the club managers rushed to finalize their nines (not tens). The presence of only eight teams meant that jobs were at a premium, and it was a buyers' market. According to the *Clipper* the previous year, "the man who can command half the salary he could in 1871 is a fortunate man."[61] After winning back-to-back championships, Boston's payroll shrank from $16,700 in 1872 to $15,800 in 1874.[62] Many

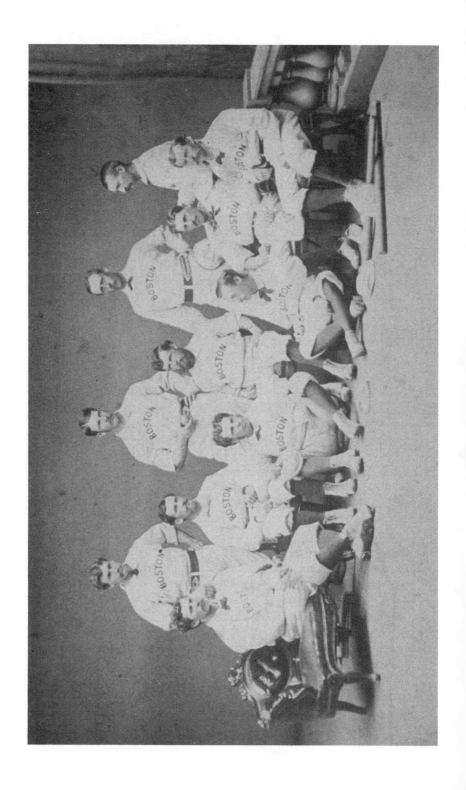

players found themselves out of a job, while others played at a reduced rate of pay. Established performers such as Al Martin, Jim Britt, and Fred Waterman disappeared from the big league scene. Virtually the entire ex–Kekionga crew from Baltimore mercifully dropped out of sight.

The champion Red Stockings maintained a pat hand. They added George Hall, power hitter and defensive whiz, to spell Harry Wright in center field. Harry, after all, had turned 39 in January. Utilityman Tommy Beals, formerly of the powerful Unions of Morrisania and the Washington Nationals, was the only other addition to the Boston team.

The Mutuals added shortstop Tom Carey, who had been cast adrift in the failure of the Lord Baltimores. The three-year-old problem at the hot corner was resolved with the addition of "Black Jack" Burdock, who had played an excellent second base for the Atlantics in 1872 and 1873. Full-bearded teammate Jack Remsen came along to replace departed center fielder Dave Eggler, who had left the team after five solid seasons. These two teamed with Jack Nelson to give the Mutuals a top-notch poker hand of three Jacks in their starting lineup. Mathews, who had spun a one hitter and a two hitter during the previous season, was retained in the pitcher's position.

Eggler, who had been a steady contributor to the Mutuals since 1869, and had batted .332 in their three NA seasons, wandered south to Philadelphia, where he signed with the White Stockings, now known as the Pearls due to a change in hosiery.[63] Eggler was one of many additions to the team that had collapsed in the final stages of the prior season. The turn-over was rendered necessary by the mass defections to Chicago engineered by Gassette and Nick Young which left only three players in the fold. Fortunately, the Philadelphia managers were able to obtain wholesale replacements from Baltimore. Pitcher Candy Cummings, playing with his fourth team in as many years, led a contingent which included hard-hitting outfielder Tom York, infielder Johnny Radcliff, and Bill Craver. Catcher Nat Hicks, fully recovered from his skirmish with Ferguson's bat, and quiet infielder Jim Holdsworth from the Mutuals completed this collection of hired guns.

The Athletics emulated Boston's policy of stability, adding only second baseman Joe Battin, formerly of the crack Easton amateur team, in place of Cherokee Fisher, who had moved on to Hartford.

The nucleus of the Atlantic team, which had shown significant improvement in 1873, remained intact. Second base, as in 1872, became a gaping

Opposite: **The 1874 Boston Red Stockings:** *(standing)* **Cal McVey, Al Spalding, James White, Ross Barnes;** *(seated)* **Jim O'Rouke, Andy Leonard, George Wright, Harry Wright, George Hall, Harry Schafer, and Tommy Beals (courtesy of Trans-cendental Graphics).**

hole in the absence of Burdock. In 1874 11 erstwhile regulars took their places at the keystone, but all were found wanting. Those admitted through the revolving door included ex–Cincinnati Red Stocking Charlie Sweasy and, of course, Frank Fleet. John Chapman, one of the old Atlantics from the halcyon days of the 1860s, returned to the Brooklyns in right field. He was a bit older (31), a touch heavier, and at least a step slower, but made an adequate showing with the bat. In his prime, Chapman had been a fine outfielder, known for the running, over the shoulder catch of long fly balls. Like Ferguson, he had been given the nickname "Death to Flying Things." The most important change in the Brooklyn alignment, however, was the release of Jim Britt, who wound up pitching for the amateur Nameless club. Britt had been punished unmercifully during the previous season (the hardest hit of any NA pitcher, according to the meticulous statistics of Athletic scorer Al Wright[64]) so his replacement by 18-year-old Tommy Bond of the Brooklyn Athletics could only be an improvement. Bond was a native of Ireland who had failed in a tryout with the Atlantics the previous season but whose main fault seemed to be throwing the ball too hard for his catcher to handle.[65] Despite leaving major league baseball at the tender age of 28 due to a sore arm, Bond racked up 234 victories in his brief career. He topped the 40-win mark 3 consecutive years, 1877 through 1879. Bond stretched the pitching rules to the maximum, delivering a very fast under-hand throw that was nearly sidearm. In 1874 he kept the weak hitting (.222) Atlantics in many games with his stellar hurling, launching them toward respectability.

Baltimore's co-op conglomeration scraped the bottom of the barrel, even in a year when available talent was plentiful. They had three Cincinnati Red Stockings on the roster, but all three (Asa Brainard, Charlie Gould and Charlie Sweasy) were on the precipitous downside of their careers. Reliable third baseman Warren White and pitcher-infielder Jack Manning provided stability, but there were slim pickings throughout the rest of the lineup. After two years in strong contention for the pennant, this Baltimore entry faced the prospect of battling Hartford and the Atlantics to stay out of last place.

Chapter 18

Going for Three

After a prosperous 1873, the financial outlook for the 1874 season was ominous. Since the 1840s, save for the Civil War period, there had been continuous economic expansion in the United States and Europe. Following the war, the interrupted westward expansion was resumed with vigor. The rich farmlands of the Midwest were exploited and their production consumed by a population increasing through a steady immigration from Europe. The country was still heavily dependent upon agriculture and the health of the economy could be measured to a great extent by farm prices and harvests.

The areas cultivated in wheat, corn, oats, rye, and barley increased from 64 million acres in 1867 to 86 million acres by 1875, with crop yields increasing 70 percent in the 12 years commencing in 1866. The increase in volume would have been meaningless, however, had the increased supply resulted in lower prices. Two unrelated factors fortuitously not only maintained price levels, but caused them to increase. The first was a postwar inflationary rise in the currency supply while the second was the Franco-Prussian War, which caused a substantial decline in European agricultural production. Thus, what would have been surplus domestic production was absorbed in foreign markets and prices were stabilized.

The economic boom was advantageous for any emerging business enterprise, and professional baseball was no exception. The sport's initial growth was fostered through sponsorship by local businessmen such as the Chicago grocer who intended to employ Albert Spalding. As their commerce prospered, the amount of money they were willing to invest in the local team increased. Likewise, the imposition of an admission charge was not feasible unless patrons were employed and able to pay the tariff. The postwar boom played no small role in the development of the professional game and the formation of the NA.

During the summer of 1873, the economic growth had come to a screeching halt. In June there had been a financial crisis in Vienna. On

September 18 Jay Cooke and Company, a Philadelphia banking house, was forced to close, sending shock waves through the financial community and precipitating a serious bank run. Plummeting stocks caused the major exchanges to suspend trading for ten days.

There had been ominous signs that the long era of prosperity was coming to an end. The United States had been importing significantly more than it had been exporting, a gap that had been steadily widening. Since the gold standard was solidly in place, and much of the international trade was based upon that precious metal, the export of hard currency was a serious concern.[1]

The banks survived and stock trading was resumed, but the economic expansion was over. Business failures mounted and prices declined, causing many of the merchants to become less concerned with the infield play of the home team and more anxious for the fate of their own enterprise. As unemployment increased, the average fan was less likely to spend his dollar at the ball grounds. While the NA had its share of internal problems unrelated to the economic situation, the Panic of 1873 reduced the league's chances of survival.

In addition to the financial contraction, 1874 saw a shift in the political direction of the country. The November midterm elections showed a reaction to the emerging scandals of the Grant administration, as voters gave the Democratic Party a majority in the House of Representatives for the first time since the antebellum period.

On December 11, 1873, General Abner Doubleday retired from active service in the U.S. Army after his most recent assignment in the state of Texas.[2] No one involved with baseball took notice of the event, not even Al Spalding, who did not take up the cause of Doubleday until more than 30 years later.[3]

Philadelphia was the site of the opening game of the 1874 season, with a resumption of the intracity rivalry between the Athletics and Pearls. A crowd including NA President Porter and Philadelphia Mayor Stokely[4] watched the Athletics try to reverse the newer club's dominance of the previous season. Much of the acrimony of 1873 was missing, however, since Philadelphia had had nearly a complete turnover of its personnel. Whereas both clubs had been composed almost completely of Philadelphians in the prior year, the Pearls of 1874 had been recruited from hither and yon, leaving the Athletics as the true "home" team. Rivalry between the opposing fans was still hot, however, as evidenced by the surprising turnout despite overcast, threatening weather.

The season started on a rather disconcerting note, considering the attempt at the annual convention to upgrade the league's umpiring standards. Captain Tom Carey of the Mutuals was chosen as arbiter for the opening game, and made a disappointing decision. In conjunction with the opposing captains, Carey agreed to play by 1873 rules rather than the new standards.[5]

Chadwick's harumph could be heard all the way to Philadelphia. Although he blustered indignantly, the powerless committees stood idly by as their carefully crafted guidelines were so unceremoniously and arbitrarily cast aside. While Chadwick, the originator of most of the new rules, "trust[ed] that the Judiciary Committee [would] act," his hope was in vain.[6] It was to be business as usual in the NA in 1874.[7]

The season was barely under way when it hit a lull in the schedule caused by that famous unpredictable New England weather. Early on the morning of April 25 the Pearls arrived in Boston to meet the two-time defending champions in what was to be the Red Stockings' opening game. After some amiable repartee between the two teams and a casual lunch, Philadelphia was dressed and standing in front of the U.S. Hotel waiting for the stage that would deliver them to Boston's Union Grounds. As they stood, they were covered by a light sprinkling of snow. The sprinkling became a storm, and there would be no game that day. Quickly — too quickly as it turned out — the Philadelphias jumped on the 3:00 P.M. train to Hartford, where they intended to play the NA's newest entry the following day.[8]

With a bit more foresight, managers Gillingham and Jacobs might have realized that Hartford is not that far from Boston, and if it was snowing in Boston it was likely also to be snowing in the former metropolis. Sure enough, when the Pearls arrived at Hartford's field in the South Meadows section, they found six inches of snow awaiting them.[9] "Being baseballers and not snowballers,"[10] as the *Hartford Courant* reminded its readers, Philadelphia scratched its plans to return to Boston (much to the disgust of Harry Wright[11]), got back on the train and returned to home base.[12]

Hartford, meanwhile, now planned to open the season on April 29 at Boston. As they were about to embark, a telegram arrived from Wright warning that the field was still unplayable, but would be ready on the morrow.[13] On April 30, Hubbell heard that it was snowing, and postponed the trip indefinitely.[14] For his caution, he received a scathing letter from Wright, who admitted to cold and high wind, but declared that there had been no snow and the field had been playable. He had now spent advertising money for naught on two days.[15]

Hartford's new team still remained unchristened. As luck would have it, the Hartfords had commenced operations during the coldest April Connecticut had experienced since formal record keeping began.[16]

The wanderings of the Philadelphias had been pointless, expensive, time-consuming and, like all travel in that era, uncomfortable. Intercity travel was done by train or boat, while the trek from hotel to playing field was made in relative comfort by horse-drawn coach. Comfort was indeed relative, for regardless of the method of conveyance, there was no escaping the city streets, which were built for neither comfort nor speed. Dirt, macadam, and cobblestone were the primary surfaces in use, with the latter prevalent in the well-traveled sections of major cities. Riding from hotel to park over cobblestones in a coach was bound to heighten the pregame jitters of any athlete with a naturally nervous stomach. Fortunately, New York City began to substitute granite for cobblestone in 1869.[17]

The advent of professional baseball in the late 1860s coincided with a dramatic increase in the availability and ease of rail travel. George Pullman introduced his trademark sleeping car just after the end of the Civil War in 1865. The dining car made its first appearance three years later, followed by the parlor car in 1875.[18] Following the completion of the transcontinental railroad at Promontory Point Utah, passengers could journey from Philadelphia to San Francisco in but a week's time at the cost of $140.[19] Despite the increased comfort, long distance travel remained arduous and something to be avoided if possible. It was no surprise that NA teams in Rockford, Fort Wayne, and Keokuk had short-lived major league tenures.

Getting the players to the game was the first step. They, however, paid no admission fee. It was more important to get the fans to the grounds. Some brought their own carriages, which could often be parked in foul-territory or deep in the outfield. However, the majority relied on their feet or public transportation. It was crucial, therefore, that a club locate its grounds within easy walking distance of the central city or directly on an accessible streetcar line. Horsedrawn trolleys first appeared in the larger cities in the 1850s and carried up to 40 passengers, bringing spectators over their steel rails in relative economy.[20] Extra cars would be put on the line for important games. Newspapers published the preferred streetcar (and, in New York, ferry) routes to unfamiliar ballgrounds.

After conquering weather and travel, Hartford appeared to be a threat to the Red Stockings, as they won their third straight by trouncing Baltimore 22–2, scoring 18 runs in the last 4 innings. Baltimore had a gaping hole behind the plate, as regular catcher Charles Snyder had been rendered hors de combat in New York.[21] The current occupant of the catcher's position was Williams/Selman, who was charged with a combination of 11 errors and passed balls.[22] On May 11 Hartford again beat the Canaries soundly, this time by a 16–6 score, with Selman once more contributing heavily to the Hartford cause.

Hartford was not alone in embarrassing Baltimore. Boston had administered fearful drubbings on consecutive days in early May, winning by a combined score of 42–7. On a tour spanning May 4–13, Baltimore lost nine straight by the combined score of 160–39. It had been felt prior to the season that the new Baltimore co-op entry was but a shadow of the strong 1872 and 1873 teams. The 1874 Canaries did not disappoint the prognosticators, losing 12 of their first 13 games and dropping like a rock to the bottom of the standings. At the end of May Selman and Sweasy were dropped from the squad, the former for "overindulgence in the flowing bowl" and the latter merely for substandard play.[23] Sweasy had come from Cincinnati in 1871 with a sparkling reputation for infield play, but had taken ill as soon as he reached Washington and had not been the same since. Although only 23 in 1871, Charlie was plagued by poor health and an indifferent attitude and was effectively washed up, although he popped up with a number of teams through 1878. The 2 players were replaced by the returning Snyder and by 19-year-old shortstop Joe Gerhardt, who had appeared with the Nationals in 1873.

The financial problems incurred by the 1873 stock club plagued its successor both off and on the field. Tom York, one of the former Baltimore players who filed suit against the club, served as umpire in one of the new club's games. York apparently vented his spleen, and was accused of extreme partiality toward Baltimore's opponent.[24]

In Brooklyn the Atlantics were making big news. There had been improvement from 1872 to 1873, but the addition of young Tommy Bond made the team truly competitive once again, as they defeated Boston twice in the early going. The first victory snapped a 13-game season-opening Boston win streak.

Fortunately for Harry Wright, no team seemed willing or able to step forward to take advantage of his momentary stumble. Hartford was demonstrating that its early run was an illusion, as they were beaten soundly by the Red Stockings in Boston. Pitcher Cherokee Fisher was already embroiled in disciplinary squabbles. Fisher's penchant for firewater, which had been at least partially responsible for his intraleague wanderings, was to be as much a bane to Gershom Hubbell as it had been to Fisher's previous employers.[25] Behind their first-string hurler, the Nutmeggers had only that prodigious loser, Bill Stearns, whose ability was clearly not enough to make the new entry competitive.

Half a continent away, the reconstituted White Stockings had begun the season fully expecting to present a strong challenge for the pennant. The 1871 entry had led the pack for a large part of the season and, many felt, would have won the pennant had it not been for the untimely intervention of Mrs. O'Leary's cow and the disastrous aftereffects. The 1874 roster was filled with the remnants of the 1873 Philadelphia White Stockings, who seemingly had the pennant well in hand until the murky incidents of September and October. Given the available talent and the capable management of Nick Young, Chicago backers were justified in their high hopes for the new team. An encouraging 4,000[26] turned out for the first home game in nearly 3 years.

The team was unable to satisfy the fans' expectations as it got off to a sluggish start. Jimmy Wood's health problems had clearly been an unsettling factor. The inherent disadvantage of training in the chilly Midwest was perhaps another cause of the team's slow break from the gate. With a 4–5 record they embarked on a tour through the east, where they hoped to fatten their record against the likes of Baltimore, Hartford, and the Atlantics, while testing their mettle against the contenders.

In the event, the tour proved the undoing of the team. After winning two of the first three games to even their record at 6–6, Chicago played a pair of matches with the Pearls. Both games drew well, with interest in Philadelphia peaked due to the return of the prodigal sons in opponents' uniforms. The second game was a runaway, despite a 6–1 Chicago lead entering the fourth inning. The *Clipper* referred to "bad and allegedly suspicious errors" on the part of Cuthbert and Zettlein which allowed Philadelphia to take the lead in the fifth.[27] Philadelphia scored in each of the last six innings en route to a lopsided 15–6 victory. Zettlein was victimized for 17 hits by his former team.

Young and Gassette were sufficiently concerned about the play of Cuthbert and Zettlein to remove them from the lineup the following day when the team moved on to the Union Grounds to play the Mutuals. Tom Collins, a youngster who had been the winning pitcher in a June 8 victory over Boston, stepped into the box in place of Zettlein, while Peter Standguard was summoned from the west to stand guard at second base. Collins was wild, as was to be expected of a player plucked from the amateur ranks. Adding to the difficulty was the fact that catcher Fergy Malone's hands were not in top condition. Nor was his attitude. He soon tired of chasing Collins's errant heaves and made no more than a perfunctory attempt to flag them down.

The first inning started poorly. Dick Higham led off with a single and continued on to second base when Fred Treacey could not find the handle. One out later, Joe Start lifted a lazy fly ball to right field. John Glenn dropped it. Bobby Mathews followed with a single and the rout was on. Eight runs later, Collins was finally able to retire the side. It was all downhill after that. Appropriately, on the anniversary of Napoleon's defeat at Waterloo, the White Stockings went down to an ignominious 38–1 pasting, the worst defeat ever sustained by a professional club.[28]

The *Clipper* reported spiritless and inept play, an opinion confirmed by the box score which showed an astounding 36 errors. Even allowing for the fact that wild pitches, passed balls and walks counted as errors, 36 in 9 innings was a formidable total. The Mutuals did their part, cracking 34 hits off Collins and Davy Force, who came in to pitch in the third. Davy fared no better than Collins, yielding 15 total bases in the fifth and 7 earned runs in the sixth. The offensive outburst, like the defensive effort, was one-sided. Mathews held Chicago hitless until the seventh, and to only two harmless safeties for the entire game.[29]

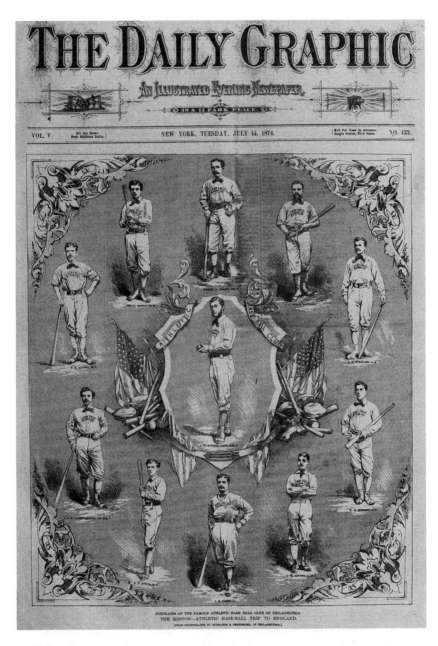

The 1874 Philadelphia Athletics: *(center)* **Dick McBride,** *(clockwise from top)* **Wes Fisler, Al Reach, John McMullin, Mike McGeary, Al Gedney, John Clapp, Adrian Anson, John Sensenderfer, Ezra Sutton and Joe Battin (courtesy of Transcendental Graphics).**

Although the debacle represented the nadir of the road trip, the journey was becoming reminiscent of the Cleveland 1872 tour which culminated with an eight-man team and the beginning of the end for the Forest Citys. On June 20, when Chicago returned to the Union Grounds to take on the erratic Atlantics, Gassette decided to reinstate Cuthbert and Zettlein rather than subject his team to another embarrassment. Malone went to the bench as a result of his injured hands and lackluster performance.[30] His replacement, Terry Connell, was little better, being charged with a combination of seven errors and passed balls. The Atlantics won easily 10–3, with Bond firing blanks for eight innings.

The Athletics were beginning to show signs of awakening after a slow start. They reversed the results of the 1873 season, dominating the season series with Philadelphia by winning nine of ten. In the early weeks of the season the Athletics were fielding a lineup of Mike McGeary behind the plate, Adrian Anson at third base, Ezra Sutton at short and John Clapp in right field. McGeary was an adequate backstop and shortstop, but Clapp was an outstanding receiver. Sutton was one of the top third basemen in the league, but was clearly out of his element at short. He had an exceptionally strong arm and, unlike Hatfield's, it was accurate.[31] The heavy-hitting Anson, even in his youth, was not the most agile of athletes and was a defensive liability at third. The fielding of rookie second baseman Joe Battin was suspect as well. With this lineup, the team had been relatively unimpressive, losing even to Baltimore. By mid–June manager Reach and captain McBride had realigned their troops into a more effective arrangement. McGeary was moved to shortstop and Anson to right field, enabling Clapp and Sutton to return to their natural positions. With this alignment, the team seemed to jell, moving ahead of the Mutuals in the race for second place. Converted pitcher Johnny McMullin led the way offensively, and finished the season with a league-leading .387 average. John was also hitting for power, slugging home runs versus Hartford and the Atlantics, and spraying out extra base hits with great frequency.

The Athletics' confidence was the result both of their own success and of some misfortune on the part of Boston. The Red Stockings had been hit with a rash of injuries reminiscent of 1871, including the knee and ankle miseries of George Wright and the disability in varying degrees of Ross Barnes and Tommy Beals. Harry, who had intended to be a spectator in 1874, was pressed into service in center field, and wound up playing in 41 contests, no mean feat for the bearded one at his advanced age.

In mid–July, the two teams prepared for their European journey with a pair of contests, one in each city. The crowd at Philadelphia was reported as nearing 10,000,[32] although that number would have seriously strained the capacity of the Jefferson Street facility. Attendance was no doubt increased by the return of George Wright and the fact that the meeting was billed as the farewell game for the two teams prior to their departure for Europe.

Hartford, which needed all the help it could get, was the beneficiary of some unusual circumstances which resulted in a much needed victory. The Athletics were scheduled to stop in the Connecticut city on July 14 on their way from Boston to Philadelphia. Preoccupied with their preparations for the impending journey to Europe, they sent a telegram to Hubbell indicating that, with regrets, they would be unable to appear on the 14th. They suggested a postponement until their return to the United States in mid–September. Hubbell was unsympathetic. He claimed a win by forfeit, which was his best chance of upending the second place Philadelphia team.[33] For once, the NA officials, hopefully uninfluenced by Hubbell's position as vice president, agreed and awarded the victory to Hartford.

It was quite possible that the Red Stockings and Athletics would show the English some estimable batting skills. During the first ten days of July players from both teams had put on a remarkable display of power for that era of the dead ball and the distant outfield fence. Both, surprisingly, came against the Atlantics' superb Tommy Bond. On July 7 catcher John Clapp hit two home runs to lead the Athletics to a 5–2 win.

On July 9 Boston punished the young Atlantics' hurler for four circuit blasts in a 14–0 rout. Jim O'Rourke and venerable Harry Wright were responsible for the entire total, hammering back-to-back home runs in consecutive innings. Harry's second round-tripper involved a bit of luck, as the ball skipped fortuitously through a hole in the right field fence.[34]

The home run was not emphasized or thought to be a particularly admirable feat in the 1870s, particularly by Chadwick. The *Clipper* repeatedly claimed that any well-muscled lout could knock the ball all over the lot, while true batting skill was demonstrated by the "scientific" hitter who sprayed the ball around and was capable of the elusive fair-foul. "Wee Willie" Keeler of the Orioles powerhouse teams of the Gay '90s would have been the toast of the town in Chadwick's eyes, while Babe Ruth would no doubt have been dismissed as a brainless slugger unversed in the "strategic points" so beloved by the sportswriting purist. Boston's four-homer game, a remarkable feat, went completely without mention in the Clipper, which could only lament the poor fielding on both sides.[35]

Chapter 19

Not Cricket

The steamship *Ohio* chugged out into the Atlantic on July 16 with 23 ballplayers aboard, along with nearly 40 other members of the party, including stockholders, reporters, and various hangers-on.[1] An enthusiastic crowd had gathered at the Christian Street Wharf to wish the party godspeed. Many sailed down the river into Delaware Bay, following the ship and shouting good wishes to the players. The wharves of Chester were lined with people who hailed the vessel and waved their encouragement.[2]

The most notable absentees among the traveling party were the iconoclastic James White of Boston, who had remained in the United States at the request of his family,[3] and Al Reach, whose growing sporting goods concern could not survive his lengthy absence. In White's place went John Kent, a long-limbed amateur first baseman from Harvard who had never played pro ball.[4] Kent sailed from New York two days after the main party and joined the Americans in Liverpool.[5] Harry Wright also decided to take kid brother Sammy, not because of his baseball skills, but due to his ability as a cricketer. Most of the Americans were novices at the British sport, while the three Wright brothers had learned the game from their father, the professional of the renowned St. George's Club.

During the 11-day trip across the ocean, Harry Wright attempted to relieve the boredom by giving cricket instruction as well as could be managed in the limited confines of the ship. Otherwise, the men passed the idle hours by playing cards, shuffleboard, and chess.[6] This is what was reported. Nineteenth-century ballplayers being what they were, it is likely that an abundant supply of liquor was brought aboard to speed along the chess and shuffleboard.

The voyage was marked by agreeable weather, and the players' land legs sufficed to maintain their health at sea. Only Sutton, Barnes, and Sensenderfer turned even a pale shade of green, although George Wright spent the entire trip complaining of seasickness.[7] Finally, on the evening of July 27, the *Ohio* docked at Liverpool, and the Americans were greeted

158

with a rude surprise. Expecting a gala welcome from their British hosts, they were met by two ex–Philadelphians who had recently immigrated to Liverpool.[8]

The Americans spent two days in the dreary industrial city reacquiring their land legs, changing their dollars into pounds, and wandering around in virtual anonymity. None of the citizens had any inkling who the Americans were or why they were in Liverpool.

On July 30, the two teams went to the playing field at 2:30 P.M. to lay out the grounds for their first game. Roughly a dozen spectators were on hand. Tim Murnane and Tommy Beals, who were tending the ticket booths, sat idly awaiting the crowds Harry Wright had envisioned. By the time the game started, roughly 500 were in attendance, far less than might have been expected for a routine championship game in the United States.[9]

The Athletics won a high-scoring, ten-inning thriller by the score of 14–11. The second game went to Boston 23–18, before a disappointing crowd numbering fewer than 200. When reports of these two games reached Chadwick, he wrung his hands, having been nervously hoping for his beloved low-scoring games.[10] For the British, accustomed to cricket scores in the hundreds, a 23–18 contest *was* a low-scoring affair, but Chadwick still felt that the two teams had not put their best foot forward.

Others were more concerned about the pitiful level of interest. A letter received from Liverpool from Samuel Hague, the manager of a local minstrel troupe,[11] laid out a number of possible reasons for the lack of enthusiasm for the American tourists. First, Hague reminded the American readers that baseball was an unfamiliar sport to the British, creating a natural roadblock to acceptance. He further felt that Allcock had not held up his end of the bargain, failing to place advertising in the local papers, either in Liverpool or Manchester, and took issue with the statement made by the *Clipper* correspondent[12] that the British were not particularly fond of sports. On the contrary, said Hague, the British were crackers about any form of athletics and a well-orchestrated publicity campaign would have generated an assemblage of 25,000.[13] His estimate was undoubtedly optimistic, but everyone was disappointed at the meager gatherings which watched the first two games of the tour.

Much of the blame seemed to settle on the English promoter. A second American expatriate from St. Louis described Allcock as a "fat, good-natured, lazy but gentlemanly person who had never seen a game of baseball played in his life."[14] He went on at length to describe the lack of publicity and advertising, for which he blamed the small attendance at Liverpool and other stops. The British preoccupation with the cricket games undoubtedly detracted from the baseball exhibitions.

Wright had been quite concerned with the ability of the Americans to make a respectable showing at the foreign sport. For that reason, he brought

THE AMERICAN BASE-BALL PLAYERS IN ENGLAND—MATCH BETWEEN THE RED STOCKINGS AND THE ATHLETICS, PRINCE'S GROUND, BROMPTON.—[See Page 755.]

his brother Sam on the trip and had unsuccessfully attempted to persuade some talented American cricketers to join them.[15] Failing in that, Harry had scheduled a number of practice games with American cricket clubs[16] in the anxious hope that some familiarity with the sport could be acquired in a relatively short period of time.

Heartily sick of the dreary city of Liverpool and disappointed at the underwhelming reception, the entourage took a one-hour train ride to Manchester, where the population was more enthusiastic. The players disembarked from the train at about 1:00 P.M. on August 1 and went directly to the Old Trafford Cricket Grounds, where a crowd of approximately 2,000 watched the Athletics prevail in a 13–12 cliffhanger. Wes Fisler had four hits for Philadelphia, including a home run, while George Hall hit a round-tripper for Boston. The crowd was decidedly more abundant and enthusiastic than that drawn from the lukewarm population of Liverpool, and included the American counsel and George W. Taylor of Lord and Taylor fame.[17]

The next stop was London, which proved to be the climax of the trip. The tourists arrived on Sunday and, Sunday ball being verboten, spent the day seeing the sights.[18] In the capital the Americans experienced the reception they had expected when they walked down the gangplank of the *Ohio*. When they arrived at the Lord's Cricket Grounds the following day, the players were greeted with a large banner proclaiming "Welcome to England," and a dozen other flags, including the Stars and Stripes, fluttering in the breeze. There were 5,000 denizens of the British Isles crowded into the ground to see this strange game of "base ball."[19] Either by design or good fortune, Allcock had scheduled the opening game in London on a Bank Holiday, on which virtually the entire city was excused from work.

Unfortunately, it was not a skillful exhibition that these Londoners saw. Joe Battin, in particular, had a rough day, committing 4 of the Athletics' 11 errors. The Red Stockings laced four home runs off McBride and buried Philadelphia by an embarrassing 24–7 margin. The turf at Lord's was so hard that any drive hit into the gaps between the outfielders skipped past them for a home run. In addition to the four Boston blasts, Adrian Anson connected for the Athletics. In the two games at Liverpool, nine home runs had been hit, a figure much higher than that acheived in domestic NA contests.[20]

London was the high watermark of the trip. Not only was the attendance far beyond that realized in any other city, but the social highlight occurred when the Marylebone Club hosted the Americans at a sumptuous banquet.[21]

Opposite: **Woodcut of Philadelphia Athletics and Boston Red Stockings playing in England during their 1874 tour (courtesy of Transcendental Graphics).**

Despite the sloppy play, the English press was quite curious about this new, fast-paced game which took but a fraction of the time needed to complete a cricket match. Much to Spalding's disgust, the press insisted that baseball was nothing but an evolution of rounders (a British game) and recalled that Frederick, the Prince of Wales, had played a game of "baseball" back in 1748.[22] They were also unanimous in their opinion (echoed by the Americans upon their return) that baseball would never rival cricket in England, regardless of its attributes.

The *London Daily News*, the *London Sportsman*, and the Liverpool journals all published detailed explanations of how the American game was played, for the benefit of the spectators who planned to attend the matches.[23] The article in the *London Sportsman*[24] bore many of the clichés that appeared ad nauseam in the *Clipper*, and appears to have been ghostwritten by the *Clipper* correspondent traveling with the two teams.

In any event, readers of the *Sportsman* trekked to Lord's hoping for a 1–0 game featured by "scientific" batting and slick fielding. They must have shaken their heads sadly when Anson, Spalding, Leonard, O'Rourke, and George Wright rapped the ball past the outfielders for home runs. Regardless of any predispositions, the British were uniformly impressed by the Americans' skill in fielding and throwing. This fascination appeared repeatedly both in the British press and in the reports of American journalists. The dominant skills in cricket were bowling and batting, while the average practitioner took little time to hone his fielding talents. Thus, the abilities of the Americans, which in present-day baseball would be viewed as shockingly primitive, were marveled upon.

The trip to Paris was canceled, purportedly due to the lack of a suitable playing field.[25] The Edinburgh and Glasgow games likewise never came off. Dick McBride and Wes Fisler made the trip to France nonetheless, going AWOL for a short journey across the Channel.[26] Harry Wright, ever mindful of the need for discipline, kept such a tight watch on the Red Stockings that none of them were able to visit the Continent.[27] For them, travel was restricted to England and Ireland, as the tourists moved from London to Sheffield, Manchester again, and Dublin.

Both the Red Stockings and Athletics found ample opportunity for shopping and sightseeing. English clothing was a prime commodity, although the *Clipper* reporter dismissed the taste of the players with the caustic observation, "about the only thing I can say in favor of the various garments is their cheapness."[28] Jim O'Rourke and Al Spalding invested heavily with the haberdashers while Count Gedney appropriately was "giving his undivided attention to diamonds."[29]

The British hosts, for the most part, treated the visitors well, touring them about the beautiful English countryside during their free time. The irreverent Americans consistently made sport of what they considered stodgy British culture and tradition. Various royal personages were referred to as the "Juke" or "his royal nibs"[30] and American slang triumphed over the king's English. Historical significance was far too trivial for the tourists, as reported on the trip through Wales on the way to Dublin. The Americans' train passed a number of old castles in various states of decay, "many of which are doubtless remembered in history, but which a party of irreverent, fun-loving Yankees had neither means nor time to identify."[31]

As the trip went on and the bleak financial results became apparent, the ballplayers' hostility to the British grew correspondingly. They contrasted the uncomfortable English trains with the cozy Pullmans[32] and belittled the natives' efforts to play baseball.[33] The failure of the trip was attributed not to the ballplayers, but to their hosts. "English people, with their slower perceptive faculties, do not pick up the intimation of coming events so naturally as their more rapid American cousins and there is little wonder that the advance agent, who is a genial, honest Englishman but who lacks the snap and vim of a successful American business agent, should have failed to stir up public interest in the affair."[34]

In addition to the baseball exhibitions, there were marathon cricket matches (are there any other kind?) with 18 Americans generally doing battle with a regular 11 man British team. Due to the handicapped team sizes, the Americans more than held their own on the cricket field, despite their lack of familiarity with the game. The three Wright brothers were generally the top performers, but O'Rourke, Spalding, and Leonard showed latent talent on occasion. Harry Schafer excelled as a wicket keeper, which was surprising in light of his less than remarkable fielding skills at third base. Sensenderfer, by all accounts, was the most hapless cricket player.[35]

Although the Americans were victorious at nearly every stop, finishing with a 6-0-1 record, the manner in which they played was decidedly not "cricket." Rather than judiciously "blocking" balls endangering the wicket, the baseballers whaled away at any pitch within reach of the bat. Spalding was an egregious and unrepentant offender in this regard.[36] The British looked askance at this uncouth form of batting despite — or perhaps because of — the success of the Americans. "A blind, slogging, batting style," they called it, although they excepted the three Wrights and O'Rourke from this reprobation.[37]

Harry Wright, who had strong roots in the sport, was a bit embarrassed, and made attempts to coax the Americans to play in the British fashion. Spalding, who in his classic work *America's National Game* took every opportunity to poke fun at British customs and mannerisms, scoffed and continued his wild swinging.

The British, for whom cricket was the main attraction of the entire expedition, were somewhat embarrassed to lose at their own game to the

Americans. They claimed that the local teams the visitors had defeated were second-rate combinations employed because most of the top players were away on holiday.[38] They also analyzed the play of the Americans as though they were professional cricketers.[39]

The success at cricket was satisfying, but didn't compensate for the continuing lack of interest. Although the Americans were well received in Richmond, the cities between London and Dublin proved largely a disappointment. Bad weather, including numerous days of rain, dogged the entourage and no doubt depressed attendance, as did the fact that the tour had taken place in late summer, when many of the British were vacationing. On their second visit to Manchester, the players were made rudely aware of the lack of pomp which accompanied their visit. After eating a rather simple lunch prior to the game, they were asked to pay three shillings per head. The following day they fared even worse, as the Manchester Cricket Club lunched while the Americans watched.[40]

The final games were played at Dublin on August 25 and 26. The hotel accommodations in Ireland were poor and the ragged ground was in sharp contrast to the lush fields encountered in England.[41] Once again the crowds were disappointing, as a total of 1,500 attended the 2 games. James Lawrence of Dublin had given the teams a financial guarantee to cross the Irish Channel, and spared no effort in advertising and promotion. This was not a repetition of the anonymous arrival in Liverpool. Unfortunately, the games were in direct competition with the Baldoyle horse races, which siphoned off a portion of the anticipated attendance and caused Lawrence to suffer a substantial loss.[42]

There was no shortage of entertainment for those who did attend. The Duke of Abercarn, Lord Lieutenant of Ireland, condescended to hit a few pitches lobbed to him by Dick McBride, much to the delight of queen's subjects. The Americans (18 strong, of course) soundly defeated the Dubliners in a 2-day cricket match and then challenged the Irish to a game of baseball with the same 18-man odds. They could not find 18 Irishmen willing to embarrass themselves at this strange game. When only six stepped forward (including the Earl of Kingston), the two Wright brothers and John Kent joined them to form a nine-man team. This hybrid combination got five outs per inning but still (not unexpectedly) bowed by a 12-6 score to the American professionals.[43]

Following this lighthearted exhibition, the Americans divided into two teams captained respectively by McMullin and Spalding. This was the final game of the tour, followed by an immediate departure to Queenstown, from whence the entourage set sail for the United States on the *Abbotsford*.

Financially, it had been a losing proposition, with most crowds falling within the 1,000 to 3,000 range. Boston lost roughly $700 after deducting costs, and the Athletics, with much heavier traveling expenses, lost $1,800.[44]

The Boston losses negated their stateside profit and resulted in a break-even year. The Athletics, whose payroll was $4,000 less than Boston's and who derived $1,000 in ground rent from the Philadelphia club, made a profit of $800 for the season. The figures include proceeds from members' tickets, without which both teams would have suffered a loss.[45]

Although Spalding, the European financial backers, and the American journalists were gravely disappointed, the showing should not have been a complete surprise. A strange game with unknown players could hardly be expected to draw more patrons than were attracted to the British cricket tours of the United States. Even though the latter game was familiar to most U.S. residents, attendance at the cricket matches was invariably modest. Other than curiosity, there was little to bring the British and the Irish to see the offerings of the European tour.

In many ways the journey of the Red Stockings and Athletics was like the National Association itself. Things did not go as well as planned, there were numerous disappointments, and the results were far from perfect. But it was a first. The NA was the first professional league and the European junket was the first time foreigners had been exposed to American baseball. In that regard it was successful, irrespective of the financial results and the lack of overflow crowds.

There were also indirect financial benefits. The two farewell games had drawn extremely well and the two welcome home games to be played upon arrival would do likewise. Having been to Europe enhanced the prestige of the two teams and hopefully led to increased attendance for the remainder of the season as well.

As ambassadors, the two teams proved themselves worthy. Wright had been careful and wise in his choice of the Athletics as the companion team, since the two clubs reflected the highest level of character and respectability among the NA entries. Bringing the Mutuals to England, for example, might have proven an unmitigated disaster. Much to the relief of everyone (and to the surprise of the British, who harbored the stereotype of the "goat-bearded Yankee" with abominable habits[46]) the players behaved as perfect gentlemen throughout their stay. There was no public drunkenness, no late carousing, and not a single incident which caused the slightest embarrassment to the party.

The return ocean voyage was difficult, as the ship encountered four days of rough seas and a violent storm. One of the steerage passengers (not one of the baseball party) died of consumption and had to be buried at sea. The last days of the journey, however, were marked by pleasant weather and bored passengers, as the players were nearly unanimous in having had their fill of Europe and sea travel.[47]

The *Abbotsford* arrived at the Christian Street Wharf in Philadelphia at 7:00 P.M. on September 9 to a rousing welcome from a crowd including

James White, who was at the dock to welcome his teammates. When Johnny McMullin, leading both teams, bounded down the gangplank, the multitude erupted in a joyous shout. July 16 and September 9 had perhaps been the highlights of the trip, as the send-off and reception in the United States far outdid anything experienced abroad.[48]

On September 10 the two teams did what they had been doing every day for nearly a month: they played a game of baseball against each other. This game, however, was a championship contest and more hotly contested than the fraternal exhibitions that had taken place overseas. It was so hotly contested, in fact, that umpire Theodore Bomeisler had to be afforded police protection from the irate Philadelphia partisans following Boston's narrow 5–4 win. Although Bomeisler had a well-earned reputation as an impartial, competent arbiter, the Athletics and their fans had taken issue with the reversal of an "out" call on an attempted steal of second by Boston's Andy Leonard.[49]

Two days later the teams traveled to Boston on the New York Express over the Albany Road, where they were greeted with strains of "Yankee Doodle Dandy," "When Johnny Comes Marching Home," and (for Harry Wright) "Hail to the Chief."[50]

Following the home-and-home encounters, the wreckage of the NA schedule was resumed. The absence of the two teams had left a tremendous void in the eight-team league, which was operating with the fewest number of entries in its five-year tenure. The interruption was not aided by Harry Wright's decision to barnstorm throughout the East immediately prior to the European expedition, nor by the "farewell" and "reception" games between the two teams.

Having failed to conquer Europe, the Red Stockings and Athletics now returned to the relatively mundane endeavor of forcing the capitulation of the Philadelphia Pearls and the Mutuals, the only remaining contenders for the flag.

Chapter 20

The Mutuals Repulsed

While the cats were away, the mice had played. In the touring teams' absence, two scandals had developed, although both had fizzled out harmlessly in the time-honored NA tradition.

The first incident occurred on August 5 at Chicago and, not surprisingly, featured the Mutuals. Betting on the game was heavy and, inexplicably, much in favor of the homestanding White Stockings, despite the Mutuals' dominance of the season series. The *Chicago Daily Tribune* confided that the reason for the heavy action on Chicago could be traced to a member of the Mutuals (management?) who went on a drinking binge the previous night with one Mike McDonald. McDonald allegedly led the betting on game day due to inside information gleaned from the drunken slurrings of his New York confidante.[1]

A second reason for the bettors' infatuation with the White Stockings was the rumor circulating before game time that Bobby Mathews was ill and unable to pitch. Mathews did pitch, however, and held a 4-2 lead after five innings. When New York took the field for the top of the sixth, Nealy Phelps entered the game in right field and Hatfield occupied the pitcher's box. Johnny was an inexperienced hurler who rarely played the position and was immediately touched for the tying runs. The White Stockings pushed across the winning run in the top of the ninth, having held the Mutuals scoreless since the second.

Although Alex Davidson of the Mutuals claimed that Mathews was suffering from an acute strain in the groin area, a claim substantiated by a letter from A. J. Baxter, M.D., the preponderance of bets falling on the Chicago side of the ledger cast suspicion upon Mathews' sudden removal. Innuendos or — in the case of the *Chicago Daily Tribune* — shrill accusations were cast in the Mutuals' direction once more. The *Tribune* referred to the incident as a "palpable and unblushing fraud" which disgraced the game of baseball.[2]

Only Mathews truly knew the condition of his celebrated groin, and

167

the debate died quickly. The key issue, ignored at the time, was that only the presence of open wagering at the grounds gave Mathews's retirement any significance. In the absence of heavy betting, the Mutuals would have no apparent motive for removing their star pitcher were he healthy. So long as open gambling with well-known odds was tolerated, doubt would be cast even upon those actions which were blameless. Yet, the ineffectual committees continued to waffle, fearful that a prohibition of gambling would slacken interest in the game and hurt attendance. As the *Clipper* ceaselessly pointed out, interest and attendance would be stimulated if the public was confident that games were on the up-and-up and uninfluenced by gambling elements. The Mathews incident did nothing to make this chimera a reality, and died out as quickly as it had emerged — without investigation or resolution.

The second murky affair smoldered much longer, and was the subject of much intense scrutiny. Umpire Billy McLean came forward with a startling revelation. Prior to a Philadelphia-Chicago game of July 15, McLean (according to his testimony) had been approached by Johnny Radcliff, who told him that he (Radcliff) had wagered his last $350 on Chicago. The money had allegedly been given to Radcliff's brother Samuel to bet in Philadelphia, although the game was to be played in Chicago. Radcliff offered to split his winnings with the umpire if McLean would swing a few crucial calls in the White Stockings' favor. He confided that teammates Cummings, Hicks, Craver, and Mack were also on the take. McLean's testimony further stated that during the game Craver brushed past Chicago pitcher Zettlein and told him, "If you cannot win this game, you cannot win any. You have got it all your own way." The umpire felt that Radcliff and his alleged co-conspirators played poorly, with numerous misplays appearing less than accidental.[3]

There were a number of holes in this argument. First, although the game had been played in mid-July, McLean did not come forward with his affidavit until August 20. Second, there was no record of Samuel Radcliff betting any money on the game in question,[4] although the possibility of using an unknown third party as a conduit always existed. Third, although Chicago won the game handily 10–3, the box score indicated that Radcliff was not charged with a single one of Philadelphia's eight errors. Craver, also indicted by McLean, was charged with a team-leading three, while Hicks made one and Mack none. Cummings, who McLean claimed was lobbing quite hittable pitches to his opponents, was roughed up for 17 hits, lending credence to the arbiter's accusation in that instance.

All of the accused issued vehement denials, Radcliff doing so by means of an affidavit in which he seriously impugned the character of McLean.[5] On September 8 the club members met to hear the report of the committee assigned to investigate the allegations and examine witnesses. Unfortunately, unanimity had not been achieved and the stockholders were subjected to three separate renderings of the facts. The initial conclusion, submitted by W. W. Dougherty and John McCormick, was that Radcliff was guilty as charged, but the others could be charged only with inept and indolent play—disgraceful but not criminal. They urged Radcliff's expulsion from the club. W. H. Redheffer and E. Rollins, however, heard the same testimony but concluded that all hands, including Radcliff, were guiltless. J. Fleishman, who had initially agreed with Dougherty and McCormick, now declared that the evidence was so contradictory and confusing that he had no idea whether the players were culpable.

With the committee firmly astride the fence, the stockholders voted 26–15 to adopt the Dougherty-McCormick findings, which resulted in the expulsion of Radcliff as of September 1 and no action against the other players.[6] As always, however, there was a job available for a skilled ballplayer, no matter whether he consistently used those skills to his team's advantage. After remaining on the sidelines for the last two months of the 1874 season, Radcliff was signed by the maiden Philadelphia Centennials for 1875. In the expanded 1875 Association, there were jobs for all, honest and dishonest alike.

With the top two teams absent from mid–July through mid–September, the soft underbelly of the NA was mercilessly exposed. Only six teams remained in the United States, with Baltimore, Hartford, and the Atlantics less than competitive and not an attractive draw. The dog days of August had always been poor ones for NA attendance, but now crowds in excess of 1,000 were a rare event. Part of the problem was, as in 1872, the troubling frequency with which the rivalries were contested. Philadelphia played Chicago on July 15, 18, and 20. The intracity rivalry between the Atlantics and Mutuals was played out on August 25, 29, and 31. The *New York Times* did not deign to send its correspondent to the Union Grounds for any of the three encounters, an indication of the lack of interest in the metropolitan area.

Although Philadelphia fans had their Pearls, Boston partisans were without hometown ball for two months. In an effort to ease their misery, Hartford and Philadelphia scheduled games at Boston for August 12 and 13. Despite their good intentions, the two teams added to the suffering of the local fans, showing them a brand of baseball the faithful had never seen from their champion Red Stockings. On the 12th, only 500[7] turned out to see a sloppy 23–10 Philadelphia victory featuring a total of 39 errors, 28 of which were committed by Hartford. Mercifully, the game scheduled for August 13 was rained out.

The Boston game did not represent the only indignity heaped upon the Hartfords in July and August. The team which had started the campaign with such promise was plummeting toward the cellar. Only the inept

Canaries kept them from reaching it. As is the case with nearly all losing teams, the camaraderie began to unravel. Bill Boyd, the team's leading batter at .382, abruptly left the team in early August to accept a better offer from the Brooklyn Fire Department.[8] Apparently, he foresaw little job security with the Hartford franchise. Cherokee Fisher attempted to drown the sorrow of his eventual 14–21 record in heavy spirits and again drew the ire of President Hubbell, along with a suspension. Although the harshness of the action was applauded by the *Clipper* as a step toward making the game more respectable, the hiatus lasted but a single day before Fisher was reinstated on a probationary basis upon payment of a $50 fine.[9] The fact that Hartford's only other available pitcher was Bill Stearns might have had something to do with Fisher's rapid reappearance.

Fisher's personal problems, shortstop Tommy Barlow's lengthy illness, and Boyd's defection took a heavy toll on the Hartford franchise. The team skidded badly as the season wound down, feeling the sting of the local press,[10] which had praised the team in May when it was in the midst of its early season winning streak. The local fans likewise abandoned the cause, as late season crowds typically numbered less than 500.

Despite the problems the Nutmeggers were experiencing with basic baseball skills, they found time to practice cricket, run much publicized foot races (won by Lip Pike),[11] and put Hubbell (who had at one time been a catcher for the old Charter Oak team[12]) in right field for an exhibition game against the Clippers of Bristol, Connecticut.[13] These diversions took their toll on the regular NA schedule (such as it was). Between June 22 and July 22, the team played only seven championship games, rendering the fulfillment of their quotas with each team a near impossibility.

The Atlantics, like Hartford, suffered through some difficult days as summer dragged on. Captain Ferguson, often known to berate erring teammates on the field, was the culprit himself on two occasions versus the Mutuals. His wild throws cost the Atlantics both contests, and left the fiery field leader no one to scold but himself. In the loss to New York on August 25, old "Death to Flying Things" was charged with six errors, experiencing great difficulty with Bouncing Things. The following day both offense and defense broke down in a 23–1 embarrassment at the hands of Philadelphia. Candy Cummings who, like the girl with the curl on her forehead, was either very good or horrid. He was very good, hurling a two-hitter at the hapless Atlantics. Only 3 weeks earlier, Cummings had been reached for 17 safeties by the weak-hitting Hartfords. In June, during an "on" day, he fanned ten White Stockings with his baffling curve.

Cummings's inconsistency, combined with his propensity for jumping from team to team and the regularity with which he found himself at the center of controversy, led more suspicious types to hint that there was more to the curveballer's mysterious off days than met the eye. The whole Philadelphia team, in fact, was approaching the Mutuals in terms of questionable effort. The late season collapse in 1873 had set the stage for 1874 rumors of spiritless play by the new edition, culminating in the expulsion of Radcliff. Many felt that he was not the only perpetrator.

When the Athletics and Red Stockings disembarked at the Christian Street Wharf, the Mutuals were the only other team that remained in contention. The opportunity to play all their games against mediocre opposition (or worse) had brought out the best in New York. They pulled out a series of four games against the Atlantics, with much needed help from the aforementioned Ferguson misplays. They downed the struggling Hartfords and the White Stockings three times apiece.

In 11 the only setback suffered by the Mutuals was the suspect 5–4 loss to Chicago on August 5, in which Mathews pitched only 5 innings. From a 17–16 record on July 16, they surged to a 27–17 mark and third place on September 7. Chadwick had always insisted that the Mutuals were a match for any team when their efforts were on the up-and-up. Granted, the opposition was second rate, but New York was no longer beating themselves. Mathews pitched with his usual skill, and the team yielded only 38 runs during the 11-game span. Given that each team in the league averaged 7.5 runs per game in 1874, the Mutuals' average of 3.5 allowed was quite respectable.

On September 7, when Boston and Philadelphia were more than halfway across the Atlantic on their return trip, the rise of New York was reflected in the standings shown below.

	W	L	Pct.	GB
Boston Red Stockings	30	8	.789	—
Philadelphia Athletics	23	11	.676	5
New York Mutuals	27	17	.614	6
Philadelphia White Stockings	22	20	.524	10
Chicago White Stockings	22	21	.512	10½
Hartford	12	21	.364	15½
Brooklyn Atlantics	9	28	.243	20½
Baltimore	7	26	.212	20½

Despite the Mutuals' surge, Boston maintained a comfortable margin. In order to win their third consecutive pennant, the Red Stockings needed only to avoid a total collapse in the final seven weeks of the season.

They were barely able to do so. Throughout the rest of September, the Mutuals inched closer and closer to Harry Wright's stumbling frontrunners. As the campaign wound down, Harry had benched George Hall and was playing every game in center. Yet the Mutuals continued to gain ground, setting up a pair of crucial confrontations beginning on September 22.

For unknown reasons, Harry Wright, rather than Spalding, was in the pitcher's box when the first game began. Spalding came in from center field in the fifth, seeking to protect the 4–3 margin which Harry had passed on to him. Albert was not up to the task, as the Mutuals took the lead with five runs in the next two innings. Boston battled back and tied the game in the eighth on a "rattling hit" by Ross Barnes that scored Harry Schafer. In the top of the ninth, the Mutuals' Jack Burdock, who had allowed Boston to tie the game on his error, atoned with a double. Pitcher Mathews singled him to third, from whence he scored on a sacrifice fly by Higham. Mathews held the one run lead in the bottom of the ninth and the Mutuals were 9–8 winners.[14]

On September 24, the two teams moved to Boston to continue the series. This time Spalding pitched a complete game, but Boston was able to score against Mathews only in the fifth inning, when their five runs were the product of throwing errors by Start and Burdock.[15] By that time New York had already tallied six times en route to an 8–5 triumph. By September 28 New York was hot on Boston's trail, having picked up eight games since mid–June and five since early September.

	W	L	Pct.	GB
Boston Red Stockings	35	13	.729	—
New York Mutuals	36	17	.679	1½
Philadelphia Athletics	28	15	.651	4½
Philadelphia White Stockings	25	21	.543	9
Chicago White Stockings	26	30	.464	13
Hartford	13	26	.333	17½
Brooklyn Atlantics	13	30	.302	19½
Baltimore	7	31	.184	23

The Red Stockings had won just 5 of their last 11, while the Mutuals continued on a torrid pace, having won 20 of 21. The *Clipper*, however, pointed out a telling statistic. Of New York's 36 victories 28 had come at the expense of Hartford, Baltimore, Chicago, and the Atlantics. Boston, on the other hand, had shown much more proficiency against the first division teams, with 21 of their 35 wins coming against Philadelphia, Chicago, the Athletics, and the Mutuals.[16]

New York's weakness against the top teams haunted them when they played the Athletics on October 3. The streaking Mutuals were expected to prevail easily over the crippled Philadelphia team, which was missing catcher Johnny Clapp and second baseman Wes Fisler. Thirty-four-year-old Al Reach was inserted in the lineup in right field, while seldom-used Tim Murnane filled in at second. Even the hometown Athletic fans expected the Mutuals to stretch their winning streak to 17.

If Mutual fans were disappointed by the 6–4 loss to the Athletics, they were devastated by the embarrassing 4–2 setback at the hands of the cellar-dwelling Canaries two days later. The *Clipper* reported that during a fifth inning defensive breakdown the Mutuals "indulged in a general growl all around."[17]

The Baltimore win took place on the morning of October 5. In the afternoon, in the second half of a rare doubleheader, the Mutuals took revenge by manhandling the Canaries 17–1. What was perhaps more astounding than New York's stunning loss was the meager attendance of 200[18] for an important championship game. Key amateur games were attracting crowds numbering in the thousands. Did the fans know something that caused them to stay away in droves? Were the Mutuals up to their old tricks in the middle of a pennant race?

Whatever the cause, the consecutive defeats put the Mutuals in a difficult position, for Boston was beginning a tear. Inexplicably, the *Clipper* had all but counted the defending champions out of the race for the second year in a row, despite the fact that the Red Stockings were in first place, based upon winning percentage. Below the standings, which showed Boston in the lead by two and one-half games, Chadwick commented that "as our readers will see, the Reds are not likely to win the pennant this season."[19] The man who had championed the European tour now reported that Boston was cursing it for having ruined their pennant hopes.[20] By September 30 Boston had 20 games to play, New York 17. Chadwick reckoned that Boston would be lucky to win 9 of their 20, while predicting that the Mutuals would not lose more than 2 or 3. "If they keep playing like they have in September and Boston shows no improvement, the Mutuals will succeed."[21]

The *Hartford Courant* viewed the standings differently, declaring on October 9 that "careful scrutiny shows the Athletics[!] have the best chance to win,"[22] Their chance was fleeting, as the *Courant* declared three days later, "[the] Athletics will do no better than third place."[23]

In the event, both Chadwick and the Courant were wrong. Boston rounded the turn into October in high gear. After downing Baltimore easily and uneventfully on September 28, the Red Stockings suffered an unlikely defeat at the hands of the pesky Atlantics. Brooklyn once again proved the Red Stockings' undoing, taking on 8–0 lead before the home team awoke. In the sixth inning Atlantic catcher Henry Kessler suffered a severe thumb injury and had to retire to the sidelines. Being on the road, the Atlantics had no substitute available. Bob Ferguson took his old position behind the plate, center fielder F. McGee moved to the infield and left fielder Eddie Booth and right fielder Jack Chapman closed in to cover the flanks of an unoccupied center field. Playing nine against eight, Boston rallied to close the margin to 9–5. In the ninth, Kessler patched himself together and stood in center field as the last line of defense. The Red Stockings picked up three more tallies but fell a run short.[24]

The following day the same teams took the field again, although other than from their uniforms the teams bore no resemblance to the nines that had played the day before. Boston hit the ground running with 2 runs in the first and didn't ease up until breaking the Atlantics' backs with 13 runs in the top of the seventh. There were 31 Atlantics errors, including 5 by a Boston amateur player named Snow who was pressed into service when Kessler was again incapacitated with a finger injury. Cal McVey and Jim White each accounted for 5 of Boston's 27 hits in a 29–0 rout.[25]

Harry Wright's charges wound their way south toward another confrontation with the Mutuals by way of Hartford, stomping the locals twice. In New York the Red Stockings first faced their nemeses, the Atlantics, who had beaten them three times at Boston, more than any other team. Once again, Brooklyn gave the champions all they could handle. With the score knotted at three in the eleventh inning and the October darkness closing in, a light rain began to fall. With two out, Tommy Bond at first, and Harmon Dehlman at the plate, the rain picked up in intensity. Time was called, but shortly the skies cleared and the players took the field once more. All the players except Dehlman, that is. He dawdled around the clubhouse, then deliberately sought out his bat and sauntered slowly toward the plate. By the time he was ready, the skies opened again, removing all hope of finishing the game.[26] While the contest went into the book as a tie, it was a great moral victory for the Atlantics, as shown by their eagerness to bring the game to an indecisive end. Once again, the erratic Brooklyn team had thwarted the mighty Bostons. On that same day the Mutuals were throwing a masterful 3–0 shutout at the Athletics to move within two and one-half games of the lead.

On October 9 the Red Stockings and Mutuals collided again at the Union Grounds. Prior to the game, the standings were as follows:

	W	L	Pct.	GB
Boston Red Stockings	39	14	.736	—
New York Mutuals	39	19	.672	2½

The game drew the largest crowd seen in Brooklyn in some time, nearly 5,000.[27] In the second, Jack Remsen blasted a ball over Harry Wright's head in center to drive in two runners, both of whom had reached on fielding errors. After Boston had cut the deficit to 2–1, Dick Higham reached on a throwing error by Harry Schafer, his second key miscue of the game. Two runs scored when a relay from the outfield escaped Schafer, making him liable for a total of three unearned runs. Boston pulled to within one run in the seventh and missed a chance to tie the score as George Wright was cut down at the plate on a snappy Remsen-Burdock-Higham relay. Mathews held on to the 4–3 lead and New York moved to within a game and a half of the greatly concerned Red Stockings.[28] What had seemed to be a runaway prior to Boston's European departure was now a red-hot two-team race as the season moved into its final three weeks. Unfortunately, there were no more games scheduled between the two contenders who, in that era, could not even get the satisfaction of scoreboard watching. They played out the string separately. With Boston again two and one-half games in front, the Atlantics returned to the spotlight. Having wreaked havoc unto Boston earlier in the season, they decided to do likewise to the Mutuals. On October 17, with the Mutuals favored 100–15,[29] a six-run rally reminiscent of the old Atlantics wiped out a 1–0 New York lead. The final score of 9–2 reflected the Atlantics' easy dominance of the affair.

Two days later Tommy Bond spun a 5–0 whitewash of the Mutuals on the same day that Boston was defeating the Athletics 14–7 at Philadelphia. The 18-year-old hurler threw the finest game of the year, and perhaps the finest game in the 4-year history of the league. Entering the ninth inning, the Mutuals had yet to get their first hit. When Higham and Allison went down meekly, 500 fans trained 1,000 eyes on Joe Start as he strode to the plate. Old Reliable lashed a solid double to left to spoil Bond's opportunity for immortality. Although New York added one more hit, the shutout was preserved on a fine running catch by Jack Chapman in right field.[30]

The three and one-half game margin was enough for the Red Stockings. After a loss to (guess who?) the Atlantics, Boston finished with six straight victories to pull away from the Mutuals. New York, which had played much of its schedule while Boston was in Europe, took the field only once following Bond's near no hitter. They forfeited two games to Philadelphia rather than incur the expenses of traveling to that city. The two teams had a "home team take all" arrangement for gate receipts and, having realized the receipts from their home games, the Mutuals declined to return the favor.[31]

When the ledgers were closed on November 1, the Red Stockings had won their third straight pennant by a comfortable margin.

	W	L	Pct.	GB
Boston Red Stockings	52	18	.743	—
New York Mutuals	42	23	.646	7½
Philadelphia Athletics	33	23	.589	12
Philadelphia White Stockings	29	29	.500	17
Chicago White Stockings	28	31	.475	18½
Brooklyn Atlantics	22	33	.400	22½
Hartford	17	37	.315	27
Baltimore	9	38	.191	31½

Despite a reasonable semblance of a pennant race, the lack of overall competition was becoming more noticeable with each passing year. For the third consecutive campaign, Boston had a team batting average greater than .300. Their .327 mark, although second to the Athletics' .331, was more than 50 points above the league average. Their 10.5 runs per game far outdistanced the Philadelphia Pearls, who were second with 8.19. After the tense pennant race of 1871, there had been little excitement in subsequent Octobers. The closest margin had been in 1873, when the race featured the total collapse of the Philadelphia White Stockings following the early signing of their players by Chicago.

There appeared to be no end in sight for the Boston dynasty. They had the best manager in Harry Wright, who brought his men to a level of teamwork in total contrast to the petty bickering found throughout the remainder of the league. On the field the Red Stockings boasted four future Hall of Famers in Spalding, O'Rourke, and the Wright brothers. They had steady veterans at every other position. The Mutuals had made a valiant charge in the second half of the season before falling short. After replacing Captain Tom Carey with Dick Higham — an unlikely choice as field general — New York won 23 of 30 games, a .767 clip. The Athletics played steadily, as always, but could not compare to Boston in terms of talent. The veterans of the 1860s were gone or fading, replaced by mediocrities such as Joe Battin and Tim Murnane. Their best was no longer good enough.

The mediocre teams were often accused of not giving their best, whether or not it was good enough. The Philadelphia and Chicago teams had been shrouded in suspicion at various times during the season. Chicago's horrendous 38–1 drubbing by the Mutuals, their defeat of the Mutuals occasioned by the mysterious removal of Mathews, and their win over a questionably motivated Philadelphia nine were all low points of the season. Although much negative press accrued from these incidents, Johnny Radcliff was the only victim of disciplinary action, and his expulsion was to be short-lived. Once again, journalists and league officials had fretted over the possibility of gambler-controlled outcomes, but virtually all alleged perpetrators were allowed to escape scot-free.

At the other end of the standings, Baltimore had reached the end of the line. They failed to complete the season, playing their last game on October 15. The city would not see major league ball again until 1882, the first season of the American Association.

Among the also rans, perhaps the most optimistic at the season's end were the Atlantics. The champions of the 1860s had reentered topflight competition in 1872 with a sorry 8–27 mark. The following year showed an improvement to 17–37. In 1874 the addition of Tommy Bond gave Brooklyn their first solid hurler since George Zettlein and brought them up to a nearly respectable 22–33 record. Both Boston and New York could testify to the tenacious play of the rejuvenated Atlantics, who had been particularly effective in October, winning 8 of 11. Brooklyn had beaten the champion Red Stockings three times on their home ground. Hopes were high for 1875.

Chapter 21

Going West

During the first half of 1875, a single event captivated the American public, particularly in the Northeast. Henry Ward Beecher was a liberal Congregational minister whose spellbinding oratory had earned him a national reputation. In 1870 Elizabeth Tilton, wife of Beecher's protégé Theodore Tilton, confessed to her husband that she had engaged in adulterous behavior with the famous minister over a two-year period. Tilton, perhaps embarrassed by the knowledge of his cuckolding, kept his own counsel and made no attempt to obtain justice from Beecher.

A feminist journal somehow got wind of the story and published it, pointing smugly to Beecher as a hypocrite who failed to practice the moralistic values he so fervently preached. With the story now public knowledge, Tilton filed a $100,000 lawsuit against his former mentor. From the start of the trial on January 11 to its conclusion with a hung jury on July 2, the public craved every titillating syllable emanating from the courtroom. More than two million words of spoken and written testimony were entered into the record, with large sections reprinted verbatim for the readers of the *New York Times* and other publications.[1]

While Tilton and Beecher sparked the public imagination, two events dominated the interlude between the 1874 and 1875 baseball seasons. The first was the rush of new entries into the league. From a low of 8 teams in 1874, membership swelled to 13 before the next season started, sending salaries back up as the competition for playing talent became more intense.

The year 1875 also saw the emergence of the west (now the Midwest) as a force in major league baseball. At that time there were few population centers between the Mississippi River and the West coast. George Custer and his more successful comrades were still attempting to clear the red man from the plains, restricting the white man to the Chicago–St. Louis line.

Baseball had originated in New York City and, for the first 20 years of its existence, stayed rooted in the New York–Philadelphia area. The Atlantics, Eckfords and Athletics were the dominant teams of the 1860s.

Prior to the Civil War, the game of baseball had been introduced to St. Louis by easterner Gerry Fruin[2] and by 1860 the city was represented in the old National Association.[3] In 1869 the first serious challenge from the west was mounted by Harry Wright and his invincible Red Stockings. The urge to imitate success was no less pressing then than now, leading Chicago to hire a team of easterners to take the field the following year.

After the tragic fire of 1871, the west was without major league ball until the reestablishment of a Chicago nine in 1874 by Gassette and Nick Young. In the spring of that year, Chicago had prepped for the championship season with a series of exhibition games in St. Louis against the top amateur teams, which had provided the professionals with a serious test.[4] Throughout the summer of 1874 baseball fever abounded in St. Louis. By winter, the natives had organized not one but two professional teams.

The teams were distinguished by the color of their stockings, brown and red. The wearers of the brown hose were by far the superior entry and often went by the generic name St. Louis. They were composed of eastern imports, led by 39-year-old Dicky Pearce, first baseman Harmon Dehlman, and outfielder Jack Chapman of the Atlantics. Lip Pike of Hartford, Ned Cuthbert of Chicago, and Joe Battin, who had played a shaky second base for the Athletics, rounded out an experienced lineup for the first year team. Pike, never reticent, offended many in Hartford with his constant boasting of the havoc his new team would wreak on the old.[5]

The battery for the 1874 Eastons, pitcher George Bradley and catcher Tom Miller, arrived in St. Louis intact after a struggle with Hartford over Miller's contract (see Chapter 22). The Eastons, a semipro powerhouse which had posted victories over the Atlantics, Athletics, and Philadelphia in 1874, contributed heavily to the NA ranks. Joe Battin, Denny Mack, Jim Devlin, Chick Fulmer, Bill Parks, John Abadie (of the newly-formed Philadelphia Centennials), and Miller and Bradley were all Easton alumni.

St. Louis also introduced 18-year-old pitcher-outfielder Jim Galvin to professional baseball. Although Galvin appeared in only 12 games, posting a 4–2 record, the seeds were planted for a National League career that would net Pud Galvin 361 major league victories and a place in baseball's Hall of Fame. The Browns were reminiscent of the 1872 Lord Baltimores, a maiden team with seasoned performers. Like Baltimore, St. Louis was expected to contend for the pennant. The team played at a field known as Sportsman's Park, which had been the site of baseball games since 1866. The same plot of land, under four different structures, would continue to play host to the sport for a century, until Busch Stadium was opened in 1966.[6] The city also added a new feature to professional baseball, as games in St. Louis could be played on Sunday.

The Red Stockings, a blasphemous incarnation of that hallowed name, were not of the caliber of the Brown Stockings. Charlie Sweasy, whose

Cincinnati background inspired perpetual hope in his numerous employers, came west to captain the new team. The remainder of the cast was unspectacular, drawn mostly from the St. Louis area. The players were local and — although they had played together for several seasons — mostly wet behind the ears. Third baseman Trick McSorley was only 16, while some of his teammates had barely passed 20.

The team was not only without success on the ball field, but seemed otherwise star-crossed as well. With no apparent causal relationship, an unusual number of the Red Stockings suffered an early death. The life expectancy of those born in the 1870s was 45,[7] a term severely shortened by the high level of infant mortality. More than 100,000 infants under the age of 1 year perished in 1870 alone.[8] The life expectancy of those reaching adulthood was therefore much greater than 45. Even considering these limited expectations, the Red Stockings had far less than their share of good luck. Of the 11 men who played for the Red Stockings in 1875, the date of death is known for only 7.[9] Outfielder Art Croft was the first to depart, in 1884 at the age of 29. He was followed by right fielder Tom Oran in 1886, Packy Dillon in 1890, Frank (Silver) Flint in 1892, and pitcher Joe Blong in the same year at the age of 39. Only teenager McSorley, who passed away in 1936 at the ripe old age of 77, and Sweasy, who expired in 1908, survived into middle age.

The players had one other thing in common. None of them were very good. Only Flint, a tough catcher who became a mainstay of the championship Chicago teams of the 1880s made any lasting imprint on major league baseball. His performance in 1875 (.086) provided no foreshadowing of his future prominence.

The Westerns of Keokuk, Iowa, were the fourth and final western entry. The Westerns were a going concern, having been in existence for several years. Keokuk compiled a 23–9 record in 1874, primarily against amateur competition. Four of their losses were to the Chicago White Stockings.[10] Declaring themselves champions of Iowa,[11] they set their sights on the championship of the United States. Their ballpark and roster were more suited to a pursuit of the Iowa championship. Built on a cornfield and known as Walte's Pasture, the field was bounded — rather, encroached upon — by Pleasant Lake. The lake was not so pleasant for the outfielders who are reported to have tumbled in while in hot pursuit of a long fly ball.[12]

Most of the ballplayers were holdovers from 1874. The left side of the infield, third baseman Wally Goldsmith and shortstop Jimmy Hallinan, were refugees from the 1871 Kekiongas. Former Chicago White Stocking Joe Simmons was the captain and center fielder. Most of the remaining players were unknowns, and all were inexperienced, with Goldsmith the elder statesman at 25. The Westerns had a strong hurler in Mike Golden, a 23-year-old flamethrowing righthander.

There was almost an informal western division among the four NA clubs. Although all were ostensibly in pursuit of the defending champion Red Stockings, the primary preseason goal of the St. Louis Browns seemed to be to defeat Chicago, the preeminent western entry. The Westerns and St. Louis Reds likewise set their sights on the White Stockings, who were just as determined to remain kingpins of the unofficial division.

Eastern teams also rushed to join the fray. Hicks Hayhurst, former manager of the Athletics, having witnessed the pecuniary success of the Philadelphia White Stockings, felt that the city could support a third team, and formed the Centennials. With the advent of the Pearls in 1873, interest in baseball — rather than being split between the two local entries — benefited from a synergy engendered by the intense intracity rivalry. Attendance had been sparked in particular by the upstart Pearls' dominance of the series and, for a while, the league in their first season.

Would three be a crowd? Hayhurst, who had managed the Athletics to their 1871 pennant, thought not and announced a 25 cent admission price for all games to stimulate attendance.[13] In an effort to provide immediate fan identification, Hayhurst signed well-known professionals George Bechtel, Bill Craver, Johnny Radcliff (after his reinstatement by the Judiciary Committee) and Fred Treacey, all of whom had made their mark in Philadelphia with the Athletics and or Pearls. The only other player with professional experience was outfielder Len Lovett, who had pitched (and lost) one game for the ill-fated Elizabeth Resolutes. All of the other players were local amateurs or semipros, including first baseman John Abadie of the Eastons. As there was no room at 25th and Jefferson, Hayhurst secured a field at nearby 24th and Ridge St.[14]

Washington, whose Nationals had been in the league in 1872 and 1873, put forth a team for the 1875 season. There were some names familiar to Washington fans. Outfielder John (Holly) Hollingshead was back once more, as was hapless pitcher Bill Stearns who, true to form, lost 14 of his 15 decisions. Aside from Hollingshead and Stearns, only second baseman Steve Brady, who had hit .336 in 25 games with Hartford in 1874, and Art Allison, the former Cleveland outfielder, had significant major league experience. The *Boston Advertiser* opined that only two of the Washington players were of major league caliber and, since they included Stearns among the two, their estimate may have been generous.[15]

The final new entry was the New Haven Elm Citys, captained by former Cincinnati and Boston first baseman Charlie Gould. Like the 1872 Middletown Mansfields, New Haven planned to take advantage of their status as a way station along the New York-Hartford-Boston route. With $3,000 of financial backing behind him,[16] manager Billy Arnold went in search of players, a scarce commodity given the 13-team field. There were a couple of false alarms. Announcements were made concerning the signings of veterans Jim Holdsworth and Johnny Radcliff,[17] only to have the players deny having signed. Tommy Barlow, the former Atlantic and Hartford performer, signed, breached the contract, and eventually had the matter settled by the Judiciary Committee.[18] As the start of the season approached, Arnold had yet to complete his roster.

The team he wound up with was unremarkable. Gould, of course, would play first. Sammy Wright, the younger brother of George and Harry, was contracted to play shortstop. Although his older brother claimed that Sammy was a better fielder and harder worker than George[19] and the *Clipper* felt that Sammy would "undoubtedly become as famous as his two brothers,"[20] the youngest Wright stole away quietly after an unimposing .175 average and mediocre defensive play marked his only full season in the majors. John McKelvey of Rochester, New York, was the opening day third baseman and later the regular right fielder. Although McKelvey did a workmanlike job for the Elm City club, his claim to fame is as the last survivor of the NA rosters. He passed away in May 1944 in Rochester, the city of his birth nearly 97 years earlier. Johnny Ryan, who had set the league record with 12 outfield putouts for the Baltimore co-op team the previous season,[21] was the regular left fielder and a part-time hurler. Jim Tipper, formerly with Middletown and Hartford, completed his trifecta as the center fielder for the third Connecticut pro team. The regular pitcher was Fred Nichols, a talented little curveballer from the Bridgeport amateur team T.B.F.U.S., who possessed an excellent pickoff move.[22]

Hartford, which had limped in seventh in an eight-team field in its first season, took drastic steps during the off-season to move into the upper echelon. Although the team had been an artistic failure, there remained enough funds in the coffer to allow the final 1874 stock installment to be used to procure players for 1875.[23] Management made wholesale roster changes, principally at the expense of the two New York teams. From the Atlantics they procured the two key players from the prior season, Bob Ferguson and Tommy Bond. The Mutuals grudgingly contributed Doug Allison, Tom Carey, Jack Burdock, and Jack Remsen. Burdock firmed up a middle infield that had been woefully inadequate in 1874. He was quick, aggressive, cocky, and had a fine throwing arm. Powerful Tom York and Candy Cummings completed a team that was poised to challenge Boston's supremacy. Not only did the club possess the finest one-two pitching punch in the circuit, they prevented the other teams from employing the talented Bond or Cummings against them. The former's presence was particularly uplifting due to his four victories over Boston for the 1874 Atlantics. Bond's overall earned run average had been second only to that of McBride.[24] Hartford had improved immensely, relegating the Mutuals to the middle of the pack after New York's strong finish of the previous year. The Atlantics, sixth in 1874, were destined for as yet uncharted depths.

Chapter 22

The Force Case

The second major development of the off-season involved a number of contractual disputes which eventually wound up in the lap of the Judiciary Committee. Player-management negotiations were often complicated by the undereducated condition of the players. Only half of the country's school-age children attended classes and many of these students appeared only sporadically. Children as young as six were employed as factory help and most offspring helped support the family as their primary responsibility. In New York City, the early center of baseball activity, it was estimated that 100,000 school-age children were employed.[1] The average citizen had a mere four years of formal schooling.[2]

Four years was enough to teach the basics of reading, writing, and arithmetic; however, many adults, including professional ballplayers, spent less than four years in school. A number were illiterate and had to have their contracts read to them before signing. To one incapable of reading, the written word certainly has a lesser degree of sanctity. In the winter and summer of 1875 the sanctity of the contract would be at the center of two crucial controversies that would eventually result in the final collapse of the tottering NA.

Contract difficulties had predated the NA. Two notable incidents involved players who would later be the subject of much suspicion in the Association, John Hatfield and John Radcliff. Hatfield's troubled history dated to 1869, when he agreed to sign a contract with Cincinnati, accepted an advance on his salary and left town, then returned to New York and signed with the Mutuals. In addition to his salary advance, Hatfield left the Midwest owing various merchants, whom he never repaid. The Red Stocking shareholders held a formal meeting, weighed the evidence, and solemnly expelled Hatfield from the club.[3] John was a mainstay of the Mutuals through 1874 and was smack in the middle of all the suspicious play perpetrated by the club. After retiring from professional baseball, Hatfield moved to St. Louis where he sold mutual betting pools.[4]

Johnny Radcliff had tarnished his reputation as early as 1868, when he deserted the Athletics late in the season to go to New York with the intention of joining the Mutuals. The directors of the Athletics raised $500 and dispatched a committee to New York to retrieve the renegade infielder. Upon finding him, they gave Radcliff a portion of the money to clear up some debts. Leaving his debts unpaid, Radcliff pocketed the money and returned to Philadelphia to finish out the season. The directors now were forced to send money to President Wildey of the Mutuals to repay the advance given to Radcliff and to pay the shortstop's bills once and for all.

Upon returning to Philadelphia, Radcliff (who apparently was illiterate) was read a contract for the following season and agreed to the terms. At the time he was discussing the Athletics' offer, however, he had a railroad ticket to Cincinnati in his pocket. Disembarking in the latter city, he signed with the Reds, who later voided his contract after discovering the earlier agreement with the Athletics.[5]

While Radcliff's conduct was far from admirable, he can be excused if he felt no guilt. The Athletics paid his bills, gave him a bonus, repaid his advance, and offered him a new contract, all after he had jumped the team. In 1874 Radcliff had been expelled by Philadelphia for throwing a game, but again was exonerated by the Judiciary Committee and signed by the Centennials. He had obviously seen no reason to change his behavior, nor had he been given any.

Following the NA's first season, pitcher Candy Cummings became the center of a raging controversy, as at least three teams bid spiritedly for his services for the following season. In November 1871 it was announced that he would not turn pro, but would remain with the semipro Brooklyn Stars.[6] Nothing could have been farther from the truth.

According to the Haymakers' version of the story, Troy had dispatched Lip Pike to Brooklyn in late September with instructions to sign the star of the Stars. Pike held discussions with the young right-hander and telegraphed back to HQ that Cummings was ready to sign if he received $300 on the spot. Pike's superiors replied that he should have Cummings sign a contract and the money would be sent. On September 26 a contract was executed, calling for a salary of $2,000 in 12 equal installments. Two days later Pike returned to Troy (with the signed document) and announced that Cummings now wanted $400 in advance, saying he owed the Star club money and needed to repay them before leaving their employ. The pitcher also telegraphed asking the Haymakers to send both copies of the contract so he could compare them to make certain that there were no discrepancies between the two. Suspecting (probably accurately) that he intended to destroy the original, the Haymakers told Cummings they would meet with him in New York during the first week in October and let him examine the original in their presence.

They met and Troy (remember that this is their version) tendered the $400 advance, which Cummings refused, claiming he wanted to show the contract to his wife. The Haymakers again suspected treachery and would only allow Cummings to take a copy to his wife. Their suspicions were heightened by rumors that Reach and Porter of the Athletics were in town attempting to convince the fickle hurler to sign with them.

Arrangements were made to meet again after Mrs. Cummings had had her say, but the pitcher failed to put in an appearance. Later that evening, the Haymakers sent an emissary to Cummings's home. Cummings once more refused the $400 and informed Troy that they should find another pitcher for 1872 as his address would be Philadelphia. He accused the Haymakers of reneging on their agreement by failing to pay the agreed upon advance. Cummings claimed that the Haymakers were $4,000 in debt and were unable to come up with the money.

The Athletics had, according to their version, signed Cummings in good faith, with no knowledge of his prior Troy arrangements. This may have been the case, but it was highly unlikely. Not only had Cummings been negotiating with the Haymakers, but there were rumors that he had signed a contract with the Atlantics, and yet other sources claimed that he had re-upped with the Stars.

In any event, the Athletics decided to disentangle themselves from the morass by canceling their contract. This left the field wide open for the Haymakers but Mrs. Cummings, like Ned Cuthbert's recalcitrant spouse a year earlier, had stated that Brooklyn suited her much better than Troy. Therefore, Troy was out.

The Mutuals, who had heretofore played no part in the unfolding drama, now entered the picture. With great dispatch and minimal fanfare, New York got Cummings's name on a contract, apparently with his wife's approval.[7] The *Clipper* felt that the Mutuals had obtained a mixed blessing. It hinted that Cummings had been a bona fide prima donna ("monarch of all he surveyed"[8]) with the semipro Stars who would need to be broken of this habit to become merely one of nine with the professional Mutuals.

The careful reader will note that negotiations between Troy and Cummings began in late September, when the season still had more than one month left. Although players were technically forbidden to sign new contracts prior to November 1, the rule was largely ignored (a "dead letter" according to the *Clipper*[9]). This was a custom that resulted in a certain awkwardness in the final weeks of each season. A player appearing with, say, the Mutuals against the Athletics might have signed to play with the Athletics for the following year, creating an understandable conflict of interest. It also created a certain lack of enthusiasm among those who knew they had been dropped from next year's nine.

Dennis Mack of the defunct Rockford team was the object of another contract controversy in the same year. When his signing with the Athletics was announced, Harry Wright appeared waving a contract Mack had signed with the Red Stockings. Again a family member—in this case Mack's father—played a key role. According to the player, the senior Mack would not allow his boy to play outside of his native Philadelphia. Wright, although feeling that the additional money offered by the Athletics played more of a role than any parental admonition, graciously conceded, releasing the first baseman from his obligation.[10]

By 1875 the number of contractual disputes had escalated. At the annual convention the haggles fell into two categories.[11] The first concerned those against whom disciplinary action had been taken in 1874. According to NA rules, any player who had been expelled by a club was ineligible to play with any other NA organization. Bill Stearns had left the Hartford nine a few days prior to the end of the season (without permission and while owing money to his landlord and several local merchants) and had been summarily dismissed. The futility of expelling someone who had already departed voluntarily is evident unless future sanctions against AWOL players were consistently enforced. This was not evident to the Judiciary Committee which quickly reinstated Stearns, supported by the logic that the pitcher had already lost income through his desertion of Hartford without pay and through the cancellation of his 1875 contract by Chicago. Based upon this dubious reasoning, Stearns was back in action, much to the delight of opposing batsmen.

A more flagrant invitation to flaunt the league regulations was issued by means of the reinstatement of the unrepentant Radcliff. The Philadelphia club had investigated and found sufficient evidence to warrant an immediate expulsion of the accused. William McLean, probably the most reliable umpire in the circuit, had provided the principal testimony against Radcliff. Yet, despite the repeated statements echoing the league's revulsion toward gambling and the lack of any new exculpatory evidence, Radcliff was made eligible for the 1875 season, ostensibly because the charges had not been brought in the proper manner. Bill Boyd, who had deserted Hartford for the Brooklyn Fire Department, was suspended, but reinstated when the Atlantics raised a howl of protest.

With these issues disposed of tidily, the committee moved on to consider cases involving the validity of certain player contracts. It must be remembered that the committee deciding these issues was the Judiciary Committee appointed at the 1874 convention which had convened the previous March. Unfortunately, despite the myriad of issues confronting them, the gentlemen of the committee (Young of Chicago, Hubbell of Hartford, Hadel of Baltimore, Porter of Boston and Reid of Philadelphia) had canceled a scheduled January 8 meeting which might have given them an opportunity to deliberate deliberately.[12]

The presence of Hadel on the committee pointed out yet another shortcoming of the administrative machinery. The members elected at one convention served through the next convention. Given the attrition rate of NA franchises, there was a relatively significant chance that, like Hadel, the committee member would represent a team no longer in existence. Baltimore had disbanded the previous October and had no intention of fielding a team in 1875. On the positive side of the ledger in this regard was Hadel's impartiality, a precious commodity as the drama of the committee's actions unfolded.

One case under study was that of Tom Miller, the catcher of the Easton amateurs, who had batted .500 in a four-game trial with the Athletics. St. Louis, hot on the trail of both Miller and batterymate George Bradley, signed both to 1875 contracts for $1,200 each in October 1874. While Bradley's document was fine in all its particulars, Miller's contract was not properly witnessed.[13] Upon discovering the error and the resulting invalidity of the contract, the catcher signed a second contract with Hartford. Miller's heart, as it turned out, was in St. Louis, and he signed a legitimate, properly witnessed contract with the Browns. Legitimate, that is, except for the existing contract with Hartford. The Browns attempted to circumvent this inconvenient impediment by antedating the contract to November 2, an embarrassing episode explained by St. Louis President Bishop as due to the team's preprinted contracts, all of which were dated November 2. Bishop had paid no heed to the warnings that Miller was already under contract to Hartford, attributing them to mere rumor.[14]

The Judiciary Committee, almost surprisingly in light of their other decisions, ruled that the Hartford contract, the first to be executed legally, was the binding document. Such clear logic was inconsistent with the earlier rulings. Hartford realized the liability of using a reluctant performer, and promptly released Miller to the Brown Stockings. Everyone applauded Morgan Bulkeley's sense of sportsmanship and generosity. No one mentioned that Hartford's recent signing of Doug Allison had rendered Miller's presence unnecessary.

The final case was a thorny one, and was the cause of much ill feeling, with the ramifications dragging on until well after the start of the season. Davy Force was a top-flight infielder who had led the league in batting in 1872. His ability far exceeded that of the others who were on trial before the Judiciary Committee, and thus his case attracted more attention and was more hotly contested by the clubs vying for Force's services. The facts of the Force case were as follows.[15] Force, while under an 1874 contract to Chicago, signed an 1875 pact with the White Stockings dated September 18, 1874. He also signed with the Athletics by means of a document dated December 5. Both the White Stockings and Athletics laid fervent claim to his services with Force himself indicating a desire to play with the latter.

While the facts were relatively simple, the issues were many. Force's 1874 contract did not expire until March 15, 1875. The NA forbade a player under contract with one team to sign a new agreement before the first contract had expired. Notwithstanding the prohibition, newspapers routinely announced signings for the next season as early as August. The announcement by Chicago's Norman Gassette of the mass signing of the 1873 Philadelphia White Stockings had been made in a letter of August 21,[16] more than two months prior to the end of the championship season. The detrimental impact upon the old team was obvious. In late 1873 Washington's Tommy Beals was held out of an important late season game with Boston since he had already signed with the Red Stockings for the following season.[17] But was a player prohibited from signing an extension with his old team? If not offered an extension, was he forced to wait until March 16 before shopping for a new team? Did the rule apply to players with co-op teams, many of whom had written contracts, or just those from salaried nines? The rules of the NA also called for all disputes to be brought to the attention of the Judiciary Committee prior to November 15. Since the Athletics did not engage Force until December 5, the White Stockings had no chance to file their claim with the committee prior to the deadline. As Force chose to align himself with the Athletics, the onus was on Chicago to take action designed to get him back. Did their failure to abide by the letter of the law prohibit the committee from taking any action whatsoever?

It was later proven that the Chicago contract had actually been signed on November 2 and had been antedated to September 18 for reasons never brought to light.[18] Even though the November 2 signing was prior to the December 5 Athletic agreement, did the alteration of the contract render it void? The five learned gentlemen of the committee decided that the antedated contract had still been signed before the Athletic pact and that Force's services rightfully belonged to the White Stockings. The ruling, which should have settled the controversy once and for all, only led to a new complication. The committee could not present its report until the general session to be held in the evening. In the meantime, new officers had been elected, including Charles Spering of the Athletics as president.

The report started badly. Having failed to convene at an earlier date, Young and his cohorts had not been able to draft a well-ordered, precise document. The rendering of the Miller decision was done in a confused manner which left the delegates wondering whether the catcher would spend the season in St. Louis or Hartford. After much discussion, the committee decided that a minority report should be prepared, distinct from the majority decision. While they trotted off to clarify the findings, the proceedings continued without them. Harry Wright introduced some minor amendments to the rules. Chadwick, still in a snit over the rejection of his ten man, ten inning rule at the prior convention, had refused to participate.

He then drew Harry's ire by claiming that he mishandled the presentation[19] although, given the relative unimportance of the changes, any lapse would not have been critical. Following Wright's amendments, the Judiciary Committee returned and issued a coherent decision on Tom Miller's contract. After all the labor pains required to produce the ruling, Hartford rescinded its claim.

Then came the long-awaited decision in the Force case. When the verdict in favor of Chicago was announced, Spering was the picture of flaming indignation. He refused to accept the committee's ruling and attempted to enlist the support of the other delegates. With or without his influence as the league's new president, he persuaded the convention to set the matter aside until morning, in effect negating the committee's directive.

The primary advantage of the overnight postponement was that new elections had taken place subsequent to the meeting of the Judiciary Committee. On the morrow Spering would get a second chance with a fresh set of faces. The 1875 Judiciary Committee consisted of Hayhurst of the Centennials, a holdover from the 1874 cast; Bulkeley of Hartford, a respected newcomer to the league's upper management; Van Delft of the Atlantics; Concannon of the Philadelphia Pearls; and Trimble of the newly admitted Westerns.

Soon after his election, Trimble informed the convention that the time consumed by his business ventures would require his declining the honor of serving on the committee. This presented an opportunity for Spering. As president, he felt entitled to unilaterally appoint Trimble's replacement. Spering fingered the most capable candidate he knew: himself. The five-man committee now contained three Philadelphians. Not surprisingly, they reversed the ruling of the 1874 committee, based upon the tenuous reasoning that any antedated contract was unenforceable and that the old committee did not have jurisdiction over the matter, since it was not brought to their attention prior to November 15.

Spering and Force were quite pleased with the amended result. Chicago was not, and found an active ally in Harry Wright. Wright could not possibly have been shocked by the early signing, since he himself had negotiated with Force prior to the end of the 1874 season.[20] He was incensed at the gross miscarriage of justice and the attempted domination of the Association by the Philadelphia teams, similar to the tactics used in the dispute over the 1873 championship. Local prejudice would make the committee not only impotent (as it had always been) but a positive force for those who controlled it. "How long will the National Association exist if the clubs violate its laws with impunity when they conflict with their special interests," he wrote angrily to Chadwick.[21]

Wright certainly resented as well the fact that his perpetual challengers had obtained an outstanding shortstop, and carried the battle well into the spring, long after the White Stockings had given up the cause for lost. Wright wrote to Hulbert that he felt it was Boston's responsibility as champions to take a stand against the blatant committee packing.[22] He outlined a series of steps to be taken in order to eradicate the new Judiciary Committee. The Boston manager would convince all the other teams to form a solid front in demanding a special meeting prior to the season which would form a new committee of representative origin. Wright would also bear witness to the agreement between Spering and Hulbert to abide by the decision of the 1874 committee. He peppered the columns of the *Clipper* with irate letters doubting whether innocent antedating due to logistical demands could invalidate an otherwise legal contract.[23]

Throughout it all, Wright retained his sense of humor. To Cammeyer he wrote, "What do you think of the new President of the Association? Is he not doing business nobly—for the Athletics?"[24] And "In regard to your list of umpires, we select Henry Chadwick first and Charles Spering second."[25]

Somehow lost in the morass was the implication of players signing with more than one organization. No mention of censure for Force, Miller or, Jack Burdock (who signed with Hartford and Chicago) was ever made.

In April Wright announced that his Red Stockings would not play any games with the Athletics.[26] He also attempted to convince the other eastern teams to join the boycott.[27] The implications of Harry's refusal to play Philadelphia had serious repercussions for the pennant race. If the teams did not complete the minimum series (now six games) neither's games would count in the standings. This would result in the disqualification of 2 contenders (including the 3-time defending champions) and the elimination from the records of the other 11 teams of any games played with the Red Stockings or Athletics.

Hartford President Morgan Bulkeley protested his team's first game with the Athletics due to Force's presence in the lineup[28] and Secretary Ben Douglas wanted to take the matter to the Championship Committee at the season's end. Wright cogently pointed out that the Judiciary Committee, not the Championship Committee, had jurisdiction over such matters and that a protest after the season, when all gate receipts had been gathered in, would be futile.[29] The Boston manager cagily brought up vague logistical matters to postpone scheduling with the Athletics,[30] but eventually realized that the other teams failed to share his venom. He reluctantly agreed to bury the hatchet and arrange games with Philadelphia.[31]

The fans did not forget the bitterness. The *Clipper* was surprised to find the New York patrons giving Force a somewhat chilly reception. During a May 11 game with the Atlantics, the crowd impartially applauded the good plays of the Athletics, with the sole exception of Force, whose "play was received with silence."[32] When the Athletics played in Boston, the partisans blistered the ears of their least favored Athletics, not limiting the direction of their abusive behavior to the opposing shortstop. Adrian Anson, an ill-tempered umpire baiter even in his youth, was the most prominent target and had to be switched from first base to center field to move him beyond range of the fans.[33]

In Philadelphia the situation took a turn for the worse, as the local fans were determined to do their Massachusetts counterparts one better. Despite the preseason acrimony attributable to the Force matter, nothing other than harsh words had marred the first five meetings. When the teams met for a fateful sixth time on June 28, Boston carried a 10–8 lead into the bottom of the ninth. To the delight of the fans, Philadelphia tied the game on an opposite field triple by Ezra Sutton. By the time Boston came to bat in the top of the tenth, it was nearly 6:30 P.M., and the police protection had slowly evaporated, as some of the gendarmerie hurried home for their evening meal. This left more than 4,000 aroused Athletic fans in control of the situation. The Red Stockings broke through for two runs in the top half of the inning and might have had more had not a fan picked up Ross Barnes's long drive to right field and relayed it to Athletics' outfielder George Bechtel, who threw Barnes out at third.

In the bottom half of the inning, with two out and two on, the spectators broke through the few remaining police officers and crowded the field. Bill Craver, who was due to bat, refused to step up to the plate until the crowd moved back. Of the seven policemen, only a few made any serious effort to restore order. Craver continued to dawdle, despite an order from umpire Charlie Gould to enter the batter's box. The crowd now completely engulfed the field. As Gould tried in vain to get the spectators off the playing surface, it began to pour. The rain did what Gould could not, but with the water coming down in sheets, the umpire was forced to call the game. Since the tenth inning was one out short of completion, the score reverted to the ninth and went into the books as a 10–10 tie.[34]

The Athletics' management was truly embarrassed by the conduct of their faithful and wrote an apologetic letter to Boston President Appolonio.[35] They proposed playing the next two games of the series on July 7 and 8, either in Boston or Philadelphia, as the Red Stockings preferred. If Philadelphia was to be the site, the Athletics offered to pay Boston's traveling expenses (including those of the club's officers) and provided repeated assurances of adequate police protection. Boston countered with a proposal stating that if a fan disturbance could not be quelled after ten minutes, the home team would forfeit.[36] The Athletics were not willing to gamble on this condition. In the event, the next games of the series were played at Boston without incident. The final vestiges of ill will arising out of the Force case appeared to have fizzled out at last. The league's tolerance for those players who violated the rules would have further ramifications, however.

Chapter 23

Going Broke

The phenomenon of the early season was the remarkable pace at which franchises dropped by the wayside. With a pennant race devoid of interest after June, most editorial speculation concerned the identity of the next team to suspend operations.

The Centennials were the first to fall. Rumors of their demise had commenced even before the season started.[1] Finally, following a 5–0 defeat at the hands of Boston on May 24, the team disbanded. Despite a nucleus of talented players, the Centennials had won only 2 of 14 games. The highlight of the brief campaign was a shocking 11–2 upset of the Athletics on May 8, while the disappointments were many, including a 20–1 loss to the same Athletics two days later. The new team had been outscored 138–70 and had answered the question regarding Philadelphia's willingness to support three teams in the negative. It would not, at least on the same day. The final game with the champion Red Stockings attracted only about 100 spectators.[2] A meeting between the same two teams two days earlier drew little better. A contributing factor to both meager turnouts was the fact that, on the same days, the neighboring Athletics were hosting Hartford in a battle of top contenders, siphoning off more than 2,000 fans of their own.[3]

On the days when the Centennials were playing without crosstown competition, attendance was really not that bad. Of the 6 games (home and away, not counting the 2 aforementioned Boston matches) for which attendance estimates were available, 4 resulted in crowds in excess of 1,000. The average for all 6 games was just under 1,000.[4] Allegedly, the financial situation was relatively stable.[5] But if the Centennials were not going to weather the season, getting out in May would eliminate the expenses associated with a western tour to St. Louis, Chicago, and Keokuk.

The stockholders also saw an opportunity to make some easy money. The Athletics were short two players due to injuries to Dave Eggler and Wes Fisler and coveted George Bechtel and Bill Craver of the Centennials. The only way the Athletics could sign either player was if the management of the Centennials released them from their existing contracts. The Centennials were willing to do just that, for a price. One of the Athletics' stockholders provided $1,500 and the releases were procured as part of the first player transaction in baseball annals.[6] With two of the team's finest players gone, there was no hope of continuing the season.

Whatever the reason, the Centennials' fling was over. The *Clipper*, prescient as always, informed its readers that the junior Philadelphia entry was "the first of the 1875 teams to retire."[7] Apparently they were expecting others to follow in short order. They would not be disappointed.

The remaining Centennial players scrambled to find employment. Second baseman Ed Somerville and catcher Tim McGinley signed with New Haven, which had gaping holes at nearly every position. Veteran Fred Treacey caught on with the Philadelphia Pearls while infielders John Abadie and George Trenwith later made token appearances with other teams. The others were forced to go the amateur or semipro route.

The identity of the second deceased entry came as no surprise to knowledgeable observers. In the NA's first season both Fort Wayne and Rockford suffered from their isolated location, small populations, and mediocre talent. Teams fraught with the latter two maladies had been able to survive only by existence in a heavily traveled eastern route taken by most of the touring ball clubs. Hartford had survived its first season, and even tiny Middletown had supported a team well into August. Chicago and St. Louis, despite geographic isolation, boasted sizable populations and talented ball clubs assembled at no little expense.

Keokuk struck out, coming up empty on all three counts. Their season began with an unpromising 15-1 defeat at the hands of Chicago in front of the home folks. In the third game of the season, the Westerns gained what would stand as their only win of the year, a solid 15-2 victory over the St. Louis Reds. Despite talent that was less than overwhelming, Keokuk proved to be a scrappy group. Of their 12 losses, 6 were by 2 runs or less, including a 10-inning 7-6 setback at Chicago and a rain shortened 1-0 defeat by the Mutuals in their final game on June 15. The pitching and defense, the twin downfalls of cellar-dwellers of past seasons, were not bad at all. The Westerns allowed an average of 6.8 runs per game, only slightly above the league average of 6.3. The reason for the Westerns' sorry 1-12 mark could be traced directly to the lack of any offensive punch whatsoever. The team batting average was a paltry .167, with strapping left fielder and future National League star Charles Jones leading the way with a mediocre .250 mark. Only three of the ten regulars were able to poke their noses over the .200 level, while six were sub-.150 swingers.

In a letter to the *Clipper* following their dissolution, the Keokuk management referred to John Carbine as "the boss first baseman in the country." They speculated that he would finish out the 1875 campaign as the regular for the first place Boston team.[8] Harry Wright elected to pass on "The Boss" in view of the fact that he brought up the rear of the straggling Western averages, with 2 hits in 39 trips to the plate, an embarrassing .051 mark.

Boston had scheduled games in Iowa for June 10, 11, and 12. After posting a 6–4 win on June 10, they decided that more money could be made in Chicago, and left Keokuk early on June 11. Harry Wright wanted to arrive in Chicago rested for the game with the White Stockings, and therefore decided to allow an extra day for travel.[9] The Western trip of the Red Stockings had been grueling, but it turned out to be immensely profitable, bringing home gate receipts in excess of $17,000.[10] Two additional games in Keokuk were unlikely to add substantially to that total. Since the games had been scheduled, the Westerns were entitled to claim forfeits and were credited (at least temporarily) with two additional wins in the standings. Under the peculiar NA custom, however, the forfeits were expunged when the Westerns disbanded but, in any event, they were Pyrrhic victories.

If Boston was unable to draw, would teams such as New Haven and Washington be able to cover the expenses of traveling to Iowa? Apparently they reached the conclusion that they could not, for the Westerns were finding it increasingly difficult to schedule home games. Chicago left with $68 for two games and vowed not to return.[11] By June 15 the club management saw that the handwriting was clearly on the wall and made the decision to disband the team while it was still solvent. According to the managers, the players were paid in full to the date of disbandment.[12] They scattered hither and yon, Hallinan and Barnie to the Mutuals and the battery of Golden and Quinn to Chicago, where Golden proved a more than adequate backup to Zettlein.

The perils of a trip to the west so readily envisioned by Keokuk's reluctant opponents were realized by the Washington team. While in St. Louis at the tailend of a dismal tour on July 5, the team set the telegraph wires humming with a report that their business agent, D. W. Bruce, had absconded with all of the treasury funds, leaving them desolate and penniless 1,000 miles from home.[13] Later, the team scorer cast some doubt on the story, which had been vehemently denied by Bruce.[14] From all indications, the tale had been planted by the players in an effort to find enough good samaritans to foot the bill for the trip home. Rather than the cloak-and-dagger story which initially hit the wires, it appeared that Washington's demise was due to the more pedestrian cause of unappealing play resulting in sparse crowds and dwindling gate receipts. It is unlikely that there were any funds with which to abscond. Whatever the cause, the Nationals were history with a record of 5–23.

This left only New Haven and the two St. Louis entries among the new teams that had started operations in 1875. The Reds of St. Louis were alive only in that they had not officially disbanded. They did not play a game after July 4 and left St. Louis only twice, venturing as far as Keokuk and Chicago. After the season, the *Chicago Tribune* reported that the St. Louis managers had indicated in March that they had no intention of traveling east, but wanted only to get as much gate money as they could from visiting NA teams.[15] But, like the Westerns, they could not promise a large enough draw to make it worth the while of the top teams to deign to play them. Their final 4–15 record included wins over the Westerns and Washington. By season's end the team's top players had deserted for greener pastures and the Red Stockings were reduced to challenging semipro competition.

New Haven's continued existence was more of a tribute to their staying power than to their ability. After losing their first 15 games, the Elm Citys were able at last to break into the victory column with a 9–2 win over Washington on May 31. The talent was skimpy, and even the Cincinnati aura exuded by Captain Gould was not enough to overcome the lack of hitting and fielding ability. Pitcher Fred (Tricky) Nichols was perhaps the team's strongest performer, allowing New Haven to avoid the routs that were commonplace among second division entries.

As the season wore on, Gould acquired McGinley and Somerville from the defunct Centennials, which upgraded the lineup somewhat. The team began to jell as the season progressed, managing to add six more victories to the initial win to finish the campaign with a rousing 7–40 mark. Gould demonstrated little managerial ability and was jettisoned in mid-season in favor of George Latham. The uncontested highlight of the season was a shocking upset of Boston on July 2. The competition for the year's low point was much more intense. The Atlantics posted their only two victories of the year at the expense of New Haven, which was also the victim in four of the five Washington wins.

Despite all the on-field catastrophes which befell the team, the nadir was reached off the field at the Tecumseh House in London, Ontario. The team found itself at the Tecumseh House in the midst of a swing through Canada, the object of which was to accumulate victories and gate receipts, both of which were needed desperately. What happened at the hotel was never proven, but when the players left, it was noted by innkeepers Conklin and Moore and by several of the New Haven players that Billy Geer and Henry Luff had substantially more luggage upon departure than upon arrival.

Ballplayers being somewhat less than reputable guests, the proprietors decided to inventory the players' rooms after they had checked out. To their chagrin, they discovered that an expensive coat that had been located in a room adjoining that occupied by Geer and Luff was missing. They wired this unwelcome bit of intelligence to the Elm City directors, who passed it on to the New Haven chief of police. On September 13 two of New Haven's finest, Officers Brewer and Reilly, located the two players in a Chapel Street bar and placed them under arrest. The rooming house occupied by Geer and Luff was entered and the room they shared searched.

The gendarmerie found a veritable warehouse. There was a wide selection of coats, including a fine black broadcloth model with an identification tag inscribed "D. MacKensie-Sarna, Ontario." This was the garment that had been described in detail by Moore. A meerschaum pipe, also thought to be contraband, was discovered on the premises; but a revolver, thought to have been stolen in New Haven, was nowhere to be found. The inventory of coats, however, was sufficient evidence to keep Geer and Luff sharing a cell in the pokey rather than the room at Chaplain's.[16]

Their stay there, however, was a short one, as the case was continued and both men were released on bail. Remarkably, Geer umpired a game between the Atlantics and Mutuals on September 25.[17] Although the NA had employed some shady characters in the arbiter's position, this was the first time an accused criminal out on bail had filled the bill.

The troubles had not finished accumulating. When the incriminating evidence was uncovered in New Haven, a hotel keeper in Wyoming, Pennsylvania, remembered that after the Elm City nine had left his establishment, a number of items had been missing. Among them was a box of handkerchiefs which were marked with the name of the owner, J. W. Grover. When the police had searched Geer's room, they found a number of handkerchiefs bearing Grover's name, along with others belonging to Julius Crane and James Wilson, neither of whom was a roommate of Luff and Geer.[18]

Both players were acquitted of the charges, although Luff's later statement was less than flattering to Geer. Luff claimed that he was an innocent victim in the whole affair, his only crime consisting of being the roommate of a player who had been caught with a cache of stolen property.[19]

While the two players caused management momentary late-season embarrassment, the team's on-field performance was a continual source of humiliation. Two of New Haven's early losses were to the emasculated Atlantics. On April 26 a ninth-inning tally gave the Atlantics a 3–2 victory, followed by a solid 14–4 win exactly one month later. The second win was marked by a combined 30 errors by the 2 teams,[20] but raised Brooklyn's record to 2-11. This represented a disappointing start for the team that had made such steady progress over the past three years. Despite the loss of a number of key players, many had remained optimistic that the proud Atlantics would continue the upward trend. On March 19 the *New Haven Register* opined that "[President] Van Delft, assisted by Charles Pabor, has got together quite a respectable force to maintain the well-earned reputation of this old organization."[21]

While the Atlantics might have seemed a formidable opponent in New

Haven, the rest of the league discovered that Brooklyn's offense did not rank with the league's best. By season's end the Atlantics would be the victim of 8 shutouts in 44 games. One or two run efforts were also commonplace, as the team averaged a meager three runs per game. Outfielder Al Gedney of the Mutuals pitched against the Atlantics and beat them 9–2, while Hartford's Tommy Bond held Brooklyn to but one hit on August 19.

The Atlantics were not the only team experiencing woes at the plate. Indeed, the composite batting average would indicate that the entire league seemed to have forgotten the art of hitting. From 1871 through 1874 the league batting average had hovered between a low of .273 and a high watermark of .277 in 1873. In 1875 the league mark plummeted astonishingly to .250. While the average team had scored 9.8 runs per game in 1871 (aided no doubt by Troy's liberal use of the lively ball) the 1875 entries averaged only 6.3 tallies per contest. The 50 shutouts during the season easily eclipsed the previous high of 15 in 1874. To Chadwick's undisguised delight, the league witnessed its first 1–0 game, with Chicago the victor over the St. Louis Reds on May 11. Other 1–0 games followed, including a Chicago-Hartford match which entered extra innings tied 0–0, another first. The latter team, with the stellar combination of Bond and Cummings, led the league with 13 whitewashes.[22]

There had been no major rule changes during the off-season that might explain the sudden drop-off in offensive output. Admittedly, pitchers and fielders were becoming more proficient with each passing year, as batters were resigned to seeing a swift underhand snap throw rather than the "square pitch" of the 1850s and early 1860s. But this had been a gradual trend, not a one season phenomenon. A more plausible reason for the overall league decline was the rapid expansion experienced in the league's final year. From nine 1873 entries and eight in 1874, the league ballooned to thirteen teams of various abilities in 1875. While modern day expansion has led to offensive outbursts by the established teams against overmatched pitching staffs, the results in 1875 were very different.

Rather than requiring nine or ten sound arms, the NA managers needed to find but one workhorse of reasonable skill. Most of the new entries had done so. Golden, Blong, Bechtel, and Nichols were all pitchers of some skill, who outlasted their ill-fated teams in major league ball.[23] Finding nine or ten competent batsmen was a much taller order to fill, and many managers returned from scouting trips nearly empty-handed. The sorry averages of the Westerns (previously chronicled) were not atypical of those posted by their fellow neophytes. The six teams which occupied the bottom six rungs of the NA ladder posted the following team batting averages:

St. Louis Reds	.181
New Haven Elm Citys	.203

Washington Nationals	.183
Philadelphia Centennials	.228
Keokuk Westerns	.167
Brooklyn Atlantics	.192

The composite average of the six teams was .194. Considering that most of the players employed by these teams were new to the major league scene, their ineptitude appears to be the overriding reason for the drop in the league batting average.

The established teams essentially maintained their previous pace. Boston, which had led the league in 1874 with a .327 mark, once again paced the field with a nearly identical .326 average. The top seven teams, including the six holdovers and the St. Louis Browns—who employed such veteran performers as Lip Pike, Dicky Pearce and Ned Cuthbert— combined for a .266 average, only nine points below the previous year's standard.

While the *Clipper* raved over the improved standard of play in 1875, as measured by the volume of its beloved low-scoring games, the decrease in run production was more readily attributable to inexperienced batters than to skillful pitching or fielding.[24]

Chapter 24

An Early Challenge

While the stragglers dropped like flies, the top two contenders left the gate at breakneck speed. Hartford had evolved from a team of journeyman veterans to a collection of established regulars like Doug Allison, Candy Cummings, and Captain Bob Ferguson.

Thanks in part to some fortuitous scheduling, the Hartfords started the season with an exhilarating winning streak that caught the fancy of the Connecticut fans. An enterprising local merchant caught the fever and sold cigars known as "Captain Bobs," in recognition of the fiery field leader.[1]

Captain Bob (the man, not the cigar) fattened his team's record at the expense of inferior competition. The Centennials, New Havens, Mutuals, Washingtons, and Philadelphias fell in rapid succession, all at Hartford. On May 13 Hartford faced its first serious challenge of the season. They were equal to the task, foiling the Athletics with a dramatic ninth-inning rally. "The Hartfords are a never say die crowd," the *Hartford Courant* boasted after Ev Mills and Candy Cummings contributed two-run singles during a five-run inning.[2]

An easy win over the Athletics two days later and two wins over the Atlantics in New York brought Hartford's record to 12–0. But despite their red-hot start, Hartford had been unable to shake the Red Stockings.

Boston roared through the opening games in a fashion which indicated that the latest model was even stronger than the three previous championship teams. Only two additions had been made to the prior year's team. Jack Manning, an 1873 Red Stocking who had spent 1874 in exile with the co-op Canaries, rejoined the team as first baseman, right fielder, and backup pitcher. Manning had a pitching delivery that taunted the rules by coming dangerously close to a sidearm throw.[3] He allowed Spalding to rest more frequently and racked up a 13–3 record in spot duty.

The second new Red Stocking was George Latham, the opening day starter at first base. Latham was a 23-year-old, stockily built Canadian who sported a thick black mustache.[4] He had written to Harry Wright inquiring about a position with an eastern team. Harry surprised the young man by offering him a three-month trial with his own champion Red Stockings at the princely sum of $70 per month.[5] If Latham, whom Wright had seen perform only twice,[6] exhibited satisfactory ability, Boston would sign him to a three-year contract (each year to be at management's option, of course).[7] Despite a .321 average, Latham found himself in New Haven by June.

One of the keys to Boston's continued success was the versatility of their players. Early in the season Harry decided that he would not have substitutes per se, but would rotate his lineup, resting each of his players periodically. In addition to being the league's premier pitcher, Spalding played a passable center field and in 1877 became the regular first baseman for the National League Chicago White Stockings. White took an occasional turn in the outfield, while Barnes filled in at short during George Wright's troublingly frequent absences due to injury. The real handymen were McVey, Leonard, O'Rourke, and Beals. All could play any infield or outfield position, while McVey and O'Rourke were quite capable behind the plate. The ability to shift the lineup in the event of injury was invaluable, given the limited roster size. The regularity with which Harry Wright moved his men around made them familiar with positions other than their own, so that an injury would not result in a raw recruit filling the void.

The Boston manager was unique among NA field leaders in his approach to pitching strategy. He was a reasonably talented backup hurler who relied almost exclusively on a change of pace. Wright sometimes rested Spalding in the latter stages of one-sided games and finished them himself. The acquisition of Manning allowed for even greater flexibility in shifting the pitching chores. Over the 5-year duration of the NA, a total of 35 saves were credited to the league's relief pitchers. Of these 29 belonged to Boston, including 12 by Wright himself.[8]

Occasionally, Wright was wrong. He sometimes shifted players to positions they were incapable of filling competently. Rather than stubbornly compound the mistake, as the Mutuals did with Hatfield, Harry invariably moved the player back to his original spot. Harry Schafer, who had played third base in 1871, was moved to left field early in the following season to make room in the infield for newcomer Andy Leonard. Although he had played the outfield for the Athletics as early as 1867,[9] Schafer was a natural infielder and Leonard was a much better outfielder, due to his powerful and accurate arm. After some early season fielding adventures, the switch was soon undone.

Boston had the advantage of having played together longer than any other team and benefited greatly from Wright's incomparable leadership. Harry, at 40, was now officially retired from the playing field and was devoting his full efforts to the management of the champions. Perhaps his greatest talent was the ability to assemble a team that was able to work well together, a rare entity in the freewheeling Association. He arranged for most of the players to live in close proximity to each other during the season[10], and monitored their behavior so closely that, while on the European trip, Wright roused the troops early for breakfast and "look[ed] sharp at the layabeds."[11]

Wright pioneered the long term contract, preferring by 1875 to sign his top performers for a three-year engagement.[12] As noted above in the case of Latham, only the player was bound. Management could end the contract by releasing the player. Even-tempered in his own manner, the Red Stocking captain was in direct contrast to hotheads like Ferguson and Jimmy Wood, whose on-field tantrums often divided their teams. For the most part, the Boston players mirrored their leader's temperament. When the old Cincinnati team split, Harry took the players whose integrity and consistency set them apart from the others, letting problem children such as Sweasy, Brainard, and Allison depart to the Olympics. The only dependable player allowed to cast his fate with Washington was Leonard, a mistake rectified a year later when Harry brought the outfielder to Boston. Ross Barnes was a touch conceited,[13] but Wright kept his ego under control and got some fine performances from the second baseman.

Not surprisingly, most of the players Wright chose not to keep wilted quickly without his leadership. Brainard's career ended in 1874, and the hurler posted an 11–41 record in his final three years. Sweasy played little with any of his NA teams. Although he appeared in one Boston game in 1873, Sweasy was not held in high esteem by Wright. Harry cautioned Hadel of Baltimore against signing the second baseman in 1874, citing his erratic behavior and the negative influence he had asserted on the other players, particularly Andy Leonard ("came very near ruining him").[14] Hadel ignored the well-intentioned advice and paid for it, releasing Sweasy early in the season for lackluster performance.

Allison's play declined markedly from the standard he had set in Cincinnati. In 1872 the *Troy Whig* was quite critical of a perceived lack of effort on the catcher's part.[15] The vitriolic *Chicago Times* was more opinionated, declaring after a July 4 game at Chicago that "Allison caught as lazily and threw as stupidly as a player ever caught or threw before."[16]

A pioneer in the development of strategy, Wright's teams executed the hit and run, hit behind the runner and always gave up an out for a run. Boston outfielders backed each other up and always threw ahead of the runner. After leaving Boston, the manager was the first to adopt the pregame ritual of batting practice and fungo hitting to the outfielders.[17]

The harmonic blend of personalities and strategies created a brand of play known as the "Boston Plan." Unlike the hated Yankee dynasty of the 1950s, the Red Stockings were loved and cheered throughout the country,

Harry Wright, manager of the Boston Red Stockings (circa 1879) who won the NA championships in 1872–75 (courtesy of Transcendental Graphics).

often to the detriment of the home team. The value of the Plan was demon-strated following the defection of Boston's "Big Four" to Chicago for the 1876 campaign. Minus his biggest stars and the nucleus of his team, Wright captured consecutive pennants in 1877–78.

   In addition to his skills as a field general, Harry was a shrewd business manager. He knew the value of his championship team as a drawing card in distant cities and drove a hard bargain when negotiating for his share of the gate receipts. From the league teams he generally demanded one-third of the receipts and, should a weaker team desire the dubious pleasure of a trouncing from the Red Stockings, they were asked to fork over as much as 60 percent of the gross, typically with a minimum guarantee of $100 to $300.[18] Hard cash was the only form of payment for, as Harry drily informed a Canadian team that had offered "other attractions," "We are not much on cognac, etc. and I can assure you we prefer a good game and big gate receipts to 'Hail Columbia,' 'Won't Go Home 'til Morn,' and all that sort of thing."[19]

The expense side of the ledger was monitored with an equal degree of fastidious attention. When traveling, Wright budgeted the princely sum of $1 per day, per man, for room and board.[20] He negotiated with railroads and chose hotels carefully. Boston traveled by rail at discounted theatrical rates,[21] and had their travel expenses reimbursed by the home team whenever possible. No detail was too small for his attention. The material to be used for uniforms (Spalding procured some quality English flannel on his visit to Great Britain),[22] the type of soil to be used on the base paths,[23] all fell within Harry's purview. He subscribed to newspapers in virtually every league city to keep abreast of developments[24] and recommended that other managers subscribe to the *Boston Herald* to follow baseball in Boston.[25]

Scheduling was one of the most important tasks of any manager, and Wright excelled at this aspect of his job. Back-to-back home and home series maximized excitement and attendance. Holidays were optimized. His correspondence with other managers and the proprietors of playing fields was voluminous and almost always resulted in a profitable arrangement for the Red Stockings. Even when things did not turn out so well, Wright attempted to make good his losses. The deficit from the European trip was deducted from the salaries of the players in the following season. Jim O'Rourke strenuously objected to the idea of sharing the risk and threatened to sit out the season rather than perform for a lower salary. After a lengthy and (from Harry's side) stern correspondence, O'Rourke decided to swallow his pride and come to Boston.[26]

The champions played the inaugural game of the 1875 season, shutting out New Haven 6–0 in the first game in the history of the latter franchise on April 19. Continuing south, Boston invaded virgin territory by taking on Washington in Richmond, Virginia, at the Richmond Fair Grounds on April 29 and May 1. These were the first major league games ever played south of the Mason-Dixon line. Although baseball had thrived in certain areas of the South, particularly New Orleans, most of the region had been too occupied with mending the devastation wrought by the war to spawn baseball organizations.

The Virginians greeted the Red Stockings with the same degree of warmth with which they had greeted Abe Lincoln just ten years earlier. The field was fenceless and rough and the crowd was boisterous and unruly.

Boston retaliated with 22–5 and 24–0 pastings of the new Washington team and a healthy guarantee from local promoter A. B. Sturgis.[27]

By May 15, there were three undefeated NA teams:

	W	L	Pct.	GB
Boston Red Stockings	14	0	1.000	—
Hartford	10	0	1.000	2
St. Louis Brown Stockings	5	0	1.000	4½
Philadelphia Athletics	8	3	.727	4½
Chicago White Stockings	4	2	.667	6
Philadelphia White Stockings	7	5	.583	6
New York Mutuals	3	4	.429	7½
Philadelphia Centennials	2	8	.200	10
St. Louis Reds	1	4	.200	8½
Keokuk Westerns	1	5	.167	9
Brooklyn Atlantics	1	6	.143	9½
New Haven Elm Citys	0	8	.000	11
Washington Nationals	0	11	.000	12½

Once again the disparity between the haves and have-nots is striking. By season's end, only the top seven teams would be able to complete their minimum quota of six games with each other. The *Boston Globe* expressed the obvious sentiment that "people are getting tired of seeing these one-horse clubs play. The sooner the leading clubs in the country devise some means to bar these weak clubs from entering the championship arena, the better it will be for their interests and for the game generally... [these teams] have no possible show of winning the pennant or even making a respectable showing."[28] The New York correspondent of the *Chicago Tribune* also lit into the tailenders with unconcealed vitriol. He stated that the group most eager to see these teams expire would be the reporters who, unlike the fans — who were free to avoid the games — were forced to attend the lackluster encounters. He comforted his western readers with the knowledge that they would be spared from the likes of the Atlantics, New Havens, etc. since it was unlikely that any of the teams would have sufficient funds to make the trek. He noted drolly that many in New York were considering a donation of funds to send the Atlantics west, on the premise that they would be unable to earn the funds for the return trip.[29]

Such plaintive cries continued to fall on the deaf ears of the NA hierarchy. Chadwick advocated limiting entrants to stock clubs and increasing the entry fee to $25,[30] a strategy of doubtful efficacy.

A second area of disparity was the number of games played by the respective entries. While Boston had taken the field 14 times, St. Louis, whose record was likewise unblemished, had only 5 victories. The western teams had fewer opportunities to schedule games until touring started in earnest and the eastern teams came west and vice versa. The St. Louis Browns had only Keokuk, Chicago, and the neighboring Reds with which to compete in the initial weeks of the campaign. These clubs had agreed among themselves not to play any championship games prior to May 1 and not to play any eastern teams before June 1.[31]

Boston and Hartford were scheduled to meet for the first time in Hartford on May 18. On May 17, with Hartford playing the Atlantics in Brooklyn and Boston playing the Athletics at home, Hartford management nervously monitored the telegraph wires. A clash of two undefeated teams was a once per season draw which could provide a substantial boost to the year's finances. A loss by either team would certainly remove the luster from the confrontation. While the Atlantics were a relatively safe bet to oblige with a loss, the Athletics usually provided tough competition. Fortunately, both Hartford and Boston prevailed, setting up the grand match in the Insurance City on the following day. Given Harry Wright's nose for finance, he probably welcomed the challenge provided by Ferguson's upstart crew. A runaway pennant race provided peace of mind, but not the remunerative paydays such as that realized on May 18.

The city of Hartford had been ablaze with baseball fever all spring. One local family habitually took the cushions from their church pews to the ballpark to render the bleachers more comfortable.[32] The rabid Hartford fans purchased all reserved seats in the pavilion well before game day. All railroads serving the city added extra cars for the expected arrivals from Boston, Providence, New York, and nearby Springfield. Ferguson also made all possible preparations, using reserve catcher Bill Harbidge against the Atlantics in order to spare the hands of first stringer Doug Allison.[33]

Hartford stockholders were not disappointed when the big day dawned. The pregame attendance prediction of 6,000 proved conservative. Nearly all of the local factories closed down to allow the workers to attend, a rare treat for those who traditionally worked six-day weeks. Without Sunday baseball, this was their only opportunity to see major leaguers in action. By the time the game started, the stands were packed and thousands more were standing within roped-off areas just beyond the outfielders. In total, over 9,000 had paid their way into the Wyllys Avenue grounds.[34]

For six innings, the game was all that everyone had expected.[35] Boston scored three times in the first after the floodgates were opened by a controversial call by umpire Al Martin, the former Eckford pitcher, who ruled that Ev Mills had failed to touch first base after taking a throw from short on McVey's routine grounder. Two innings later, Martin struck again. After Ross Barnes had scored on Leonard's infield out, Martin silently, almost privately, called time and then called play again in the same respectful manner. Unfortunately, none of the spectators and few of the players heard him. Among those who failed to hear time called was Jim O'Rourke, who had rounded second and continued on to third. He and virtually everyone else in the ballpark were astonished to hear him called out for failing to retouch second after time had been called.

Spalding, who was always willing to extend a helping hand to the umpire, raced from the bench to dispute the call. Boston's reputation and Harry Wright's encyclopedic knowledge of the rules often allowed them to intimidate the unskilled umpires. In a game at Philadelphia in 1874, one spectator became so impatient with Spalding's time-consuming disputes that he took the sign placed in the grandstand which read, "Don't Dispute the Umpire" and turned it around so that it faced the players.[36]

On at least one occasion, the umpire asked for the opinion of a Red Stocking player before ruling. In a Boston-Athletic game in 1872 a Spalding pitch glanced off the bat of a ducking Denny Mack, hit his body, and rolled out toward the mound. With so many contact points, the umpire became confused. He asked George Wright what the rules provided in such an instance. George stated without hesitation that the double play turned by the Red Stockings should stand. It did.[37]

At times the Red Stockings' intimate knowledge of the rules caused other headaches for the beleaguered arbiters. The code specifically stated that it was illegal for a player to catch a ball in his hat. In another game with the Athletics, with runners at first and second, Wright, at the urging of the clever Spalding,[38] caught a Fergy Malone popup in his hat. He knew, of course, that this was not an out. The runners, not knowing what to do, stayed put, allowing Wright to start an easy double play. In this case, however, he was unable to sway the umpire, who tried to block out the entire episode by allowing Malone to bat again.[39]

So it was that, when Spalding came out to argue, Martin not only failed to send the Boston captain packing, but seemed to welcome the proffered advice. The 2 men thumbed through the rule book for a full 15 minutes while the crowd waited restlessly. "Read it out loud!" "Pass it around and let us all read it!"[40] they shouted at Martin and Spalding as the two men remained huddled in an animated conference. Not surprisingly in light of Spalding's earnest lobbying, Martin ruled that O'Rourke should return to second base as if the entire incident had not occurred. The Hartford crowd turned ugly. The fans did not feel any better after McVey rocked a solid liner to center which scored O'Rourke with a run that gave the defending champions a 5–0 advantage.

The *Hartford Courant* had called the Hartfords a "never say die crowd" and the players showed their mettle in the fourth. Doug Allison singled to left. Burdock followed with a ground ball to O'Rourke at third base. Jim had virtually no experience at third prior to the 1875 season. His arm was extremely powerful, as demonstrated in a number of contests, but was woefully inaccurate. His fielding in the early season games had been quite shaky.[41] Now, in his haste to start a double play, O'Rourke fired the ball over Barnes's head into right field, allowing Burdock to reach second and the slow-footed catcher to lumber to third. Hartford let loose a flurry of hits and Ev Mills tied the game with a two-run single placed neatly over the head of George Wright.

The score remained tied until the bottom of the seventh, when George Wright plated one run with a single and O'Rourke produced a second with an infield grounder, in the finest tradition of the Boston Plan. The two-run lead was enough for Spalding, who set Hartford down meekly in the eighth and ninth. His mates added three meaningless runs in the bottom of the ninth for the eventual 10–5 victory.

Harry Wright led his team back to Boston that same night into the midst of a wild celebration that must have reminded him of the glory days in Cincinnati. By the time the train arrived, carrying both victor and vanquished, 300 to 400 supporters, including a 20-member German marching band, had assembled to escort both teams to club headquarters. It was quite a procession, with the band in the lead playing "Hail to the Chief," followed by approximately 50 avid fans carrying brooms in the manner of rifles. After a brief celebration at headquarters, the two teams moved on to Siever's Hotel for further libations, and then retired, for they had a game to play the following day.[42]

The Boston crowd nearly outdid their Hartford counterparts in the field of enthusiasm. A crowd of 6,000 overwhelmed the 6 ticket takers and packed the Union Grounds.[43]

The first game however, seemed to have crushed the spirits of the Hartfords. Boston breezed to a 13–2 conquest, apparently having weathered the previous night's gathering better than their guests. The second consecutive win solidified the Red Stockings' hold on first place and raised doubts as to whether Hartford's record had been merely the result of a prolonged homestand against inferior competition. The loss to Boston marked the beginning of their first road trip of the season, and Hartford's inability to beat Boston was the bane of their first two seasons of major league competition. In 1874 they had not posted a victory until October 30, a 9–8 squeaker fortunately halted by darkness after seven innings. In 1875 they would not beat the champions until October 29.

The St. Louis Browns had a strong start, defeating the rival White Stockings twice, the second time before a crowd estimated at anywhere from 10,000 to 20,000.[44] They were the reigning champions of the western division. On June 5 they upset the eastern division champions 5–4 in St. Louis. When the final out was recorded, nine innings of tension were released as the jubilant fans poured onto the field to transport the players away on their shoulders.[45] The season was but a month old and their new team had not only beaten Chicago, but had inflicted the first loss of the season on the champion Red Stockings. Although St. Louis was erupting with glee, Harry Wright stated that he had hardly expected to finish the season without a loss[46] and it was still Boston that was in first place on June 7.

	W	L	Pct.	GB
Boston Red Stockings	26	1	.963	—
Hartford	19	5	.792	5½
Chicago White Stockings	11	3	.786	8½
St. Louis Brown Stockings	9	3	.750	9½
Philadelphia Athletics	16	6	.727	7½
Philadelphia White Stockings	12	10	.545	11½
New York Mutuals	9	10	.474	13
Washington Nationals	4	14	.222	17½
St. Louis Reds	2	8	.200	15½
Brooklyn Atlantics	2	13	.133	18
Keokuk Westerns	1	10	.091	17
New Haven Elm Citys	1	19	.050	21½

Chapter 25

A Little Chin Music, Maestro

Following their initial defeat in St. Louis, Boston continued their western tour by traveling to Chicago, where they lost to the White Stockings 2–0 on a brilliant three-hitter by Zettlein. Four days later the Red Stockings retaliated with a vengeance, gaining a 24–7 victory in a contest featuring 15 Chicago errors, including 6 by Dick Higham.

This raised that perennial NA concern, the integrity of the games. The uncertainty of sporting events aside, how could a team that wins 2–0 with a superb effort one day lose a 24–7 laydown to the same team less than a week later? How could Zettlein be overpowering on one occasion and a batting practice pitcher the next? It was as difficult to believe 100 years ago as it is in retrospect today. The *Clipper* pulled no punches when dicussing the suspicious play of some of the teams. They isolated Philadelphia, Chicago, the Mutuals, and the Atlantics as teams whose cyclical performances defied all explanation.[1] It was barely possible for the Atlantics to throw a game, for they were heavy underdogs every time they took the field. The other three teams played erratically enough to come through when least expected and fail miserably after having inspired a ray of hope.

The failure of teams to play up to the level of their abilities arose from two sources. The first was a proclivity to on-field bickering, which Chadwick referred to as "growling" or "chin music." Unlike most forms of music, chin music led to extreme disharmony. Leading practitioners of this art were Nat Hicks, Jack Nelson, and Bob Ferguson. Hartford fans, who had been gleefully smoking their Captain Bob cigars when the team was on its early season hot streak, were ready to ignite the real thing as the team began to fall off Boston's pace. In mid–July, following a 7–0 defeat at the hands of Boston and a 9–1 loss to the Mutuals, the *Hartford Courant* carped that "Captain Ferguson is complained of justly by his own men and by spectators for too much talking on the field. There is the impression that

209

the club would work in better harmony if he were less disposed to shout at players. Moreover, his own playing is not up to the standards of the others in the nine, and it was displayed in a most aggravating manner yesterday."[2]

The *Chicago Tribune* was even more brutal. "[Ferguson] is the best man to run a club—into the ground—that I ever saw," wrote the paper's New York correspondent.[3] He went on to call the Hartford captain a bully and a tyrant and gave numerous examples to support his claims. There were many. Not only had Ferguson physically threatened gamblers (which was probably to his credit) he had also challenged reporters who wrote stories which failed to meet his approval.[4] Ferguson was irascible, high strung, and had an embarrassing habit of chewing out his charges right on the playing field. Al Spalding later described him as "tactless" and "lacking in diplomacy," and claimed Ferguson "knew nothing of the subtle science of handling men by strategy rather than by force."[5] Following his own retirement in 1877, Spalding had employed Ferguson to captain the Chicago team the following year. After finishing fourth in a six-team league, Bob was jettisoned in favor of Adrian Anson.

When the team was winning, the fans took the view that Ferguson was an emotional, "take charge" leader. When his team was mired in the throes of a deep slump as the unfortunate Atlantics often were, the fans joined the players in their conviction that Bob's on-field histrionics were divisive and counterproductive. This pattern would follow the fiery field general for the rest of his career, which ended in 1887 as manager of the American Association New York Metropolitans.

Despite the lack of peace on the field, there was no evidence that Hartford was engaging in any underhanded play. With the suspicions that cloaked the entire league, however, no team was safe from journalists questioning their integrity. The team could "field well enough if they want to," inferred the *Hartford Courant*.[6] In a classic case of the pot calling the kettle black, the *Chicago Tribune* confided to its readers that "the Hartfords are not a success as a baseball nine (due to) a pernicious element."[7]

The Mutuals remained the maestros of chin music. Many who were now contaminating the league with their obnoxious behavior—such as Ferguson—received their initial training in New York. Even with the departure of renowned carper Johnny Hatfield, the Mutuals retained their reputation for disharmony on the field. Unlike Hartford, however, their play was tainted with the suspicion that some of their key errors were not accidental. In fact, slick-fielding first baseman Joe Start may have frustrated his less honorable mates by preventing additional skullduggery with his fine snags of errantly thrown balls.[8] Intentional errors, and the resultant sold games, could be traced to a handful of performers, most of whom were known to the public and, to Chadwick's unending consternation, to the team managers as well.[9] Yet they continued to engage these players year after year.

The travails of John Hatfield and John Radcliff have been well documented. Radcliff's fellow Centennial, Bill Craver, had first been accused of running afoul of the rules in 1870 when he was with Chicago. He played with three different teams that season, including a final stop at Troy. Chicago's attempt to have Craver expelled for violating his contract was thwarted because the matter had not been properly brought before the Judiciary Committee.[10] With the Haymakers, he was involved in the dead ball/lively ball arguments of 1871 and was a named party in the incident which led to Radcliff's expulsion in 1874. The Athletics-Baltimore affair of 1872 and the 1875 Athletics-Boston fiasco both featured Craver in a prominent role.

Throughout the existence of the NA, Craver never wanted for employment, despite his sullied reputation. His ability and a spunky temperament, which allowed him to play through injuries, a requisite skill in those pre-equipment days, made him a sought-after commodity. Yet, throughout his tenure there were veiled and not-so-veiled references to his questionable blatant errors. In 1876 Craver was savagely beaten by a gambler, apparently the result of a double-cross.[11] No attempt was ever made to discipline him until 1877, when National League President William Hulbert barred Craver along with three Louisville teammates for dumping games. No one in the NA had been willing to act with such decisiveness. It appeared as though only a full confession would satisfy the strict standards for incontrovertible truth that the Judiciary Committee required.

The temerity of league officials was compounded by their partisan bias, much discussed during the recital of the Force case. Members of the committee were often dealing with players from their own teams, whose expulsion would likely damage that team in the standings. In 1875, when so much of the dirty business was centered in Philadelphia, three of the five members of the Judiciary Committee were from that city. Under these circumstances, the high jinks continued. At the end of August 1875 Mike McGeary of Philadelphia accused teammates Zettlein (now with the Pearls after his release by Chicago) and Fred Treacey of fixing a game with Hartford. His only evidence was the poor play of both and information from a third party that his two comrades were on the take. Zettlein and Treacey countercharged that it was McGeary, not they, who was involved in skullduggery. They claimed that Jack Burdock told them confidentially that McGeary had approached him and offered $1,000 to throw the game, as he had a substantial sum wagered on his own team. McGeary was further accused of attempting to arrange an earlier Atlantic-Philadelphia game and a match with the amateur Doerr team.[12]

One week later the charges were heard and all three players were acquitted. The entire matter was chalked up to personal animosity and the season continued.[13] On October 23, only a week before the end of the campaign, the Charmer stormed off the field during a game and refused to continue, claiming that his teammates were throwing the game.[14] Zettlein's assertion was given credence by the charge of some of the Philadelphia directors that telegrams had been sent from the road instructing gamblers how to place their bets.[15] Clarification was often needed, as not everyone was working from the same script. It was alleged that in one sordid encounter, both Philadelphia and Chicago were attempting to throw the game to the other.[16]

Zettlein was pitching for the Pearls after having obtained his release from Chicago following an ongoing dispute with one-legged manager Jimmy Wood.[17] One will recall that Zettlein had been followed by controversy for the past three years. In 1873 he was a key member of the Philadelphia team that had folded en masse following their recruitment by Chicago for the subsequent year. With the White Stockings, he had been suspiciously held out of the infamous 38–1 loss to the Mutuals in which the team had been accused of lying down. He had had a stormy parting with Wood, and now found himself immersed in controversy shortly after arriving in Philadelphia.

Treacey had followed the Charmer nearly step for step. They had been teammates in Chicago in 1871, Philadelphia in 1873, Chicago in 1874, and now Philadelphia once more in 1875. In the interim, Treacey had been with the ill-fated Centennials, along with Radcliff and Craver, when they mysteriously closed up shop in May. Now with his third club in the past two years, he found himself in hot water along with his pal Zettlein. The birds of a feather had often flocked together. In 1872 the Baltimore entry included Craver, Hall, Radcliff, and Higham.

At about the same time in 1875 that the Charmer was released by the White Stockings, the Chicago management also decided that they had had their fill of Higham and asked him to find employment elsewhere.[18] It was rumored that he was betting against his own team.[19] The White Stockings had polarized into a "Hastings clique" and a "Higham clique."[20] Higham found a new team without the least difficulty. The Mutuals, ever on the qui vive for unsavory characters, snatched him up instantly to play second base for them. Higham was yet another whose sordid reputation was well advertised, but never prevented him from being signed by an NA club.

Higham's explosive temper brought him into conflict with others of a similar ilk, including catcher Nat Hicks. In July 1874 the two had a direct confrontation in Brooklyn. When last seen at the Union Grounds the previous year, Hicks was dealing with the business end of Bob Ferguson's bat. He was now fully healed and ready to battle his old team, the Mutuals. New York was captained that year by the equally irascible Higham, causing the *Clipper* to observe puckishly that it was "quite a treat to see how charmingly the amenities of social life are observed by these model generals when they meet on the diamond field in battle array." Hicks and Higham were described as "two of the sweetest tempered men in the fraternity."[21]

The conflict between the two antagonists came to a dramatic denouement. The game was a seesaw affair which went into extra innings tied 9–9. In the tenth, with Higham at second, Joe Start laced a single to center. Higham chugged around third carrying the go-ahead run. Dave Eggler uncorked a strong, accurate peg to the plate and Hicks positioned himself squarely in front of the precious dish. Higham, perhaps sensing the opportunity of a lifetime, crashed headlong into the Philadelphia catcher. Hicks went sprawling head over heels and momentarily took leave of his senses. While he lay prone and helpless near the plate in a scene similar to Ernie Lombardi's famous "snooze" in 1939, two more runners, including the alert Start, circled the bases and scored. Higham and the Mutuals won this battle 12–9.[22]

Higham's later banishment from the umpiring profession came as no surprise to those who had followed his career closely. In addition to his frequent changes of allegiance—voluntary and otherwise—and his questionable play, Higham's umpiring had been a cause for concern. In an 1872 Mutual-Mansfield game, Middletown complained bitterly about Higham's partiality and the umpire himself was reported to have boasted of his unfair decisions. Even the Mutuals admitted that they had been the beneficiaries of much unwarranted largesse.[23]

In addition to inherent dishonesty, the motivations for selling games were many. The lifestyle of the nineteenth-century ballplayer was an unstable one. Some players, such as the Wright brothers, held gainful employment during the off-season. Most did not, and did not budget their salaries to cover the winter months. Many of the latter were tempted to make their additional income through illicit means. Gambling was an accepted way of life for many players, as the long railroad trips taken during the season were conducive to marathon card games, frequently for high stakes.[24]

Bribery was often a much more reliable source of income than that received from the clubs. There was little risk involved in taking money from gamblers, given the league's lax enforcement of its code of rules. Salaries were a less dependable income source. By the end of the 1875 season the usually reliable Athletics were reputed to be $5,000 behind in salary payments, not having met payroll for six weeks, while the Pearls were $3,000 behind.[25] Co-ops still paid their players on an irregular basis. As had been the practice for three years, some of the 1875 Mutuals were paid regular salaries, while others were paid from a percentage of gate money.[26] This was undoubtedly one source of their incessant bickering. Even among the salaried class, injury brought with it the risk that salary payments would be stopped. A further source of salary interruption was the insolvency and or demise of a team. Such a fate befell 4 of the 13 entries in the NA's final season. All in all, accepting bribes was likely to be a safe, steady source of income for a professional ballplayer.

After five years, the pattern was clear. In shady situation after shady situation, the same cast of characters lurked at or about the scene of the crime. The names of Zettlein, Radcliff, Craver, and others appeared again and again in connection with alleged "hippodroming" schemes. The 1873 Philadelphias became the 1874 Chicagos, with the same rumors following them halfway across the country. As Chadwick so cogently pointed out to the managers and stockholders, the hippodroming problems would continue until the managers drove the point home by refusing to offer contracts to known connivers and blackguards.[27]

Chadwick was not so naive as to attempt an appeal to good sportsmanship and fair play. He pointed to the monetary losses accruing to the teams whose efforts on the field were thought to be less than wholehearted. He talked about the difference in Philadelphia's 1875 gate receipts ($16,000) and those of Boston ($37,000),[28] the league's pillar of respectability. What he did not mention was the impact that Boston's sparkling 71-8 record may have had upon the attendance figures and the handsome profit of $2,400[29] realized in that year. This oversight notwithstanding, the point was valid. By the end of the 1875 season the drawing power of teams such as the Mutuals, Philadelphias and White Stockings was virtually nil. Fans were reluctant to gamble a 50 cent admission price when they couldn't be assured of seeing an honest game.

In addition to the growlers and the fixers, two other character types contributed to the league's sordid image. The first was the "revolver," the player who failed to acknowledge the sanctity of the contract. Force and Miller were two celebrated examples, but there were many others. Once again, the players' guilt must be equally shared with league officials, who allowed the Force case to be manipulated by Spering to his own and Force's advantage. Further, the instability alluded to above encouraged players to take a dollar whenever presented with the opportunity. Finally, as was brought out so vividly in the free agent madness of the 1990s, it takes two to contract. Harry Wright, in a letter to William Hulbert discussing the multiple contracts of infielder Jack Burdock, wondered why the players should respect the rules when it was obvious that the managers did not.[30] The players surely couldn't be blamed if they had been tempted to break their existing contract with the offer of more money.

The final brand of undesirable was the drunk, of which there were many, as alcoholism was quite common among NA players. Mutuals shortstop Jimmy Hallinan was accused by the *Clipper* of missing a key game due to an acute hangover.[31] He was forgiven his indiscretion upon paying a $50 fine. Charley Hodes was signed by Chicago for the 1871 season only upon the pledge that he would abstain from drinking.[32] A number of players, such as Cherokee Fisher, Bill Lennon, and our old friend Williams/Selman were suspended or released for persistent alcoholism, while the erratic habits of others (particularly Mathews and Higham) led to the inference that they shared a similar problem. Fisher had been suspended twice by Hartford in 1874 and once by Philadelphia the following year.[33] Philadelphia was his fifth team in five seasons. Mathews began drinking heavily during his stint with the Kekiongas and was unable to shake the habit.[34] His life fell apart when his baseball career was over and he ended his days in an insane asylum.[35]

None of these issues was new. Gambling and revolving had been recognized as evils from the first days of the NA's formation. In 1875, however, the gambling issue seemed to reach epidemic proportions, with repeated suspicions of hippodroming reported in local papers. Expectations of foul play ran so rampant that every key error was questioned and every controversial umpiring call examined for purchased bias.

Boston's fourth straight pennant, this one by a lopsided margin, called the competitiveness of the league into question, while the failure of nearly half the starting field to finish the full quota of games cast doubts upon the league's credibility. For five years these problems had festered. Committee action (or inaction) was not going to solve the problem, and no strongman could assume power under the diffused NA structure. It was clearly a time of crisis, with no ready solutions at hand.

Chapter 26

A Stunning Secession

The final blow came from a most unexpected source. It was not the Mutual or Philadelphia players who brought the NA down, but the revered Red Stockings of Harry Wright.

Near the end of the 1874 season there was a great deal of speculation that the champion Red Stockings would disband at the end of the schedule.[1] Throughout the following year, the rumor had persisted that Harry and George Wright would return to Cincinnati, which had spurned them five years earlier.[2] There was no truth to the claim, which Harry had persistently denied. But now the nucleus of the Red Stockings was about to desert Harry.

In mid–July, with Boston comfortably ahead of the second-place Athletics, came the stunning announcement that Spalding, White, McVey, and Barnes had signed with Chicago for the 1876 season. While lunching at Taunton prior to a game with the local amateurs, McVey casually mentioned to his manager that he would not be playing in Boston the following season. Wright thought he was joking until Jim White told him it was true and divulged the entire transaction.[3]

Only in 1873 had there been a wholesale defection from one team to a competitor in mid-season. Chicago had been the culprit in that instance as well, with disastrous results. Would history repeat itself and, if so, could the league survive a second such black eye? The four Red Stockings were not from the same mold as the 1873 Phillies, many of whom had been involved in shady escapades before and after the event. White was a paragon of virtue, aside from a hardheaded stubbornness that showed itself on occasion. Spalding was the circuit's premier entrepreneur, while Barnes and McVey had no prior stains upon their reputation.

Another factor which led to the belief that the season would be concluded honorably was the motivation of the players in accepting the Chicago offers. Money was a factor for sure. Another significant motivation, however, was the players' desire to return to the west. Spalding, in particular, had wrenchingly rejected lucrative offers in the past to remain with Harry Wright.[4] In late 1874 rumors had circulated that he would go to Chicago and be replaced in the Red Stockings lineup by Mathews.[5] Spalding and Barnes were Rockford boys, while White had started with Cleveland, and McVey, an Indianapolis native, with Cincinnati.

White's status had been shaky for several seasons. In 1872 he had used the leverage of competing offers to obtain a salary from Cleveland that was estimated as high as $3,500.[6] In both 1874 and 1875 Boston President Appolonio had been forced to make a personal visit to the reluctant catcher in order to convince him to return to the Red Stockings.[7] Chicago had offered White a $2,500 salary to play with the White Stockings in 1875, but James had rejected it.[8] Thus, his ultimate departure was not without warning.

Prior to the formation of the Cincinnati Red Stockings in 1869, most teams had been home grown. President Hulbert of Chicago appealed to this sense of regional pride in Spalding, telling him that he was a western boy who ought to be playing in the west.[9] To sweeten the pot, he offered an unheard of $4,000 salary to fill the positions of pitcher, captain, and manager.[10] Once Albert had agreed to terms, he became Hulbert's chief recruiter, convincing his three teammates to join him on the journey west.[11] White received $3,600 per year, while Barnes and McVey accepted $2,500 each.[12] Spalding then accompanied Hulbert to Philadelphia, where they corralled fellow westerners Anson and Sutton.[13] Anson, spurned by Chicago manager Tom Foley in 1871, was finally going to get his chance to play with the White Stockings.[14]

The fear of a late season collapse by the Red Stockings proved unfounded. They continued to pull away and coasted to their fourth consecutive pennant. The incumbent Chicago team did not finish as strongly. With most of the players knowing they were to be released at the end of the season to make way for the incoming Red Stockings and Athletics, the White Stockings staggered to a 30–37 finish after an 11–3 start.

At first, the Boston fans did not take the news well. Spalding, through his skill as a pitcher (he had 22 and 24 game winning streaks during the 1875 season) and his admirable bearing and character, had been a hero to Boston's youth. Now he was openly taunted in the streets of the city by the same young boys who had worshipped him prior to the announcement.[15] Spalding, if anyone, was considered the villain, since he had made all the arrangements. Despite the unsettling treatment and Appolonio's offer to match or beat the Chicago salaries,[16] Spalding and his fellow deserters remained firm in their desire to go to Chicago. In spite of the abuse from Boston fans, the break with management was cordial considering the circumstances. White and Spalding emphasized that they had no quarrel with Appolonio and Wright but merely wanted to better their conditions and return to the West.[17] At season's end the players (loyalists and seceders alike) were treated to a sumptuous banquet at which the departing players were sent on their way with best wishes (other than against Boston).[18]

While all appeared to have been forgiven, the brazen rupture of the rules and subsequent lack of punishment sent a clear message that the prohibition against inking players in mid-season was indeed, as the *Clipper* had claimed, a dead letter. While the signings actually served a useful purpose by evening out the competition through the breakup of the powerful Red Stockings, it was becoming clear that the league could not continue to exist on such a basis.

While the big news was being made off the field, important things were occurring within the foul lines as well. On July 28, Joe Borden, known by the pseudonym "Josephs"[19] took the pitchers' position for the Philadelphia Pearls against Chicago. Borden was a 21-year-old right-hander who weighed in at a mere 140 pounds. He had begun the season with the amateur Doerr team, joining Philadelphia when the Pearls released incorrigible Cherokee Fisher for insubordination.[20] On this day Borden pitched better than any hurler had before, holding the White Stockings hitless in a 4–0 victory. Despite a number of one-hitters, including several by Bobby Mathews, there had never been a no-hitter thrown in NA competition.

Given the *Clipper*'s infatuation with defense and low-scoring games, one would think they would have spared no adjective in the describing the first major league no-hitter. Not so. The entire game story covered one paragraph and, while the unique nature of the contest was acknowledged, Borden's name was mentioned only once. "Josephs, the young pitcher of the Philadelphias, deserves great credit for his effective delivery."[21] That was all. In the same issue there was a long, drawn out account of a tedious Mutuals-Athletics game, complete with play-by-play detail. Yet, Borden's masterpiece was inexplicably given short shrift by Chadwick.[22]

The *Clipper*'s *sans souci* attitude was not unique. After a total of seven games and a 2-4 record, Borden was replaced by Zettlein, who became available after his release by Chicago. Apparently, Borden's well-to-do father felt that playing baseball was no way for his young son to earn a living, no-hitter notwithstanding.[23] Eventually, with parental consent in hand, the youngster signed with Boston for the 1876 season as Spalding's replacement.

Borden's Boston career started promisingly, as the winning pitcher in the first National League game. Later in the season, he duplicated his NA feat by hurling a no-hitter, the first in the history of the new league.[24] By mid-season, however, Borden had a sore arm and was unable to pitch effectively. The penurious Harry Wright, mindful of the salary he was obligated to pay the young pitcher, forced Borden to earn his keep by serving in the capacity of groundskeeper. Rather than expressing indignation at this reversal of fortune, Borden cheerfully wielded the rake and shovel.[25]

Joe Start of the Mutuals also performed well in obscurity. On July 21 against Philadelphia, he pounded out three home runs and a triple, for a remarkable fifteen total bases.[26] Like Borden's no-hitter, Start's batting feat was given little mention in the press.

The Red Stockings had largely relegated the excitement of the pennant race to the quest for second and third place. The final fleeting hope of over-taking the leaders was extinguished on September 3 when the Athletics were routed 16–0 before an appalled crowd of Philadelphians. The contest was a complete runaway, as Boston scored five times in the first and twice in the second. The win gave the Red Stockings a nine and one-half game lead with less than two months to play and rendered the rest of the season anticlimac-tic. Boston had outscored its opponents 832–344 and was undefeated in 35 home games. Even third place Hartford had run up a dominating 557–341 scoring margin.

Without a post-season playoff of any kind, all teams were merely play-ing out the string after the identity of the champion was obvious. The effect upon attendance was exactly as one might anticipate. After the effective elimination of the Athletics, crowds rarely exceeded 1,000, and occasionally games between inept or suspect teams drew in double digits.

Surprisingly, the *Clipper* suggested a remedy that included a series of exhibition games for prize money between the top teams, replete with throw-ing and running contests and the like.[27] Fortunately, the suggestion was not acted upon, avoiding a repetition of the sorry tournament of 1872.

St. Louis, which would post an impressive fourth place finish, was rapidly acquiring a reputation as a collection of poor sports. The team refused to play New Haven or the Atlantics due to the limited anticipated return,[28] refused to play in any game officiated by Billy McLean[29] and became embroiled in a battle with the Athletics.[30] The Brown Stockings also stomped off the field after eight innings in a game against the nonleague Cincinnati team to protest an umpire's call.[31]

The Athletics and Hartford were also feuding. Philadelphia had tried to claim a forfeit when Hartford had canceled a game due to the death of Ferguson's father.[32] During the previous season, Hartford had refused the Athletics a postponement sans forfeit when three Philadelphia players were unable to make it to the post shortly before the team's departure for Europe.[33] The two teams refused to play each other for several months before ending the foolishness in September.

Although no one realized it at the time, 1875 saw the establishment of an all-time major league record that has endured until the present day. The mark is likely to outlast DiMaggio's 56-game hitting streak, Cy Young's 511 wins, and other seemingly unreachable standards.

When one thinks of legendarily inept teams, the 1962 New York Mets expansion franchise (40–120), the 1916 Philadelphia Athletics (36–117) or, for purists, the 1899 Cleveland Spiders (20–134) come to mind. These last placers were virtual powerhouses in comparison to the 1875 Atlantics.

Bereft of their 1874 regulars, management had made the mistake of signing players who not only possessed meager talent, but who were not overly reliable or above reproach. Frank Fleet was the regular catcher in the latter part of the season. Al Nichols, later expelled with Craver, Hall, and Devlin, played third in 32 of the team's 44 games before jumping ship to sign with Louisville. Bill Boyd, recently reinstated by the Judiciary Committee and apparently no longer happy at the Brooklyn Fire Department, was another questionable performer.

On more than one occasion late in the season, the first pitch was held in abeyance while captain Charley Pabor hustled to get nine men together to take the field. During the course of the season, the Atlantics employed no less than 35 players. The patchwork nature of the lineup is demonstrated by the fact that 14 of these men played only one game as emergency fill-ins. Local amateurs, old hands such as Al Martin and even an employee of the Union Grounds[34] took turns in the lineup. When the team played the Mutuals on September 25, Boyd was the only one in the lineup who had played for the Atlantics in the first game between the two teams in May.

In the age of the ironman hurler, Brooklyn used six different pitchers. The mainstays of the staff were 18-year-old John Cassidy (1–25) and Jim Clinton (1–12). Although Cassidy lasted the entire season, Clinton joined many of his teammates who departed after realizing that the pecuniary rewards of remaining with the Atlantics would be minuscule. The team was structured as a co-op, without regular salaries. When the poor quality of the team became known, the crowds dwindled and the pool of receipts shrank. This in turn caused the few quality players to search out greener pastures, making the team even less competitive and dropping attendance to even greater depths. Not knowing what nine players would be in the lineup, fans were unwilling to risk the price of admission to watch what amounted to a pickup nine. They could observe play of a higher caliber in the amateur games at Prospect Park. Approximately 100 diehards watched the Atlantics lose to New Haven on September 11. The *Clipper* stated morosely that there was "not the least interest in the contest . . . every game there is a different team."[35] Crowds hovered around the 100 mark throughout September as management denied rumors that the team was about to disband at any moment.[36] President Van Delft tried desperately to prevent other team managers from raiding his roster, an achievement realized only when the level of talent dropped to such a low level that other managers had no desire to sign any of the remaining players.

The rumors of dissolution were strong after a 13–2 loss to the Athletics on September 17.[37] Like the pesky relative, however, the Atlantics kept coming back. On September 30 the team played an exhibition against Josh

Hart's Theatre Comique, an appropriate matchup.[38] Although there was no indication they did so on this occasion, the members of the Theatre Comique often played in their stage costumes.[39] Fifty unsuspecting drifters turned out for this barnburner. The Atlantics finally went down for the third time following a 20–7 defeat by Hartford on October 9.

Unknown to the team's fans at the time, Brooklyn had reached the high watermark following their second win over New Haven, when the team sported a 2–11 mark. Thirty-one consecutive losses later, the once proud Atlantics, champions of the mid-1860s, ended their existence with a sorry 2–42 record, a winning percentage of .045, 51½ lengths behind the Red Stockings.

Like the St. Louis Reds, the Atlantics never had any intention of visiting the western teams.[40] They intended merely to capitalize on their New York location to shake as much gate money from their home games as possible. The team played 31 of their 44 games in New York, venturing only to Boston, Philadelphia, and the two Connecticut cities.

The remaining teams played out the string, with the Athletics wresting second place from Hartford and St. Louis. By November 1, the standings reflected a most unusual season.

	W	L	Pct.	GB
Boston Red Stockings	71	8	.899	—
Philadelphia Athletics	53	20	.726	15
Hartford	54	28	.659	18½
St. Louis Brown Stockings	39	29	.574	26½
Philadelphia White Stockings	37	31	.544	28½
Chicago White Stockings	30	37	.448	35
New York Mutuals	30	38	.441	35½
St. Louis Reds	4	15	.211	37
Washington Nationals	5	23	.179	40½
New Haven Elm Citys	7	40	.149	48
Philadelphia Centennials	2	12	.143	36½
Keokuk Westerns	1	12	.077	37
Brooklyn Atlantics	2	42	.045	51½

The records of the disbanded teams were thrown out of the "official" standings, as were those of the teams that had failed to complete their full quota of games. In the latter category were New Haven and the Atlantics, both of which had failed to make a western tour, and the St. Louis Reds, who had not come east. The disheartened New Haven management had also chosen to forfeit a game to Hartford rather than play them the day following a 10–0 loss.[41] Philadelphia had likewise fallen short of a full schedule. Philadelphia and Chicago had neglected to send a record of their games to the Championship Committee,[42] relieving that body of the obligation of including their results in the standings. The "official" standings sans the illegal games were as follows:

	W	L	Pct.	GB
Boston Red Stockings	34	5	.872	—
Philadelphia Athletics	17	16	.515	15
Hartford	18	19	.486	14
St. Louis Brown Stockings	16	18	.471	15½
New York Mutuals	5	32	.135	28

The dominance of the Red Stockings was reflected in individual statistics as well. Ross Barnes led the league in batting with a .372 mark, followed by Jim White and Cal McVey. Lip Pike of St. Louis snuck into fourth place at .342, followed by a fourth Red Stocking, George Wright. Barnes also led in base hits, followed in order by four teammates, as Andy Leonard joined the aforementioned quartet. The top five in runs scored were all from Boston. If the 1875 season represented the end of an era, it was a fine end indeed.

Chapter 27

Grand Central Hotel

As soon as the 1875 season concluded, league officials began looking forward to 1876, a campaign expected to be a special one for a special year. The year 1876 marked the centennial celebration of the signing of the Declaration of Independence, and no expense was spared in the construction of a commemorative exhibition in Philadelphia. In addition, the year marked the thirtieth anniversary of the first baseball game at the Elysian Fields.

Despite the dreadful occurrences of 1875 — the failure of so many teams to finish the season, the rumors of fixed games, the runaway pennant race, and the mid-season defections to Chicago — most insiders expected business as usual in the following season. At the annual convention scheduled for New Haven on the first day of March, it was anticipated that Cincinnati, Louisville, and an additional New York entry would join the teams that had survived 1875.[1]

The two former teams had been assembled in mid-season and acquired valuable playing experience, while backers of the latter planned to raise $10,000, sign a 20-year lease on a playing field and engage none other than Henry Chadwick as manager of the nine.[2] Cincinnati, showing disdain for its heritage, chose to name its new entry "the Blue Stockings." Other potential entries included Cleveland, Burlington, Buffalo and the Americus Club of Philadelphia.[3] The papers cynically speculated that one-third of the 1876 entries would fail to weather the season.[4]

After four years of Boston domination, many were looking forward to a more competitive race in what was known as the "Centennial Season." No one broached the possibility that, given the strength of the talent Hulbert had assembled, the league might turn out to be as unbalanced as in previous years, with Chicago replacing Boston in the van.

The level of competition aside, the other problems of the NA would not disappear with the mere passage of time. The league was dominated by the players and administered primarily with their interests in mind. After five

years the declining attendance figures had driven home to the more respectable and perceptive the feeling that a drastic change was needed. By the end
of the 1875 season, top amateur games were outdrawing the pros. The
Athletics, one of the bellwethers of the struggling league, had finished the
season in debt.[5]

The winds of change were blowing from the west, which had added a
second strong representative in St. Louis and would nearly equal the
number of eastern representatives when Louisville and Cincinnati
presented their credentials. The east-west differences were becoming more
pronounced, as the NA's decline had taken place under the auspices of the
easterners, who had dominated its management. The Force case was a clear
incidence of the westerners feeling they had been jobbed by a Judiciary
Committee packed with Philadelphians. No westerner was more parochial
than William Hulbert, one of the Chicago stockholders. It was he who convinced Spalding that his western loyalties should outweigh his acquired
allegiance to Harry Wright. The 1876 White Stockings would be composed
almost exclusively of western boys, a difficult proposition in a sport originated in and dominated by the metropolitan east.

Hulbert felt that the evils that permeated the NA (particularly the effects of gambling) were perpetuated by the easterners (even though his own
White Stockings had been prime suspects) and needed to be obliterated by
moral men from the west. The way in which the Philadelphia interests had
railroaded the Force case through the 1875 convention had only fueled Hulbert's indignation. It had also provided him with an unlikely ally in Harry
Wright, despite Chicago's brazen pirating of Boston's "Big Four."

There was one other thing. There was a rumor circulating which hinted
that the eastern teams were planning to expel the six players who had contracted with Chicago for violating the rule prohibiting mid-season signings.[6]
If there was any truth to the rumor, Hulbert would have to beat the easterners to the punch if he wanted his new assemblage of stars to take the field
legally. He was prepared to do just that. In concert with the honeymooning
Spalding, Hulbert prepared a constitution for a new government, to be
called The National League of Professional Base Ball Clubs.[7] The choice
of that name was critical and established a new direction for professional
baseball. The sport would no longer be under player control, nominally or
in substance. The players would play and the owners would manage. This
passage of control would have a number of ramifications for both parties.
With the Malthusian increase in teams in 1875 had come escalating salaries,
reflecting the forces of supply and demand. With ownership control replacing player control, salaries would be reduced and stabilized. Boston's 1875
payroll would not be equalled for the remainder of the decade.[8]

Hulbert's plan encompassed a number of proposals which would remedy many of the NA's shortcoming and, not incidentally, increase the

pecuniary return to club stockholders.[9] First, the unstable teams must be eliminated. The top clubs had been forced by the championship format to schedule all Association teams and thus play a number of games which resulted in relatively effortless victories but quite unrewarding gate receipts. The entry fee for the new league would be $100 per team, a far cry from the nominal $10 assessed by the NA. The funds would be used to establish a central league administration, rather than for the purchase of a championship banner. Those unwanted teams which were not discouraged by the increased tariff were eliminated by edict. Each league city must have a population of at least 75,000 (farewell, New Havens). No team could locate within a 5-mile radius of another league team (adios Philadelphias and St. Louis Reds). An exception to the former criterion was made to allow the inclusion of Hartford, which did not have the required population level. For those who successfully leaped these hurdles, a final obstacle was put in place. An applicant for admission must petition the existing franchise holders, and could be blackballed by two negative votes.

In addition to eliminating unwanted franchises, Hulbert saw a need to give the owners greater control over the players. The reserve clause was still in the future, but beginning in 1876 the players would be bound much more tightly to their clubs. They were prevented from negotiating with other teams while the season was in progress (this rule, of course, was not retroactive). A player could sign an extension with his own club at any time, which gave each owner an advantage in retaining his talent.

The lax morality of the old Association was attacked with a vengeance. Gambling and pool-selling were prohibited on the grounds of any club. Any player found guilty of dishonesty was to be barred for life. The NA had had the same sanction, of course, but had never shown any zeal for enforcement. As Hulbert himself would demonstrate in the Louisville scandal of 1877, the new league would show no such hesitation.

Finally, the new code addressed the sorry state of umpiring. National League games would be officiated by professionals who would be compensated at the rate of $5 per game. With his new constitution in hand, Hulbert embarked upon a divide and conquer strategy. The initial revelation of his intentions came in a far-ranging interview with Spalding published in the *Chicago Tribune*.[10] The new White Stockings pitcher expounded at length on the shortcomings of the NA and some potential solutions. Receiving favorable response to the publication of the *Tribune* interview, Hulbert went to work on the western teams, from which he expected unquestioning endorsement of his daring plan. At a clandestine four-day meeting at the Galt House in Louisville, the Chicago president obtained the support of the Cincinnati, St. Louis, and Louisville management. They gave their proxies to Hulbert and Charles Fowle of St. Louis to negotiate with the eastern clubs.

The chosen teams from the east were the Red Stockings, Athletics, Mutuals, and Hartfords. In Harry Wright of Boston, Hulbert had a ready ally. Despite the fact that Chicago had stolen Boston's top four players, Wright was well aware of the inadequacies of the existing structure. He was also cognizant of the financial havoc brought about by the inclusion of inept teams and the public disapproval aroused by uncontrolled gambling and the presence of tainted performers. Hulbert was less sure of the reaction of the other three eastern teams. Hartford was a solid entry led by reputable executives such as Morgan Bulkeley and could be expected to support reform.

The Mutuals and Athletics were the only teams which predated the NA and might be reluctant to cede the power they had wielded in the old Association. The attempted power play of the three Philadelphia teams in the Force case had played a large part in precipitating the actions of Hulbert. The Mutuals had great respect for Harry Wright. William Cammeyer, in particular, carried on quite a jovial correspondence with the Boston manager[11] and might yield to his influence. The prospect of being isolated from the top six teams might also influence the thinking of the latter two clubs.

In any event, Hulbert took no chances. He arranged to meet with representatives of the other clubs on February 2 at the Grand Central Hotel in New York City. Other than Harry Wright, the eastern representatives knew very little regarding the specifics of Hulbert's plan. The latter, in keeping with his "divide and conquer" strategy, gave each person a different meeting time, allowing him to present the plan to each man individually, rather than allowing the established easterners to join forces against him.

The meeting was anticlimactic. The need for reform was so evident and Hulbert's approach so skillfully conceived and developed that there was no serious opposition. The new league was endorsed unanimously and plans were made to commence play in April. The demise of the NA had been orchestrated quickly and bloodlessly only ten blocks from Collier's Rooms, where it had been given life only five years earlier.

As a crusading reformer, Henry Chadwick would have been expected to applaud this attempt to change the sordid ways of professional baseball. Instead, he reacted with fury at the secrecy of the affair, thinly disguising the jealous pique he felt at having been left out of the new league's formation.[12]

The veteran sportswriter and others who had likewise been left out in the cold, such as the Philadelphia Pearls and the New Haven Elm Citys, attempted a last stand against the new National League. Backers of the Pearls wondered why their team had been effectively expelled while the Mutuals, whose integrity was no more admirable, had been included in the new league.[13] New Haven stockholders pointed not to the team's sorry performance in the field in 1875 but to the fact that they had finished the season and had operated with unquestioned integrity (conveniently forgetting about Luff and Geer). They raised the issue of Hartford's inclusion.[14] But all was in vain. Prospective replacements for the seceding teams came primarily from small Pennsylvania towns that had no chance of supporting a major league franchise.[15]

It was clearly over. It would be 14 years before ballplayers would again control their own destiny in the short-lived Players' League. The formation of the National League did not result in miracles, but the institution of professional management wrought great changes in the game. The amount of erratic umpiring was diminished. The characters which filled the rosters of NA teams were either eliminated or forced to submit to the new discipline. Teams achieved a measure of stability and became "major league" in more than name alone.

While all of the changes resulted in increased efficiency, they also put the seal on the unique nature of the NA. No more Frank Fleets, Bill Cravers, Cherokee Fishers, or Frank Williams/Selmans. By 1877 a fixed schedule was in place and the comical snafus and silly quarrels were the exception rather than the rule. Teams didn't play with last minute substitutes or fold in mid-season.

Efficiency is not entertaining. Accounting is not a popular spectator sport. The National Association had its warts, was poorly run, and generated only one worthwhile pennant race in five years. But it was the first major league, a noble experiment that served a necessary function in baseball's awkward transition from an amateur to a professional sport.

Appendix

Selected Statistics

Statistical Leaders for the National Association, 1871–75

Pitching Leaders (Victories)

Al Spalding	207-56
Dick McBride	152-76
Bobby Mathews	132-111
George Zettlein	125-90
Candy Cummings	124-72
Cherokee Fisher	51-64
Tommy Bond	41-48
George Bradley	33-26
Jim Britt	25-63
Asa Brainard	24-56

Base Hit Leaders

Ross Barnes	540
George Wright	494
Cal McVey	477
Andy Leonard	471
Al Spalding	462
James White	456
Davy Force	436
Adrian Anson	430
Dave Eggler	424
Lip Pike	402

Batting Leaders
(min. 1,000 at bats)

Ross Barnes	.379
Cal McVey	.362
Levi Meyerle	.353
George Wright	.353
Adrian Anson	.352
James White	.347
Ezra Sutton	.327
Davy Force	.326
Andy Leonard	.321
Lip Pike	.321

Batting Champions

1871	Levi Meyerle (Ath)	.492
1872	Davy Force (Troy-Balt)	.412
1873	Ross Barnes (Bos)	.402
1874	John McMullen (Ath)	.387
1875	Ross Barnes (Bos)	.372

Individual Team Rosters

1871 Season

Philadelphia Athletics

P	Dick McBride (20–5)	.213
C	Fergy Malone	.317
1B	Wes Fisler	.293
2B	Al Reach	.348
3B	Levi Meyerle	.492
SS	John Radcliff	.261
OF	Ned Cuthbert	.241
OF	John Sensenderfer	.339
OF	George Heubel	.321

Boston Red Stockings

P	Al Spalding (20–10)	.265
C	Cal McVey	.419
1B	Charlie Gould	.269
2B	Ross Barnes	.378
3B	Harry Schafer	.272
SS	George Wright	.409
OF	Fred Cone	.235
OF	Harry Wright	.267
OF	Dave Birdsall	.277

Troy Haymakers

P	John McMullen (13–15)	.262
C	Mike McGeary	.244
1B	Clipper Flynn	.311
2B	Bill Craver	.303
3B	Steve Bellan	.213
SS	Dick Flowers	.303
OF	Steve King	.396
OF	Tom York	.218
OF	Lip Pike	.351

Cleveland Forest Citys

P	Al Pratt (10–18)	.254
C	James (Deacon) White	.315
1B	Jim Carlton	.235
2B	Gene Kimball	.184
3B	Ezra Sutton	.346
SS	John Bass	.275
OF	Charley Pabor	.310
OF	Art Allison	.257
OF	Elmer White	.282

Chicago White Stockings

George Zettlein (18–9)		.238
Charley Hodes		.246
Bub McAtee		.277
Jimmy Wood		.352
Ed Pinkham		.227
Ed Duffy		.231
Fred Treacey		.344
Tom Foley		.250
Joe Simmons		.201

Washington Olympics

Asa Brainard (13–15)		.200
Doug Allison		.333
Ev Mills		.273
Andy Leonard		.285
Fred Waterman		.305
Davy Force		.265
Harry Berthrong		.218
George Hall		.260
John Glenn		.301

New York Mutuals

Rynie Wolters (16–16)		.320
Charlie Mills		.248
Joe Start		.339
Dick Higham		.330
Bob Ferguson		.218
Dicky Pearce		.267
John Hatfield		.262
Dave Eggler		.313
Dan Patterson		.205

Fort Wayne Kekiongas

Bobby Mathews (7–12)		.281
Bill Lennon		.229
Jim Foran		.344
Tom Carey		.235
Frank Selman		.217
Wally Goldsmith		.209
T. J. Donnelly		.200
Bob Armstrong		.229
Bill Kelley		.211

Rockford Forest Citys

P	Cherokee Fisher (4–20)	.226
C	Scott Hastings	.233
1B	Denny Mack	.238
2B	Bob Addy	.254
3B	Adrian Anson	.352
SS	Chick Fulmer	.243
OF	Ralph Ham	.220
OF	George Bird	.214
OF	Gat Stires	.271

1872 Season

Boston Red Stockings

P	Al Spalding (37–8)	.339
C	Cal McVey	.306
1B	Charlie Gould	.256
2B	Ross Barnes	.404
3B	Harry Schafer	.262
SS	George Wright	.336
OF	Andy Leonard	.341
OF	Harry Wright	.262
OF	Fraley Rogers	.294

Philadelphia Athletics

Dick McBride (30–14)	.275
Mike McGeary	.344
Fergy Malone	.269
Wes Fisler	.327
Adrian Anson	.381
Denny Mack	.247
Ned Cuthbert	.328
Fred Treacey	.256
Levi Meyerle	.318

Lord Baltimores

P	Bobby Mathews (25–16)	.229
C	Bill Craver	.278
1B	Ev Mills	.274
2B	Tom Carey	.296
3B	Cherokee Fisher (9–3)	.205
SS	John Radcliff	.283
OF	Tom York	.269
OF	George Hall	.300
OF	Dick Higham	.339
	Lip Pike	.288

New York Mutuals

Candy Cummings (33–20)	.196
Nat Hicks	.308
Joe Start	.274
John Hatfield	.303
Bill Boyd	.254
Dicky Pearce	.188
John McMullen	.234
Dave Eggler	.346
George Bechtel	.302

Troy Haymakers

P	George Zettlein (14–8)	.248
C	Doug Allison	.319
1B	Bub McAtee	.209
2B	Jimmy Wood	.322
3B	Davy Force	.414
SS	Steve Bellan	.278
OF	Steve King	.297
OF	Charley Hodes	.231
OF	Al Martin (1–2)	.287

Cleveland Forest Citys

Al Pratt (3–9)	.261
James (Deacon) White	.336
Joe Simmons	.230
Scott Hastings	.422
Ezra Sutton	.282
Jim Holdsworth	.321
Charley Pabor	.269
Art Allison	.261
Rynie Wolters (2–6)	.221

Brooklyn Atlantics

P	Jim Britt (8–27)	.219
C	Tom Barlow	.276
1B	Harmon Dehlman	.201
2B	Jim Hall	.246
3B	Bob Ferguson	.262
SS	Jack Burdock	.250
OF	Albert Thake	.274
OF	Jack Remsen	.205
OF	Jack McDonald	.214

Washington Olympics

	Asa Brainard (2–7)	.405
	Frank Selman	.275
	Clipper Flynn	.220
	Tommy Beals	.282
	Fred Waterman	.400
	Wally Goldsmith	.225
	John Glenn	.150
	George Heubel	.125
	A. V. Robinson	.188

Middletown Mansfields

P	Cy Bentley (2–14)	.239
C	John Clapp	.306
1B	Tim Murnane	.296
2B	Eddie Booth	.336
3B	George Fields	.282
SS	Jim O'Rourke	.287
OF	Jim Tipper	.264
OF	Frank McCarton	.271
OF	Frank Buttery (3–2)	.295
	Ham Allen	.169

Brooklyn Eckfords

	George Zettlein (1–7)	.059
	Doug Allison	.299
	Andy Allison	.140
	Jimmy Wood	.176
	Jim Clinton	.188
	Jim Snyder	.275
	Count Gedney	.158
	Jack Nelson	.235
	Al Martin (2–8)	.183

Washington Nationals

P	Bill Stearns (0–11)	.255
C	Bill Lennon	.231
1B	Paul Hines	.286
2B	John Hollingshead	.311
3B	Warren White	.318
SS	Joe Doyle	.222
OF	Ed Mincher	.118
OF	Dennis Coughlin	.324
OF	Oscar Bielaski	.170

1873 Season

Boston Red Stockings

P	Al Spalding (41–15)	.317
C	James (Deacon) White	.382
1B	Jim O'Rourke	.330
2B	Ross Barnes	.402
3B	Harry Schafer	.262
SS	George Wright	.378
OF	Andy Leonard	.298
OF	Harry Wright (2–1)	.233
OF	Bob Addy	.340

Philadelphia White Stockings

	George Zettlein (36–14)	.209
	Fergy Malone	.268
	Denny Mack	.280
	Jimmy Wood	.295
	Levi Meyerle	.331
	Chick Fulmer	.262
	Ned Cuthbert	.264
	Fred Treacey	.252
	George Bechtel (0–3)	.233

Lord Baltimores

P	Candy Cummings (28–14)	.250
C	Bill Craver	.281
	Cal McVey	.369
	Scott Hastings	.256
1B	Ev Mills	.317
2B	Tom Carey	.325
3B	Davy Force	.340
SS	John Radcliff	.280
OF	Tom York	.283
OF	George Hall	.320
OF	Lip Pike	.296

Philadelphia Athletics

Dick McBride (25–21)	.255
John Clapp	.288
Adrian Anson	.353
Wes Fisler	.313
Ezra Sutton	.318
Mike McGeary	.283
John McMullen	.254
Tim Murnane	.214
Cherokee Fisher (2–2)	.255

New York Mutuals

P	Bobby Mathews (29–22)	.183
C	Nat Hicks	.212
1B	Joe Start	.252
2B	Jack Nelson	.305
3B	John Hatfield	.292
SS	Jim Holdsworth	.306
OF	Count Gedney	.254
OF	Dave Eggler	.327
OF	Dick Higham	.304

Brooklyn Atlantics

Jim Britt (17–36)	.191
Tom Barlow	.251
Harmon Dehlman	.212
Jack Burdock	.238
Bob Ferguson	.248
Dicky Pearce	.258
Charley Pabor	.346
Jack Remsen	.293
Bill Boyd	.270

Washington Nationals

P	Bill Stearns (7–24)	.171
C	Pop Snyder	.153
1B	John Glenn	.253
2B	Tommy Beals	.271
3B	Warren White	.265
SS	T. J. Donnelly	.248
OF	Paul Hines	.328
OF	John Hollingshead	.255
OF	Oscar Bielaski	.262

Elizabeth Resolutes

Hugh Campbell (2–16)	.129
Doug Allison	.275
Mike Campbell	.146
Ben Laughlin	.222
Nevins	.196
Frank Fleet (0–3)	.229
Eddie Booth	.299
Henry Austin	.226
Art Allison	.304

Marylands

P	Ed Stratton (0–2)	.167
C	Mike Hooper	.000
1B	Bill Lennon	.200
2B	Marty Simpson	.000
3B	Henry Kohler	.136
SS	Lew Say	.167
OF	John Smith	.190
OF	Bill Smith	.063
OF	Bill French (0–1)	.211

1874 Season

	Boston Red Stockings			New York Mutuals	
P	Al Spalding (52–18)	.333		Bobby Mathews (42–23)	.234
C	James (Deacon) White	.321		Dick Higham	.254
1B	Jim O'Rourke	.344		Joe Start	.290
2B	Ross Barnes	.339		Jack Nelson	.220
3B	Harry Schafer	.265		Jack Burdock	.275
SS	George Wright	.345		Tom Carey	.284
OF	Andy Leonard	.340		John Hatfield	.224
OF	George Hall	.321		Jack Remsen	.224
	Harry Wright	.307			
OF	Cal McVey	.382		Doug Allison	.270

	Philadelphia Athletics			Philadelphia White Stockings	
P	Dick McBride (33–22)	.269		Candy Cummings (28–26)	.208
C	John Clapp	.331		Nat Hicks	.257
1B	Wes Fisler	.383		Denny Mack	.203
2B	Joe Battin	.272		Bill Craver	.345
3B	Ezra Sutton	.336		Jim Holdsworth	.328
SS	Mike McGeary	.362		Chick Fulmer	.264
OF	Count Gedney	.323		Tom York	.249
OF	John McMullen	.387		Dave Eggler	.314
UTL	Adrian Anson	.367		George Bechtel (1–3)	.281

	Chicago White Stockings			Brooklyn Atlantics	
P	George Zettlein (27–30)	.186		Tommy Bond (22–32)	.217
C	Fergy Malone	.223		Jake Knowdell	.133
1B	John Glenn	.261		Harmon Dehlman	.220
2B	Levi Meyerle	.369		John Farrow	.208
3B	Davy Force	.302		Bob Ferguson	.257
SS	John Peters	.278		Dicky Pearce	.290
OF	Ned Cuthbert	.258		Eddie Booth	.237
OF	Paul Hines	.276		Bobby Clack	.157
OF	Fred Treacey	.175		John Chapman	.258
	Jim Devlin	.274			

	Hartford			Lord Baltimores	
P	Cherokee Fisher (14–21)	.229		Asa Brainard (5–24)	.239
C	Scott Hastings	.371		Pop Snyder	.190
1B	Ev Mills	.285		Charlie Gould	.225
2B	Bob Addy	.264		Jack Manning (4–14)	.299
3B	Bill Boyd	.382		Warren White	.254
SS	Tom Barlow	.312		Lew Say	.169
OF	Jim Tipper	.306		Johnny Ryan	.179
OF	Lip Pike	.346		Harry Deane	.231
OF	Bill Barnie	.196		Oscar Bielaski	.206
	Bill Stearns (2–16)	.192			

1875 Season

Boston Red Stockings

P	Al Spalding (57–5)	.318
C	James (Deacon) White	.355
1B	Cal McVey	.352
2B	Ross Barnes	.372
3B	Harry Schafer	.295
SS	George Wright	.337
OF	Andy Leonard	.323
OF	Jim O'Rourke	.289
OF	Jack Manning (13–3)	.285

Philadelphia Athletics

Dick McBride (44–14)	.265
John Clapp	.248
Wes Fisler	.276
Bill Craver	.314
Ezra Sutton	.328
Davy Force	.312
George Hall	.298
Dave Eggler	.288
Adrian Anson	.318

Hartford

P	Candy Cummings (35–12)	.183
	Tommy Bond (19–16)	.263
C	Doug Allison	.232
1B	Ev Mills	.261
2B	Jack Burdock	.283
3B	Bob Ferguson	.233
SS	Tom Carey	.254
OF	Tom York	.284
OF	Jack Remsen	.256
OF	Bill Harbidge	.216

St. Louis Brown Stockings

George Bradley (33–26)	.268
Tom Miller	.166
Harmon Dehlman	.215
Joe Battin	.263
Bill Hague	.226
Dicky Pearce	.256
Ned Cuthbert	.266
Lip Pike	.342
John Chapman	.246

Philadelphia White Stockings

P	Cherokee Fisher (22–18)	.231
	George Zettlein (12–8)	.203
C	Pop Snyder	.301
1B	Tim Murnane	.285
2B	Levi Meyerle	.314
3B	Mike McGeary	.294
SS	Chick Fulmer	.222
OF	Fred Treacey	.207
OF	John McMullen	.249
OF	Bob Addy	.263

New York Mutuals

Bobby Mathews (29–38)	.176
Nat Hicks	.233
Joe Start	.278
Jack Nelson	.187
Joe Gerhardt	.213
Jim Hallinan	.299
Al Gedney	.198
Jim Holdsworth	.271
Eddie Booth	.199

Chicago White Stockings

P	George Zettlein (17–14)	.216
	Mike Golden (7–7)	.242
C	Scott Hastings	.248
1B	Jim Devlin (6–16)	.283
2B	Dick Higham	.234
3B	Warren White	.237
SS	John Peters	.277
OF	John Glenn	.234
OF	Paul Hines	.314
OF	Oscar Bielaski	.232

St. Louis Red Stockings

Joe Blong (3–11)	.143
Frank Flint	.086
Charlie Houtz	.307
Charlie Sweasy	.167
Trick McSorley	.176
Billy Redmond	.175
Art Croft	.153
Dan Morgan (1–3)	.205
Tom Oran	.177

Washington Nationals

P	Bill Stearns (1–14)	.256
C	A. M. Thompson	.095
1B	Art Allison	.169
2B	Steve Brady	.133
3B	Herm Doscher	.160
SS	John Dailey	.208
OF	Bill Parks (3–9)	.183
OF	John Hollingshead	.227
OF	Larry Ressler	.189

New Haven Elm Citys

	Fred Nichols (4–28)	.175
	Tim McGinley	.255
	Charlie Gould	.252
	Ed Somerville	.207
	Henry Luff (1–7)	.262
	Sammy Wright	.175
	Johnny Ryan (1–5)	.150
	Jim Tipper	.147
	John McKelvey	.208
	Billy Geer	.225

Philadelphia Centennials

P	George Bechtel (2–12)	.266
C	Tim McGinley	.226
1B	John Abadie	.217
2B	Ed Somerville	.220
3B	George Trenwith	.174
SS	Bill Craver	.265
OF	Fred Treacey	.271
OF	Fred Warner	.237
OF	Charlie Mason	.229

Keokuk Westerns

	Mike Golden (1–12)	.140
	Joe Quinn	.298
	John Carbine	.051
	Joe Miller	.111
	Wally Goldsmith	.113
	Jim Hallinan	.241
	Charles Jones	.250
	Joe Simmons	.161
	Billy Riley	.147

Brooklyn Atlantics

P	John Cassidy (1–25)	.168
C	Jake Knowdell	.194
1B	Fred Crane	.210
2B	Bill Boyd	.292
3B	Al Nichols	.159
SS	Henry Kessler	.241
OF	Charley Pabor	.229
OF	Bobby Clack	.100
OF	Jim Clinton (1–12)	.120
UTL	Frank Fleet (0–1)	.216

Notes

Introduction

    1. Carroll, p. 20.

Chapter 1. Opening Day

    1. This was the required marking. There is no definitive proof that Hamilton Field was laid out in this manner.

    2. Miers, p. 27.

    3. Game descriptions can be found in the *New York Times*, May 8, 1871, and *The New York Clipper* (hereinafter referred to as *Clipper*), May 13, 1871.

    4. While baseball — even professional baseball — had been played in prior years, 1871 represented the first year in which a league had been formally organized, thereby making it the first year of major league ball. In 1969 the 100th anniversary of professional baseball was celebrated in recognition of the first openly all-professional team, the Cincinnati Red Stockings. The Reds, however, operated independently rather than as part of a league with formal championship parameters.

    5. Chadwick Scrapbooks.

    6. Ibid.

    7. "What did they take a name such as that for?" lamented the *Clipper*, the nation's most prominent sporting journal (*Clipper*, May 13, 1871). The appellation was, in fact, taken from the name of the original Indian settlement which later became the community of Fort Wayne (Lowry, p. 145).

Chapter 2. Elysian Fields to Fort Wayne

    1. The work of the Mills Commission (which endorsed Doubleday) is covered in Bartlett, pp. 4-9.

    2. Ibid., p. 10.

    3. Durant, p. 4.

    4. Ibid.

    5. Bartlett, p. 12; and Seymour, p. 15.

    6. Seymour, p. 18.

    7. Bartlett, p. 17.

8. Adelman, pp. 138–40.

9. Older histories claim that Al Reach was the first professional player. Voight (p. 15), Seymour (pp. 47–48) and other modern accounts accord the honor to Creighton.

10. This incident is reported in numerous sources and as various ailments. The preponderance of evidence indicates that the fatal injury was a ruptured bladder.

11. Adelman, p. 109.

12. Bartlett, p. 21.

13. *Clipper*, December 6, 1873.

14. *New York Times*, March 22, 1875.

15. Lowry, p. 39.

16. Seymour, p. 44; and Chadwick Scrapbooks. In other sources it is reported as $6,000.

17. Voight, p. 18; and Chadwick Scrapbooks.

18. Spalding, p. 109.

19. Voight, p. 17. While Rockford's civic pride may have received a healthy shot in the arm, the Excelsiors reaped the pecuniary rewards. With the Nationals declining to share in the receipts, Chicago pocketed all of the gate money from the estimated 8,000 fans who wanted to see if the no longer invincible Nationals could be beaten. They couldn't, at least not by the Excelsiors (Chadwick Scrapbooks).

20. Chadwick Scrapbooks.

21. Robert Smith, p. 24.

22. Voight, p. 17; and Seymour, p. 52.

23. Meirs, p. 20. Also see Adelman, p. 164, for municipal aid to Mutuals.

24. Voight, p. 27.

25. Most sources claim that the record was 57-0-1, including Voight and the Chadwick Scrapbooks. According to a footnote in Seymour, p. 57, Darryl Brock has done research indicating that the record was actually 60-0-1.

26. The records for the tour were somewhat loosely maintained by current standards. The statistics set forth herein are those commonly reported and accepted by many sources. Other sources credit Wright with a batting average as high as .630.

27. Chadwick Scrapbooks concerning miles traveled and attendance

28. Seymour, pp. 56-57.

29. Robert Smith, p. 33; Chadwick Scrapbooks; and Grace, p. 82.

30. Chadwick Scrapbooks.

31. *New York Times*, March 13, 1871.

32. *Clipper*, March 11, 25, 1871.

33. Chadwick Scrapbooks.

34. *New York Times*, March 1, 1871.

35. Chadwick Scrapbooks.

36. *Clipper*, December 10, 1870.

37. Chadwick Scrapbooks.

38. Ibid.

Chapter 3. Collier's Rooms

1. Author's observations from 1985 visit.

2. *New York Times*, March 13, 1871.

3. Davis, p. 238.

4. U. S. Department of Commerce, p. 1,118.

5. Ridpath, p. 555.
6. Ibid., p. 556.
7. *Clipper*, March 25, 1871.
8. *New York Times*, March 1, 1871; and *Clipper*, February 4, and March 25, 1871.
9. *New York Times*, March 1, 1871; and *Clipper*, February 4, and March 25, 1871.
10. *Clipper*, March 11, 1871.
11. Chadwick Scrapbooks.
12. *Clipper*, March 25, 1871.
13. A complete description of the meeting is set forth in *Clipper*, March 25, 1871.
14. Voight, p. 65.
15. *Clipper*, March 20, 1875.

Chapter 4. The Game

1. Quigley, pp. 37–38.
2. Ibid., p. 35.
3. Ibid., pp. 39–40.
4. *Clipper*, February 18, 1871.
5. Durant, p. 22; and *Hartford Courant*, May 3, 1875.
6. Quigley, p. 45 (re Hicks); and Bartlett, p. 110 (re Allison).
7. Chadwick Scrapbooks.
8. Ibid.
9. *Clipper*, May 18, 1872.
10. The rules were published frequently in *Clipper* and, since Chadwick as the driving force behind the Rules Committee, this rendering has been relied upon.
11. Fortunately, the ball-strike indicator made its first appearance in 1875 to aid in the complex calculations (*Clipper*, May 22, 1875).
12. Ibid., November 15, 1873.
13. *Clipper*, September 12, 1874; and *Hartford Courant*, September 4, 1874.
14. *New Haven Register*, July 23, 1875.
15. Chadwick Scrapbooks.
16. 1891 *Clipper Annual* quoted in Anson, p. 34.
17. Chadwick Scrapbooks.
18. 1891 *Clipper Annual* quoted in Anson, p. 34.
19. 1891 *Clipper Annual* quoted in Anson, p. 36.
20. Chadwick Scrapbooks.
21. Thorn and Palmer, p. 291.
22. 1891 *Clipper Annual* quoted in Anson, p. 36.
23. Ahrens, p. 86.
24. Lowry, p. 39.
25. Ibid., p. 68.
26. (Chadwick Scrapbooks.) Although the bare-handed fielders were far less effective than their gloved successors, a word of caution must be injected when discussing error totals. Scorers did not distinguish between balls that were "too hot to handle" and those that were not. If it was within reach, even after a long run, it was caught or it was an error. Walks, wild pitches, and passed balls also counted

as miscues, inflating error totals and reducing the number of earned runs credited
to a team.

27. *Clipper*, December 11, 1875.

28. Bartlett, p. 43.

29. Chadwick Scrapbooks.

30. Voight, p. 26.

31. The silk proved too chilly and was discarded in favor of flannel the following year (*Clipper*, March 15, 1873).

32. *New York Times*, May 2, 1872; and *Clipper*, March 23, 1872.

33. *Clipper*, May 4, 1872.

Chapter 5. The Players

1. Chadwick Scrapbooks.

2. *Cincinnati Commercial*, November 25, 1870.

3. *Boston Times*, May 15, 1875.

4. *Clipper*, January 25, 1871; and Bartlett, p. 39.

5. Spalding, p. 141.

6. Kaese, p. 7.

7. Chadwick Scrapbooks. This claim is based upon having the highest
number of hits per game among the regular players.

8. Chadwick Scrapbooks; and *Nineteenth Century Stars*, p. 10.

9. *Nineteenth Century Stars*, p. 10.

10. Harry Wright to Charles Gould, June 19, 1873.

11. *Clipper*, December 10, 1870. Again based upon the greatest number of hits
per game.

12. Chadwick Scrapbooks.

13. Chadwick Scrapbooks; and *Nineteenth Century Stars*, p. 17.

14. Voight, p. 31.

15. Wright to Benjamin Douglas, June 29, 1872.

16. *Clipper*, July 8, 1871.

17. *Clipper*, February 4, 1871. In the February 18 issue, the *Clipper* placed
Waterman as the leader; however, their own statistics showed the top batter to be
Wright.

18. Chadwick Scrapbooks.

19. *Clipper*, April 8, 1871.

20. Ibid., April 15, 1871.

21. Ibid., February 3, 1872.

22. A profile of all Athletics players is in *Clipper*, November 18, 1871, and
Boston Journal, March 18, 1871.

23. *Nineteenth Century Stars*, p. 44.

24. *Boston Journal*, March 18, 1871.

25. Ibid.

26. *Clipper*, December 21, 1872; and Chadwick Scrapbooks.

27. *Clipper*, January 14, February 11, March 4, 18, 1871.

28. Thorn and Palmer, p. 1,313.

29. *Nineteenth Century Stars*, p. 94.

30. *Clipper*, April 1, 1871.

31. See Chadwick Scrapbooks for a history of the Cleveland team.

32. *Clipper*, December 24, 1870.

33. Ibid.

34. An excellent profile of White is Overfield, "James 'Deacon' White."

35. Kaese, p. 27.

36. *Nineteenth Century Stars*, p. 122.

37. Pabor was known by the unlikely sobriquet "The Old Woman in the Red Cap," the reason for which has eluded the numerous historians who have researched the era.

38. Overfield, "Lee Allen," p. 39.

39. *Clipper*, December 17, 1870 (based upon hits per game).

40. Chadwick Scrapbooks.

41. Ibid.

42. Voight, p. 88; and *Nineteenth Century Stars*, p. 117.

43. *Clipper*, February 4, 1871.

44. Hatfield's feat is mentioned in numerous sources, including Harry Wright's letter to the editor of the *New York Mercury* located in the Chadwick Scrapbooks.

45. Adelman, pp. 175-77.

46. *Clipper*, May 13, 1871.

47. Adelman, p. 176.

48. Ibid.

49. Ibid.

50. Miers, p. 19.

51. Chadwick Scrapbooks.

52. Salant, p. 7.

53. Birthplaces were taken from the *Macmillan Baseball Encyclopedia*, as were the heights, weights and birthdates of the players.

54. *Clipper*, December 9, 1871.

55. *Clipper*, January 3, 1874.

56. Sutherland, pp. 132-34.

57. A detailed treatment of industrial working conditions is set forth in Sutherland, pp. 158-82.

58. *Clipper*, April 29, 1871.

59. Seymour, p. 25.

60. Adelman, p. 148.

61. *Clipper*, March 25, 1871.

62. Wright to Nick Young, March 28, 1873.

63. *Clipper*, May 20, 1871.

64. Wright to Nick Young, April 25, 1871; and Wright to Mutuals, May 15, 1871.

65. *Boston Herald*, October 25, 1874.

66. Wright to Mason, June 6, 1871.

Chapter 6. Play Ball

1. *Clipper*, April 8, 1871.

2. Kaese, p. 8.

3. *New York Times*, April 6, 1873.

4. *Clipper*, March 14, 1874, March 27, 1875.

5. *Middletown Sentinel and Witness*, March 2, 1872.

6. *Clipper*, March 23, 1872.
7. Ibid.
8. Ibid.
9. Ibid., March 29, 1873.
10. Ibid., March 28, 1874.
11. *New York Times*, August 20, 1875.
12. *Clipper*, April 29, 1871.
13. Ibid., March 18, May 13, 1871.
14. *New York Times*, May 30, 1871.
15. *Clipper*, February 11, 1871.
16. Ibid.
17. Allen, "The Wansley Affair," in Einstein, pp. 23–24.
18. *New York Times*, June 6, 1871.
19. Kaese, p. 9.
20. *Clipper*, April 29, 1871.
21. *New York Times*, April 30, 1871.
22. Ibid.
23. Ibid., March 15, 22, 1873.
24. Ibid., July 15, 1871.
25. Ibid., December 11, 1875.
26. Ibid., July 15, 1871.
27. *New York Times*, July 4, 1871; and *Clipper*, July 15, 1871.
28. *Clipper*, July 15, 1871.
29. Ibid.
30. Ibid., July 1, 1871.
31. Anson, p. 44.
32. Ibid., pp. 41–43.
33. Ibid., p. 62.
34. *Clipper*, February 4, 25, 1871, re Zettlein; and *Clipper*, April 1, 1871, re Mathews.
35. Anson, p. 50.
36. Lowry, p. 74.
37. *Clipper*, July 22, 1871.
38. Ibid., June 3, 1871.
39. Ibid., May 27, 1871.
40. *New York Times*, May 11, 1871; and *Clipper*, May 20, 1871.
41. *Clipper*, July 8 and November 11, 1871.
42. Ibid., May 27, June 3, and November 11, 1871.
43. Ibid., June 10, 1871.
44. Ibid., November 11, 1871.
45. Ibid., October 7, 1871.
46. *Boston Advertiser*, May 5, 1874.
47. Voight, p. 71; and *Nineteenth Century Stars*, p. 56.

Chapter 7. The First Pennant Race

1. *Clipper*, July 22, 1871.
2. Ibid., August 5, 1871.
3. Ibid.
4. Ibid.

5. Ibid.

6. Ibid., November 11, 1871.

7. Ibid., September 23, 1871.

8. Ibid., October 21, 1871.

9. Voight, p. 39.

10. Salant, p. 7.

11. *Clipper*, August 26, 1871. In *Clipper*, September 2 and November 18, 1871, it was stated that Smith had suffered a mental breakdown. A later article, located in Chadwick Scrapbooks and written in 1897, indicated that Smith was then 53 years old and in fine health. Another article stated that he entered the mercantile business.

12. *Clipper*, May 27 and August 19, 1871.

13. *St. Louis Republican*, June 6, 1875.

14. *Clipper*, March 14, 1874.

15. Ibid., August 23, 1873.

16. Grace, p. 82.

17. *Clipper*, September 16, 1871.

18. Ibid., September 30, 1871.

19. Ibid., October 21, 1871.

20. Ibid., July 15, 1871.

21. Ibid.

22. Chadwick Scrapbooks.

23. *Clipper*, September 30, 1871.

24. *New York Times*, October 9, 1871; and *Clipper*, October 14, 1871.

25. *Clipper*, October 14, 1871.

26. *New York Times*, April 24, May 2, 1872; and *Clipper*, April 6, 1872.

27. *Clipper*, October 7, 1871.

28. Ibid., October 14, 1871.

29. Ibid.

30. Ibid.

31. Ibid.

32. Chadwick Scrapbooks.

33. Sutherland, p. 212.

34. Lowry, p. 42.

35. Sutherland, p. 213.

36. Chadwick Scrapbooks, from the *New York Herald*; and *Clipper*, October 21, 1871.

37. *Clipper*, October 21, 1871.

38. Ibid.

39. Wright to Thatcher, November 7, 1871.

40. *Clipper*, October 28, 1871.

41. Voight, p. 40.

42. *Clipper*, November 25, 1871.

43. Ibid.

44. Ibid.

45. Ibid., October 21, 1871.

46. Ibid., October 28, 1871.

47. Ibid.

48. Ibid., November 4, 1871.

49. Ibid., October 28, 1871; and *New York Times*, October 25, 1871.

50. Game description from *Clipper*, November 4, 1871.

Chapter 8. The Pernicious Practice

1. *Clipper*, October 28, 1871.
2. Ibid., October 25, 1873.
3. Spalding, pp. 73–74.
4. Adelman, p. 162; and *Clipper*, August 15, 1874.
5. *Clipper*, December 10, 1870.
6. Allen *100 Years of Baseball* p. 24.
7. Chadwick Scrapbooks.
8. *Clipper*, May 1, 1875.
9. Ibid., December 16, 1871.
10. Voight, p. 38.
11. Chadwick Scrapbooks.
12. *Clipper*, February 11, 1871.
13. Ibid., September 26, 1874.
14. An account of the meeting is contained in *Clipper*, November 11, 1871.
15. Ibid., December 23, 1871.
16. Ibid., October 21, 1871.
17. Ibid.
18. *Chicago Republican* quoted in *Clipper*, December 9, 1871; and *Clipper*, April 27, 1872.
19. Adelman, p. 179; *Hartford Courant*, August 20, 1875; and Chadwick Scrapbooks.
20. *Clipper*, July 25, 1874.
21. Anson, p. 52.
22. *Clipper*, February 3, 1872.
23. Ahrens, p. 85.
24. *Nineteenth* Century Stars, p. 60.
25. Chadwick Scrapbooks.
26. *Clipper*, February 10, 1872.
27. Wright to Benjamin Douglas, March 25, April 8, 18, 1872.
28. *Clipper*, April 20, 1872 and May 4, 1872.
29. Ibid., March 2, 1872.
30. Ibid.
31. *Middletown Sentinel and Witness*, April 26, 1872.
32. *Clipper*, April 20, 1872.
33. Wright to John Clapp, January 18, 1872.
34. SABR Newsletter, January 1987.
35. *Middletown Sentinel and Witness*, May 10, 1872.
36. Chadwick Scrapbooks; and *Middletown Daily Constitution*, July 11, 1872.
37. *Middletown Press,* August 25, 1988.
38. *Clipper*, April 20, 1872.
39. Voight, pp. 84, 171.
40. *New York Times*, April 21, 1872.
41. Spalding, p. 63.
42. *Clipper*, January 25, 1871, and December 14, 1872.
43. Ibid., May 4, 1872.

Chapter 9. A Two-Tiered League

1. A full report of the convention proceedings is contained in *Clipper*, March 16, 1872.

2. *Clipper*, March 14, 1874.

3. The preference of the *New York Times* is expressed in a number of issues during the months of September and October, 1872.

4. *Clipper*, April 27, 1872.

5. Ibid., May 4, 1872. Other than a July 4, 1873, Mutuals-Atlantics game (Lowry, p. 86), the Elysian Fields were not in the news again until May, 1874, when a distraught youth named Goodwell committed suicide on the grounds. Reports indicated that Goodwell had suffered through a tormented love affair that proved significantly less than elysian. The *Hartford Courant*, May 25, 1974, stated that "he had endured the trials of life for nineteen long years."

6. *Clipper*, May 4, 1872.

7. Ibid., June 1, 1872.

8. Ibid., August 10, 1872.

9. Ibid., May 4, 1872.

10. Ibid.

11. Ibid., May 18, 1872.

12. Ibid., July 20, 1872.

13. Ibid., May 18, 1872.

14. The *Middletown Constitution* and *Daily Constitution*, along with the Stagno Collection, indicate that the game was played at Hampden Park. Lowry, who is generally well informed, does not indicate that the two teams played in Springfield.

15. *Clipper*, August 3, 10, 1872; and Chadwick Scrapbooks from *New York World*.

16. *New York Times*, April 21, 1872.

17. Chadwick Scrapbooks.

18. Ibid.

19. *Middletown Constitution*, July 31, 1872.

20. *New York Times*, July 28, August 3, 1872.

21. *Clipper*, August 10, 1872.

22. *New York Times*, September 10, 11, 1872.

23. *New York Times*, August 10, 1872; and *Clipper*, August 17, 1872.

24. *Clipper*, September 7, 1872.

25. *Middletown Constitution*, June 5, 1872.

26. Ibid., June 12, 1872.

27. Ibid., July 10, 1872.

28. *Middletown Sentinel and Witness*, July 26, 1872.

29. *Middletown Constitution*, August 21, 1872.

30. Ibid.

31. *New York Times*, May 25, 26, 1872.

32. Ibid., July 6, 1872.

33. The following year Wolters again deserted his team, the Irvingtons, earning the sobriquet "Old Unreliable" (*New York Times*, July 31, 1873).

34. *Clipper*, July 13, 1872.

35. Ibid.

36. *New York Times*, July 7, 1872; and *Clipper*, July 13, 1872.

37. *Clipper*, July 13, 1872.

38. Ibid., August 10, 1872.
39. *New York Times*, August 21, 1872.
40. *Clipper*, August 31, 1872.

Chapter 10. The Tournament

1. On May 18 as reported in *Clipper*, May 25, 1872.
2. Ibid., June 29, 1872.
3. Ibid., August 3, 1872.
4. Ibid., July 13, 1872.
5. Ibid.
6. Ibid., September 21, 1872.
7. Ibid., September 7, 1872.
8. Ibid.
9. *New York Times*, September 3, 1872.
10. *Clipper*, November 2, 1872.
11. Ibid., September 21, 1872.
12. Wright to Championship Committee, October 30, 1872.
13. *Clipper*, August 31, 1872.
14. Ibid., August 3, 1872.
15. Ibid., October 12, 1872.
16. Ibid., October 19, 1872; and Chadwick Scrapbooks.
17. Accounts of the tournament games are contained in *Clipper*, October 19, 26, 1872 and *New York Times*, October 2–11, 1872. Birdsall's injury is noted in *New York Times*, October 9, 1872.
18. *Clipper*, October 26, 1872.
19. Ibid.
20. Ibid.
21. Ibid., November 9, 1872.

Chapter 11. Financial Troubles

1. A full account of the convention is contained in *Clipper*, March 15, 1873.
2. Ibid., December 23, 1871. Voight claimed the Athletics had a profit of $150, using the *North American and United States Gazette* as his source. Thus, at best, the club's profitability was marginal.
3. *Clipper*, December 23, 1871.
4. Ibid., November 30, 1872.
5. Ibid., December 14, 1872.
6. Ibid., December 7, 1872.
7. Wright to Ross Barnes, December 22, 1872; and Wright to Jim O'Rourke, December 24, 1872.
8. *Clipper*, December 7, 1872.
9. Ibid., December 14, 21, 1872.
10. Ibid., January 25, 1873.
11. Overfield, "James 'Deacon' White," p. 3.
12. *Clipper*, February 8, 1873.
13. Subsequent Athletics financial statements include rental income from the White Stockings.

14. Chadwick Scrapbooks.

15. Ibid.

16. *Clipper*, March 1, 1873.

17. Wright to Nick Young, May 21, 1873.

18. *Clipper*, November 22, 1873. Statistics compiled by Al Wright of the Athletics.

19. Chadwick Scrapbooks.

20. *Clipper*, November 18, 1871.

21. Ibid., November 11, 1871.

22. Johnson, p. 44.

23. In 1882 Higham roused the suspicions of Detroit President William G. Thompson who felt that an inordinate number of Higham's calls favored Detroit's opponents. Thompson hired a team of private detectives to investigate. The sleuths struck paydirt quickly, uncovering a letter in Higham's own handwriting which predicted the winners of games he was to officiate. The discovery put an abrupt end to Higham's umpiring career (Allen, "The Wansley Affair," in Einstein, p. 25).

24. *Clipper*, February 1, 15, 1873.

25. The announcement of Young's marriage is in *Clipper*, November 2, 1872.

26. Ibid., March 29, 1873.

27. Lowry, p. 52.

28. *Clipper*, December 20, 1873.

29. Ibid., May 3, 17, 1873.

30. Ibid., July 26, 1873.

31. Ibid., March 22, 1873.

32. Ibid., October 28, 1871.

Chapter 12. The Umpire

1. Seymour, p. 39. In the Chadwick Scrapbooks the date is given as 1868, but contemporary accounts indicate the existence of a solitary umpire prior to 1868.

2. Seymour, p. 17.

3. *New York Times*, August 24, 1866.

4. *Clipper*, January 15, 1876.

5. Ibid., December 18, 1875.

6. *Hartford Courant*, June 26, 1874.

7. *Clipper*, May 13, 1871.

8. *New York Times*, May 6, 1871.

9. Kaese, p. 9.

10. Interview with Robert Tiemann, then chairman of Nineteenth Century Committee for SABR.

11. *Clipper*, May 13, 1871.

12. Ibid.

13. *Boston Herald* from Chadwick Scrapbooks.

14. *Clipper*, May 20, 1871.

15. Ibid.

16. Ibid., July 29, 1871.

17. Ibid., September 30, 1871.

18. The play-by-play account of the game, in its various versions, is contained in *Clipper*, June 1, 1872. The *Baltimore Gazette* and *Philadelphia City Item* are quoted in *Clipper*, June 1, 1872.

19. *Clipper*, June 1, 1872.
20. *Baltimore Gazette* quoted in *Clipper*, June 1, 1872.
21. *Baltimore Dispatch* quoted in *Clipper*, June 15, 1872.
22. *Philadelphia City Item* quoted in *Clipper*, June 1, 1872.
23. *Clipper*, June 8, 1872.
24. Ibid., August 3, 1872.
25. Game account in Ibid., June 22, 1872.
26. Ibid., July 6, 1872.
27. Ibid., June 28, 1873.
28. Ibid., June 7, 1873.
29. Ibid.
30. Ibid., August 2, 1873.
31. Chadwick Scrapbooks.
32. *Clipper*, September 6, 1873.
33. *Boston Journal*, July 14, 1874.

Chapter 13. A New Powerhouse

1. *Wall Street Journal*, February 10, 1986: "Chester's Cold Ears — The Authentic Story of a Vital Invention."
2. *Clipper*, March 22 and April 19, 1873.
3. Ibid., June 21, 1873.
4. Ibid., May 24, 1873.
5. Ibid., June 28, 1873.
6. Ibid., July 5, 1873.
7. Ibid., May 3, 1873; and Wright to Nick Young, April 11, 1873.
8. *Clipper*, April 26, 1873.
9. Ibid., July 26, 1873.
10. Chadwick Scrapbooks.
11. *Clipper*, August 16, 1873.
12. Ibid., July 13, 1872.
13. Ibid.
14. Ibid., September 7, 1872.
15. Wright to the officers of a Montreal team, May 9, 1873.
16. *Clipper*, July 26, 1873.
17. Wright to Hicks Hayhurst, June 23, 1873.
18. *Clipper*, June 28, 1873.
19. *New York Times*, May 25, 1873.
20. Wright to Resolute Club, June 19, 1873.
21. *New York Times*, August 5, 1873.
22. There are many discussions of Allison's eligibility in *Clipper* throughout the month of August.
23. *Clipper*, September 7, 1872.
24. Ibid., September 6, 1873.
25. Wright to Addy, date illegible.
26. Anson, p. 51.
27. Ibid.
28. Robert Smith, p. 26.
29. *Clipper*, August 30, 1873.

Chapter 14. The Mutuals

1. *Clipper*, June 7, 1873.
2. Primarily through their association with Tweed and Wildey.
3. See Chapter 8.
4. Adelman, p. 162.
5. *New York Times*, June 27, 1871.
6. Almost literally, as a line drive off the bat of Wes Fisler whistled past his ear, nearly decapitating him.
7. *Clipper*, June 15, 1872; and *New York Times*, June 9, 1872.
8. *Clipper*, May 31, 1873.
9. Although Bellan disappeared from U.S. baseball, he went on to make his mark as the father of baseball in Cuba. Bellan was player-manager of the Havana team from 1878–86 (*Nineteenth Century Stars*, p. 11).
10. *Clipper*, June 14, 1873.
11. Ibid., June 7, 1873.
12. Ibid., July 12, 1873.
13. Ibid.
14. Ibid.
15. *Hartford Courant*, July 11, 1874.

Chapter 15. Boston Makes a Run

1. *Clipper*, August 23, 1873.
2. Ibid., November 22, 1873.
3. The situation is discussed in detail in several issues of the *Clipper* during August, 1873.
4. Ibid., October 4, 1873.
5. Ibid., September 27, 1873.
6. Ibid., October 11, 1873.
7. Ibid.
8. Ibid.
9. Ibid.
10. Ibid., November 15, 1873.

Chapter 16. The Return of the White Stockings

1. *Clipper*, February 21, 1874.
2. Ibid.
3. Ibid., January 10, 1874.
4. Ibid.
5. Ibid.
6. Ibid.
7. Ibid., January 31, 1874.
8. Ibid., December 13, 1873.
9. Ibid., January 31, 1874.
10. Ibid., December 13, 20, 1873.
11. Ibid., December 6, 1873.
12. Ibid., January 10, 1874.
13. Ibid., November 22, 1873.

14. Ibid., March 7, 1874; and *Hartford Courant*, March 13, 1874.
15. *Clipper*, March 20, 1875.
16. Ibid., January 3, 1874.
17. Ibid., November 15, 1873.
18. Ibid., February 1, 1873.
19. Ibid., February 7, 1874.
20. Ibid.
21. Lowry, p. 52.
22. *Hartford Courant*, March 14, 1874.
23. Ibid.
24. *New York Times*, March 7, 1874.
25. Seymour, p. 77; and *Nineteenth Century Stars*, p. 65.
26. *Clipper*, August 23, 30, 1873.
27. Ibid., December 6, 1873.
28. Lowry p. 42.
29. Chicago InterOcean, July 11, 1874.

Chapter 17. A Trip to Europe

1. *Clipper*, January 3, 1874.
2. Ibid., December 6, 1873.
3. Ibid.
4. Ibid., January 28, 1871.
5. Spalding, p. 5.
6. There are many references to proposed tours in the Chadwick Scrapbooks, *Clipper*, and secondary sources.
7. Wright to A. G. Fitzgerald of Athletics, January 5, 19, and February 11, 1874; and *Boston Globe*, March 23, 1874.
8. *Clipper*, April 4, 1874.
9. *Boston Advertiser*, July 1874.
10. Bartlett, pp. 22–24.
11. Quigley, p. 44.
12. Bartlett, pp. 25–26.
13. Ibid., pp. 26–28.
14. Spalding, pp. 119–22; and Bartlett, pp. 31–32.
15. Bartlett, p. 33.
16. $2,500 per his account, more likely $1,500 (Bartlett, p. 38; and Kaese, p. 8).
17. Bartlett, pp. 118–19.
18. Ibid., p. 146.
19. Ibid., pp. 145–59, 200–218.
20. Ibid., p. 289.
21. Ibid., p. 225.
22. Ibid., pp. 272–84.
23. Ibid., pp. 290–93.
24. Spalding, p. 176; and Bartlett, pp. 59–60.
25. *Boston Globe*, March 23, 1874.
26. Bartlett, p. 61.
27. Stout, p. 83.
28. Ibid.

29. Ibid.

30. Bartlett, p. 62.

31. Wright to Allcock, March 28, May 1, 1874.

32. Wright to James Ferguson, April 13, 1874.

33. Wright to Allcock, April 6, 1874.

34. A profile of Chadwick can be found in Souders, pp. 84–85.

35. Chadwick Scrapbooks.

36. Voight, pp. 28–29.

37. Spalding Scrapbooks.

38. Wright to William Hulbert and Charles Fowle, January 24, 1876.

39. There is a plaque in the Hall of Fame which incorrectly states that the use of the term "Chicago" for a shutout originated with Cap Anson's powerhouses of the 1880s. However, the term was commonly used in the 1870s and can be traced to a shutout of (not by) Chicago by the Mutuals in July 1870 (*Clipper*, August 26, 1871).

40. *Clipper*, October 18, 1873.

41. *Chicago Tribune* quoted in *Clipper*, July 6, 1872.

42. *Clipper*, August 7, 1875.

43. *Chicago Tribune*, June 9, 1875.

44. *Cleveland Leader* quoted in *Middletown Constitution*, May 22, 1872.

45. Chapter 14, n. 1, and chapter 18, n. 23.

46. *Clipper*, January 31, 1874.

47. Ibid., February 7, 1874.

48. Ibid., December 20, 1873.

49. Ibid., April 12, 1873.

50. Ibid., December 20, 1873.

51. Ibid., February 21, 1874.

52. *New York Times*, March 7, 1874; and *Clipper*, March 14, 1874.

53. *Clipper*, March 21, 1874.

54. Ibid.

55. Ibid., December 12, 1874.

56. Ibid., January 31, 1874.

57. Ibid.

58. Ibid.

59. Ibid.

60. A complete report of the convention can be found in the *New York Times*, March 7, 1874; *Hartford Courant*, March 4, 1874; and *Clipper*, March 14, 1874.

61. *Clipper*, January 18, 1873.

62. Voight, pp. 56–57.

63. *Clipper*, April 11, 1874.

64. Ibid., November 22, 1873.

65. *Nineteenth Century Stars*, p. 15.

Chapter 18. Going for Three

1. All information on the economic situation from Noyes, pp. 1–22.

2. Spalding, p. 26.

3. The Mutuals received bad news on April 10 when they learned of the death of Charlie Mills, the old Atlantic who had been the regular catcher on the original 1871 team. Mills had retired in 1872 but had umpired on numerous occasions in 1873. It was reported that while umpiring during a rainstorm, Mills caught a hellacious

cold which eventually turned into consumption, proving fatal to the old backstop. As was the traditional tribute to their fallen comrades, a benefit game was played, with the proceeds accruing to Mills's unfortunate widow (*New York Times*, April 12, 1874; and *Clipper*, April 18, 1874).

4. *Clipper*, April 25, 1874.

5. Ibid.

6. Ibid.

7. Upon observing a meticulously umpired game a few weeks later, the *Boston Herald* coyly stated, "That captious New York reporter would have hugged himself with delight had he been present to hear the wides called" (*Boston Herald*, May 9, 1874).

8. *Clipper*, May 2, 1874.

9. *Hartford Courant*, April 27, 1874.

10. Ibid.

11. Wright to Charles Hadel, April 27, 1874; and Wright to Reid, April 29, 1874.

12. *Hartford Courant*, April 27, 1874.

13. *Clipper*, May 2, 1874.

14. *Hartford Courant*, May 1, 1874.

15. Wright to Hubbell, May 1, 1874.

16. *Hartford Courant*, May 4, 1874.

17. Sutherland, p. 178.

18. Ibid., pp. 180–81.

19. Ibid., p. 180.

20. Ibid., p. 179.

21. *Hartford Courant*, May 12, 1874.

22. Ibid., May 8, 1874.

23. *Clipper*, May 30, 1874.

24. Ibid., June 20, 1874.

25. *Hartford Courant*, July 22, 23, 1874; and *Clipper*, July 4 and August 1, 1874.

26. *Clipper*, May 23, 1874.

27. Ibid., June 20, 1874.

28. This was the most one-sided game in the history of the NA, per the Stagno Collection. As there are no comprehensive, accurate scores of prior games, this cannot be verified with total certainty, although it is strongly believed by the author to be true.

29. *Clipper*, June 27, 1874.

30. *New York Times*, June 19, 1874; and *Clipper*, June 27, 1874.

31. Sutton had honed that accuracy during winters spent in his native upstate New York. Building a snowman in the vicinity of first base, Ezra would retreat to his third base position and throw snowballs at the effigy for hours on end (*Clipper*, April 1, 1874).

32. *Clipper*, July 25, 1874.

33. *Hartford Courant*, July 15, 1874.

34. *Boston Herald*, July 10, 1874.

35. *Clipper*, July 18, 1874.

Chapter 19. Not Cricket

1. Bartlett, p. 63.

2. *Philadelphia Press*, July 17, 1874.

3. Bartlett, p. 63; and *Clipper*, July 25, 1874.

4. According to Anson, pp. 81–82, Kent later became a prolific writer. In the *Hartford Courant*, October 25, 1875, it was reported that Kent attempted suicide by jumping out a window in Newton, Massachusetts, but survived. Neither of these assertions is supported elsewhere.

5. *Boston Herald*, August 11, 1874.

6. Ibid.

7. *Clipper*, August 15, 1874.

8. *Boston Herald*, August 11, 1874.

9. Ibid.

10. *Clipper*, July 18, 1874.

11. Chadwick Scrapbooks.

12. *Clipper*, August 8, 1874.

13. Ibid., August 22, 1874.

14. *St. Louis Democrat*, September 13, 1874.

15. Wright to A. G. Fitzgerald, January 5, 1874; and Wright to Allcock, April 11, 1874.

16. Wright to St. George's Cricket Club, April 13, 1874.

17. *Clipper*, August 22, 1874.

18. Ibid.

19. *Boston Herald*, August 18, 1874.

20. The entire exhibition schedule was marked by a high level of offensive output. The Athletics' team average was .356 while Boston was not far behind at .338. McVey and Anson were the individual leaders at .453 and .427 respectively (averages are listed in *Clipper*, September 26, 1874).

21. Spalding was so impressed, he preserved the menu for posterity (Spalding Scrapbooks).

22. *Clipper*, September 12, 1874.

23. In particular, see *London Daily News*, August 11, 1874.

24. *London Sportsman* quoted in *Clipper*, August 29, 1874.

25. *Clipper*, August 15, 1874.

26. *Boston Herald*, August 24, 30, 1874.

27. Ibid., August 24, 1874.

28. *Clipper*, August 29, 1874.

29. Ibid.

30. *Boston Herald*, August 30, 1874.

31. Ibid., September 7, 1874.

32. Ibid.

33. Ibid., August 24, 1874.

34. Ibid., September 13, 1874.

35. *Clipper*, September 5, 26, 1874.

36. Spalding, pp. 180–84.

37. *London Saturday Review* in Spalding Scrapbooks.

38. *Boston Herald*, August 27, 1874.

39. *St. Louis Democrat*, September 13, 1874.

40. *Boston Herald*, August 30, 1874.

41. Ibid., September 7, 1874.

42. Ibid.

43. Ibid.; and *Clipper*, September 5, 1874.

44. Kaese, p. 14.

45. *Clipper*, November 21, 1874; February 6, 1875.
46. *Dublin Mail*, August 25, 1874.
47. *Boston Herald*, September 13, 1874.
48. *Philadelphia Press*, September 10, 1874.
49. *Clipper*, September 19, 1874.
50. Ibid.

Chapter 20. The Mutuals Repulsed

1. *Chicago Daily Tribune* quoted in *Clipper*, August 15, 1874.
2. Ibid.
3. *Clipper*, September 12, 1874.
4. Ibid.
5. Ibid.
6. Ibid., September 19, 1874.
7. Ibid., August 22, 1874.
8. *Hartford Courant*, August 11, 1874.
9. Ibid., July 23, 1874.
10. Ibid., September 7, 8 and October 1, 1874.
11. Ibid., July 22, 1874.
12. Chadwick Scrapbooks.
13. *Hartford Courant*, July 23, 1874.
14. *Clipper*, October 3, 1874.
15. Ibid.
16. Ibid., September 26, 1874.
17. Ibid., October 10, 1874.
18. Ibid.
19. Ibid.
20. Ibid.
21. Ibid.
22. *Hartford Courant*, October 9, 1874.
23. Ibid., October 12, 1874.
24. *Clipper*, October 10, 1874.
25. Ibid., October 17, 1874.
26. Ibid.
27. Ibid.
28. Ibid.
29. *New York Times*, October 18, 1874.
30. *Clipper*, October 31, 1874.
31. *Boston Herald*, October 25, 1874.

Chapter 21. Going West

1. See the *New York Times* on virtually any day the trial was in progress.
2. Robert Smith, p. 55.
3. Voight, p. 9.
4. *New York Times*, April 29, 1874; and Clipper, May 9, 1874.
5. *Hartford Courant*, July 28, 1875. Pike obviously had not endeared himself to the Hartford faithful. "Lipman is a good ballplayer, whatever else is said of him," the *Courant* stated on July 22, 1875.

6. Lowry, p. 74.

7. Sutherland, p. 127.

8. Ibid.

9. The dates of death are taken from the *Macmillan Baseball Encyclopedia*.

10. *Clipper*, December 19, 1874. The December 5 issue lists the record as 18–3; however, the more detailed context of the December 19 article renders it more credible.

11. The prior year the Westerns had made a similar claim, only to be challenged by Iowa City in a letter to the *Clipper*, June 20, 1874, claiming that a 14–12 victory on August 26, 1873, had made the team from the latter city the champions of Iowa.

12. Lowry, p. 56.

13. *Clipper*, November 21, 1874.

14. Ibid., April 3, 1875. According to Lowry, the Centennials played some of their games at the Athletics' grounds.

15. *Boston Advertiser*, April 13, 1875.

16. *Clipper*, January 23, 1875.

17. *New Haven Register*, March 10, 1875; and *Clipper*, March 13, 20, 1875.

18. *New Haven Register*, March 2, 1875; and *Clipper*, February 27, 1875.

19. Wright to Charlie Gould, March 31, 1875.

20. *Clipper*, May 1, 1875.

21. Ibid., February 6, 1875.

22. *Hartford Courant*, August 21, 1875.

23. Ibid., September 9, 1874.

24. *Clipper*, January 23, 1875.

Chapter 22. The Force Case

1. Sutherland, p. 61.

2. Ibid., p. 97.

3. The Reds printed a pamphlet containing a transcript of the proceedings. It can be found in the Chadwick Scrapbooks.

4. Chadwick Scrapbooks.

5. Letter to *Clipper* from Athletics, March 11, 1869, from Chadwick Scrapbooks.

6. *Clipper*, November 18, 1871.

7. Ibid., January 20, 27 and February 24, 1872.

8. Ibid., January 20, 1872.

9. Ibid., August 7, 1875.

10. Wright to Hicks Hayhurst, December 26, 1871.

11. The actions of the Judiciary Committee are set forth in excellent detail in *Clipper*, March 13, 1875.

12. Ibid., December 26, 1874, and March 13, 1875.

13. Ibid., December 5, 1874.

14. Ibid., December 26, 1874.

15. Ibid., March 13, 1875.

16. Ibid., August 30, 1873.

17. Ibid., November 1, 1873.

18. Ibid., March 20, 1875, letter from Athletic Club.

19. *Clipper*, March 13, 20, 1875.

20. Wright to Davy Force, September 19, 1874.

21. *Clipper*, March 20, 1875.

22. Wright to William Hulbert, March 15, 1875.

23. *Clipper*, March 20, 1875. Uncharacteristically, Chadwick, who usually took umbrage at shenanigans such as committee packing, took the side of the Athletics, comparing the Force case to the Addy case of the previous season (*Clipper*, March 27, 1875) which it did not resemble in the least. "You see how Chadwick gives it to me again in this week's *Clipper*," Wright wrote to Hulbert (Wright to Hulbert, March 18, 1875).

24. Wright to William Cammeyer, March 12, 1875.

25. Ibid., March 23, 1875.

26. *Clipper*, April 17, 1875; *Hartford Courant*, April 16, 1875.

27. *Clipper*, April 17, 1875.

28. *Hartford Courant*, May 14, 1875.

29. Wright to Benjamin Douglas, March 21, 1875.

30. Wright to Hicks Hayhurst, March 31, 1875.

31. Ibid., April 14, 1875.

32. *Clipper*, May 22, 1875.

33. Ibid., June 26, 1875.

34. *Boston Globe*, June 29, 1875; *Philadelphia Times*, June 29, 1875; and *Clipper*, July 10, 1875.

35. *Clipper*, July 10, 1875.

36. Ibid.

Chapter 23. Going Broke

1. *Clipper*, April 3, 1875.

2. Attendance estimates taken from *New York Times*, May 1, 1875, *Hartford Courant*, May 4, 24, 1875; and *Clipper*, May 1, 8, 15, 29, 1875.

3. Ibid.

4. Ibid.

5. *Philadelphia Press* quoted in *Hartford Courant*, May 27, 1875.

6. Voight, p. 58; and Bartlett, p. 73.

7. *Clipper*, June 5, 1875.

8. Ibid., June 26, 1875.

9. *Keokuk Gate City*, June 11, 1875; *Clipper*, June 19, 1875.

10. *Boston Globe*, dispatch dated June 14, 1875, from Spalding Scrapbooks.

11. *Chicago Tribune* quoted in *Hartford Courant*, May 19, 1875.

12. *Clipper*, June 26, 1875.

13. *New Haven Register*, July 7, 9, 1875.

14. Ibid., July 26, 1875.

15. *Chicago Tribune* from Chadwick Scrapbooks.

16. *New Haven Register*, September 14, 1875.

17. *New York Times*, September 26, 1875.

18. *New Haven Register*, September 25, 1875.

19. *Clipper*, October 2, 1875.

20. Ibid., June 5, 1875.

21. *New Haven Register*, March 19, 1875.

22. Stagno Collection.

23. Golden played for Chicago in 1875 and Milwaukee of the National League

in 1878. Blong was with St. Louis in 1876 and 1877. Bechtel played for the Athletics (following the aforementioned sale of his contract and for New York and Louisville in the following year, while Nichols hurled for a number of major league teams through 1882.

24. At season's end the *Clipper* published a list of all games in which the winning team scored nine runs or less, broken into categories by the number of runs scored by the winning team. One must read the *Clipper* from week to week to truly appreciate the mania with which Chadwick was attracted to the low-scoring game, regardless for the reason for the lack of scoring (*Clipper*, November 13, 1875).

Chapter 24. An Early Challenge

1. *Hartford Courant*, April 21, 1875.
2. Ibid., May 14, 1875.
3. *Clipper*, January 9 and March 22, 1875.
4. *Boston Times*, May 15, 1875.
5. Wright to George Latham, January 18, 29 and February 6, 1875.
6. *Boston Times*, May 15, 1875.
7. Wright to Latham, January 18, 1875.
8. Statistics compiled by SABR task force chaired by Robert Tiemann.
9. *St. Louis Dispatch*, June 4, 1874.
10. Voight, p. 58.
11. *Boston Herald*, August 24, 1874.
12. Correspondence with Latham, n. 5 above.
13. *Nineteenth Century Stars*, p. 10; and *Clipper*, January 23, 1875.
14. Wright to Charles Hadel, April 3, 1874.
15. *Troy Whig* quoted in *Clipper*, June 15, 1872.
16. Chicago Times quoted in *Clipper*, July 13, 1872.
17. Voight, p. 208.
18. This is demonstrated in many letters in the Wright correspondence.
19. Wright to Goldie of Guelph, July 16, 1872. This type of humor was a staple of Wright's correspondence, which sometimes disintegrated into near giddiness. After being shut out by the White Stockings in 1874, he wrote to William Cammeyer of the Mutuals, asking the latter not to mention Chicago to him, nor goose eggs. "I have not seen things, everything, anything, all things look so blue in a long while. We have had an early frost. I feel frosty" (Wright to Cammeyer, September 15, 1874).
20. Voight, p. 58.
21. *St. Louis Times*, June 7, 1875.
22. Wright to Hulbert, March 20, 1875.
23. Wright to S. Mason Graffen, March 17, 1875.
24. Wright to Frank Queen, May 18, 1871; and Wright to Douglas, April 19, 1875.
25. Wright to Hulbert, March 23, 1875.
26. Wright to O'Rourke, December 8, 31, 1874, January 29, February 8 and March 4, 1875.
27. *Richmond Dispatch*, April 30, 1875; *Clipper*, May 8, 1875.
28. *Boston Globe* quoted in *Hartford Courant*, May 15, 1875.
29. *Chicago Tribune*, quoted in *St. Louis Republican*, June 1, 1875.
30. *Clipper*, February 7, 1874, January 22, 1876.

31. *Boston Herald*, April 20, 1875; *New Haven Register* quoting from unamed Philadelphia paper, April 9, 1875.

32. *New Haven Register*, May 26, 1875.

33. Pregame preparations are detailed in *Hartford Courant*, May 17, 18, 1875.

34. Ibid., May 19, 1875; and *Clipper*, May 29, 1875.

35. Detailed descriptions of the game can be found in *Hartford Courant*, May 19, 1875 and *New Haven Register*, May 19, 1875.

36. *Boston Advertiser*, June 18, 1874.

37. *Clipper*, October 12, 1872.

38. Spalding, p. 165.

39. *Clipper*, September 21, 1872.

40. Ibid., May 29, 1875.

41. *Boston Herald*, May 6, 9, 1875.

42. Ibid. quoted in *Clipper*, May 29, 1875.

43. *Boston Globe*, May 20, 1875.

44. *Clipper*, May 22, 1875; and *Hartfort Courant*, May 12, 1875.

45. *Clipper*, June 12, 1875.

46. *Chicago Tribune*, June 9, 1875.

Chapter 25. A Little Chin Music, Maestro

1. *Clipper*, November 6, 1875.

2. *Hartford Courant*, July 15, 1875.

3. *Chicago Tribune* quoted in *St. Louis Republican*, June 1, 1875.

4. Chadwick Scrapbooks.

5. Spalding, pp. 195–96.

6. *Hartford Courant*, July 8, 1875.

7. *Chicago Tribune* quoted in *Hartford Courant*, June 2, 1875.

8. *Clipper*, November 27, 1875.

9. Ibid., November 7, 1874, and January 22, 1876.

10. Ibid., February 25 and September 2, 1871.

11. Chadwick Scrapbooks.

12. *Hartford Courant*, September 1, 1875; and *Philadelphia Times* quoted in *New Haven Register*, September 1, 1875.

13. *Clipper*, September 11, 1875; and *New Haven Register*, September 7, 1875.

14. *Clipper*, October 30, 1875.

15. Ibid., December 11, 1875.

16. Ibid., October 23, 1875.

17. Ibid., August 14, 1875.

18. *Hartford Courant*, June 30, 1875.

19. *New Haven Register*, August 23, 1875.

20. *Hartford Courant*, May 18, 1875; and *Clipper*, May 15, 1875.

21. *Clipper*, July 11, 1874.

22. Ibid.

23. *Middletown Constitution*, July 26 and August 2, 1872.

24. Voight, p. 82.

25. *New Haven Register*, October 23, 1875.

26. Voight, p. 53.

27. *Clipper*, November 7, 1874, and January 22, 1876.

28. Ibid., December 11, 1875.

29. Ibid., December 25, 1875.
30. Wright to Hulbert, December 29, 1874.
31. *New York Times*, July 17, 1875; and *Clipper*, July 24, 1875.
32. *Clipper*, October 28, 1871. Hodes passed away on February 14, 1875, his demise perhaps hastened by alcoholic overindulgence. For a game played on July 19, 1875, his name was listed in the box score as catcher for the Mutuals, a feat that would have been the ultimate in the "pluck" that Chadwick so admired. Of course, it was one of the frequent errors in contemporary box scores which vex researchers, as "Hodes" was actually Nat Hicks (*New York Times*, July 20, 1875; and *Clipper*, July 24, 1875).
33. *Clipper*, July 24, 1875; and *New York Times*, July 20, 1875.
34. Chadwick Scrapbooks. Other references to Mathews' drinking are in *Clipper*, October 21, 1871; February 28, 1874.
35. *Nineteenth Century Stars*, p. 83.

Chapter 26. A Stunning Secession

1. *Boston Herald*, September 27, 1874.
2. Ibid., July 18, 1875.
3. *Chicago Tribune*, July 24, 1875.
4. *Boston Herald*, July 25, 1875; and *Hartford Courant*, September 29, 1874.
5. *Hartford Courant*, September 29, 1874.
6. Chadwick Scrapbooks.
7. *Chicago Tribune*, July 24, 1875; and *Boston Herald*, March 22, 1874.
8. *Boston Herald*, September 27, 1874.
9. Bartlett, p. 73; and Overfield, "James 'Deacon' White" p. 4.
10. *New Haven Register*, July 30, 1875.
11. *Clipper*, December 25, 1875; and Bartlett, p. 74.
12. *New Haven Register*, July 30, 1875.
13. Bartlett, p. 75.
14. A chance he would later try to avoid following an Athletics' counteroffer (Anson, pp. 93–94).
15. Bartlett, p. 76.
16. Ibid., p. 78.
17. *Clipper*, November 20, 1875.
18. Ibid.
19. Another NA player with an identity problem, Borden had initially played under the name of "Nedrob," which is Borden spelled backwards (*Nineteenth Century Stars*, p. 16).
20. *Clipper*, July 31, 1875; *New Haven Register*, July 26, 1875; and *Philadelphia Times* quoted in *Hartford Courant*, July 26, 1875.
21. *Clipper*, August 7, 1875.
22. Ibid.
23. *New Haven Register*, August 9, 1875.
24. Borden did not receive official credit for his gem, as two walks were recorded as hits.
25. Kaese, p. 19; and Allen, *100 Years of Baseball*, p. 37. According to Allen, Borden later worked in a Pennsylvania factory, stitching the baseballs he had once thrown past opposing hitters.
26. *New York Times*, July 22, 1875.

27. *Clipper*, October 2, 1875.
28. *New Haven Register*, September 25, 1875.
29. *Clipper*, September 4, 1875.
30. Ibid., November 6, 1875.
31. *New York Times*, September 19, 1875.
32. *Hartford Courant*, May 27, 31, 1875.
33. See chapter 18.
34. *Clipper*, September 25, 1875.
35. Ibid., September 18, 1875.
36. Ibid., August 28, 1875.
37. *New York Times*, September 18, 1875.
38. *Clipper*, October 9, 1875.
39. Ibid., August 16, 1873.
40. *Chicago Tribune* from Chadwick Scrapbooks.
41. *New Haven Register*, June 16, 1875; and *Hartford Courant*, June 16, 1875.
42. *Clipper*, December 11, 1875.

Chapter 27. Grand Central Hotel

1. *Hartford Courant*, September 18, 1875.
2. *Clipper*, September 18, 1875.
3. *New Haven Register*, October 29, 1875.
4. *Hartford Courant*, September 18, 1875.
5. *New Haven Register*, October 23 and November 1, 1875.
6. Bartlett, p. 82.
7. Ibid., pp. 85–86.
8. Voight, p. 77.
9. The story of the formation of the National League and the contents of its constitution has been told in many histories, including Voight, pp. 60–68; Bartlett, pp. 82–89; and Seymour, pp. 75–85.
10. Bartlett, pp. 80–81.
11. See the Wright Correspondence.
12. *Clipper*, February 12, 1876. Years later, in 1907, when the success of the National League was assured, Chadwick softened his stance and began to use the pronoun "we" when recounting the formation of the new league (Chadwick Scrapbooks).
13. *St. Louis Globe Democrat*, February 4, 1876.
14. *New Haven Register* quoted in *Clipper*, February 12, 1876.
15. Voight, p. 67.

Selected Bibliography

Newspapers

New York Times, 1871–75 (April–November).
Middletown Constitution, 1872 (April–August).
Middletown Daily Constitution, 1872 (July–August).
Middletown Sentinel and Witness, 1872 (March–August).
New York Clipper, 1871–75.
Hartford Courant, 1874–75 (April–November).
New Haven Register, 1875 (April–November).

Baseball Books

Adelman, Melvin. *A Sporting Time*. Urbana: University of Illinois Press, 1986.
Allen, Lee. *The Cincinnati Reds*. New York: G. P. Putnam's Sons, 1948.
_____. *100 Years of Baseball*. New York: Bartholomew House, 1950.
Anson, Adrian. *A Ball Player's Career*. Chicago: Era Publishing, 1900.
Bartlett, Arthur. *Baseball and Mr. Spalding*. New York: Farrar, Straus and Young, 1951.
Brown, Warren. *The Chicago Cubs*. New York: G. P. Putnam's Sons, 1946.
Durant, John. *The Story of Baseball in Words and Pictures*. New York: Hastings House, 1947.
Einstein, Charles, editor. *The Third Fireside Book of Baseball*. New York: Simon & Schuster, 1968. "The Wansley Affair" by Lee Allen.
Kaese, Harold. *The Boston Braves*. New York: G. P. Putnam's Sons, 1948.
Lowry, Philip. *Green Cathedrals*. Cooperstown, NY: Society for American Baseball Research, 1986.
Miers, Earl Schenk. *Baseball*. New York: Grossett and Dunlap, 1967.
Quigley, Martin. *The Crooked Pitch*. Chapel Hill, NC: Algonquin, 1984.
Reichler, Joseph L., editor. *Macmillan Baseball Encyclopedia*, Fifth Edition. New York: Macmillan, 1982.
Salant, Nathan. *Superstars, Stars and Just Plain Heroes*. New York: Stein and Day, 1982.
Seymour, Harold. *Baseball, The Early Years*. New York: Oxford University Press, 1960.

Smith, Ken. *Baseball's Hall of Fame*. New York: Grossett and Dunlap, 1952.
Smith, Robert. *Baseball in America*. New York: Holt, Rinehart and Winston, 1961.
Spalding, Albert. *America's National Game*, New York: American Sports Publishing, 1911.
Thorn, John, and Peter Palmer, editors. *Total Baseball*. New York: Warner, 1989.
Thorn, John, and Mark Rucker, editors. *The National Pastime*. Cooperstown, N.Y.: Society for American Baseball Research, 1984.
Voight, David. *American Baseball* (vol. 1). University Park: Pennsylvania State University Press, 1983.

Non-Baseball Books

Davis, Burke. *The Long Surrender*. New York: Vintage, 1985.
Noyes, Alexander. *Thirty Years of American Finance*. New York: G. P. Putnam's Sons, 1900. Reprint New York: Greenwood, 1969.
Ridpath, John Clark. *A Popular History of the United States of America from the Aboriginal Times to the Present Day*. New York: Phillips and Hunt, 1886.
Sutherland, Daniel. *The Expansion of Everyday Life*. 1860–76. New York: Harper and Row, 1989.
U. S. Department of Commerce, Bureau of the Census. *Historical Statistics of the United States of America — Colonial Times to 1970*. White Plains, NY: Kraus International, a division of Kraus-Thomsen Organization, 1975.

Articles

Ahrens, Arthur. "The Chicago National League Champions of 1876." *Baseball Research Journal*, 1982. Society for American Baseball Research (hereafter abbreviated as SABR).
Carroll, Bob. "For the Hall of Fame: Twelve Good Men." *National Pastime*, Winter 1985. SABR.
Grace, Kevin. "'Bushel Basket' Charlie Gould of Red Stockings." *Baseball Research Journal*, 1984. SABR.
Ivory, Bill. "Burial Sites of Hall of Famers." *Baseball Research Journal*, 1982.
Johnson, Lloyd. "Long 1877 Duel of Zeros Put Syracuse on the Map." *Baseball Research Journal*, 1984. SABR.
LinWeber, Ralph. "Baseball Guides Galore." *Baseball Research Journal*, 1982. SABR.
Overfield, Joseph. "James 'Deacon' White." *Baseball Research Journal*, 1975. SABR.
_____. "Lee Allen." *Baseball Research Journal*, 1975. SABR.
_____. "A Memorable Year: 1884; A Memorable Performer: Jim Galvin." *Baseball Research Journal*, 1982. SABR.
Phelps, Frank. "Macmillan." *The National Pastime*, 1987. SABR.
Skipper, James K., Jr. "Feminine Nicknames: 'Oh, you Kid,' from Tillie to Minnie to Sis." *Baseball Research Journal*, 1982. SABR.
Smith, James D. "Baseball Players, Managers, and Umps Active in Four Major Leagues." *Baseball Research Journal*, 1982. SABR.
Souders, Mac. "Henry Chadwick." *Baseball Reserach Journal,* 1986. SABR.
Stout, Neil. "1874 Baseball Tour not Cricket to British." *Baseball Research Journal*, 1985. SABR.

Nineteenth Century Stars, **SABR, 1989**

The following articles from *Nineteenth Century Stars* have been utilized:

Subject	Author
Robert Addy	Joseph M. Overfield
Ross Barnes	Frank V. Phelps
Esteban Bellan	R. Tiemann and J. Jimenez
Tommy Bond	Bob Richardson
Joe Borden	Randy Linthurst
Asa Brainard	Joseph M. Overfield
John Chapman	Joseph M. Overfield
John Clapp	Frank V. Phelps
Jim Creighton	Mark D. Rucker
Jim Devlin	Frederick Ivor-Campbell
Bob Ferguson	Frank V. Phelps
Wes Fisler	Joseph M. Overfield
Davy Force	Joseph M. Overfield
Chick Fulmer	Joseph M. Overfield
George Hall	James D. Smith, III
Paul Hines	Frederick Ivor-Campbell
William Hulbert	William E. Akin
Andy Leonard	B. Richardson and J. Sumner
Bobby Mathews	James D. Smith, III
Cal McVey	Frederick Ivor-Campbell
Levi Meyerle	James D. Smith, III
Dicky Pearce	Frank V. Phelps
Lip Pike	Joseph M. Overfield
Joe Quest	R. Puff and R. Tiemann
Al Reach	Joseph M. Overfield
Joe Start	Frederick Ivor-Campbell
Ezra Sutton	Richard A. Puff
Jim Tyng	Bob Richardson
Deacon White	Joseph M. Overfield
Tom York	Richard A. Puff

Other

Harry Wright Correspondence
Henry Chadwick Scrapbooks
Albert Spalding Scrapbooks
Michael Stagno Collection

Notes on Sources

For the period 1871–75 I have relied on primary sources to the greatest extent possible. For episodes beyond these years, I have used secondary sources, particularly the fine histories of Voight and Seymour. Bartlett's biography of Al Spalding also yielded a great deal of information about the Boston pitcher, particularly his life before and after the National Asociation period.

The *New York Clipper* formed the backbone of the research due to its comprehensive day-to-day coverage of the sport. Prominent baseball men corresponded through its pages and the *Clipper* culled and reprinted significant articles from local journals. As Henry Chadwick was the principal contributor to the *Clipper,* it is presumed that strong editorial opinions were those of Chadwick.

For supporting and corroborative purposes, the Chadwick Scrapbooks, Harry Wright Correspondence and the Spalding Scrapbooks all yielded valuable information. Chadwick was a bit too liberal with the scissors in many instances, and it was difficult, if not impossible, to determine the original source. In such cases, I have merely labeled the material as emanating from "Chadwick Scrapbooks." Spalding was much more conscientious in the area of indentification, and footnotes generally indicate the original source rather than "Spalding Scrapbooks."

The *New York Clipper* has been cited as *Clipper*. The footnotes also contain numerous citations from newspapers not listed in the Selected Bibliography. These citations have been quoted in other papers or can be found in the Chadwick or Spalding Scrapbooks.

Team standings have been compiled from game scores contained in the Michael Stagno Collection unless otherwise indicated. All batting and pitching statistics — along with birthdates, heights, and weights of the players — have been taken from the *Macmillan Baseball Encyclopedia* unless stated otherwise.

For events outside the 1871-75 period which have been frequently reported, such as the 1869 Cincinnati Reds tour and the formation of the National League, I have merely indicated where the major histories have treated the incident rather than utilizing extensive footnoting.

Finally, when citing the Society for American Baseball Research publication *Nineteenth Century Stars* I have noted only the page number, rather than identifying the author of the individual segment. All authors are given full credit in the Selected Bibliography.

Index